Human Performance Improvement

Human Performance Improvement

Building Practitioner Competence

Second Edition

William J. Rothwell
Carolyn K. Hohne
Stephen B. King

ELSEVIER

AMSTERDAM · BOSTON · HEIDELBERG · LONDON
NEW YORK · OXFORD · PARIS · SAN DIEGO
SAN FRANCISCO · SINGAPORE · SYDNEY · TOKYO

Butterworth-Heinemann is an imprint of Elsevier

Butterworth-Heinemann is an imprint of Elsevier
30 Corporate Drive, Suite 400, Burlington, MA 01803, USA
Linacre House, Jordan Hill, Oxford OX2 8DP, UK

 Recognizing the importance of preserving what has been written, Elsevier prints its
books on acid-free paper whenever possible.

Library of Congress Cataloging-in-Publication Data
Rothwell, William J., 1951-
  Human performance improvement: building practitioner competence /
William J. Rothwell, Carolyn K. Hohne, and Stephen B. King.—2nd ed.
    p.   cm.
  Includes bibliographical references and index.
  ISBN-13: 978-0-7506-7996-1
  ISBN-10: 0-7506-7996-4
    1. Employees—Training of.   2. Employees—Training of—
Evaluation.   3. Performance standards.   I. Hohne, Carolyn K.   II. King,
Stephen B.   III. Title.

HF5549.5.T7R68 2006
658.3'1243—dc22

                                                              2006051912

British Library Cataloguing-in-Publication Data
A catalogue record for this book is available from the British Library.

ISBN 13: 978-0-7506-7996-1
ISBN 10: 0-7506-7996-4

For information on all Butterworth-Heinemann publications
visit our Web site at www.books.elsevier.com

Printed in the United States of America
07 08 09 10 11 12   10 9 8 7 6 5 4 3 2 1

Working together to grow
libraries in developing countries

www.elsevier.com | www.bookaid.org | www.sabre.org

ELSEVIER   BOOK AID International   Sabre Foundation

Dedication

*From **William J. Rothwell:*** This book is dedicated to my beloved wife, **Marcelina Rothwell**, and my beloved daughter, **Candice Rothwell**—the two most important women in my life.

*From **Carolyn K. Hohne:*** This book is dedicated to my life-long friend and husband **Bruce**, my daughter **Brielle**, who is as beautiful on the inside as she is on the outside, and my son **Carter**, who is an endless source of humor in my life.

*From **Stephen B. King:*** This book is dedicated to **my family**, to my wife, **Marsha King**, who is a constant source of encouragement, love, and friendship, and to my son **Jonathan Paul King**—the greatest joy in my life!

Contents

Acknowledgments

Writing a book is like putting together a jigsaw puzzle. The authors start with ideas, concepts, values, and beliefs in much the same way that someone who begins putting together a puzzle starts out with a box filled with pieces that are disorganized. The authors must then form these odds and ends into something coherent. Now that we have completed the puzzle, we would like to thank the many people who helped us in that task.

First, the authors thank each other. Despite busy work schedules, we were able to come together and work effectively long enough to see this project to completion. That is no small achievement, and it deserves recognition of the time it required and the dedication it demanded.

Second, the authors would like to thank the following people:

- *Daryl Hunt, Xiaoli Cao*, and *Will Hickey,* who helped conduct research on resources suited to building HPI competencies in the original first edition of this book. *Xiaoli Cao* also helped with the difficult task of tracking copyright permission requests on the first edition, and the authors wish to thank her for her diligence and persistence in doing that.
- *Yi Xue,* who helped conduct research on resources suited to building HPI competencies in the second edition of this book.
- *Tobin Lopes,* who also did most of the work in updating the resources at the back of the second edition.
- *Gao Lin,* who did most of the work in tracking down the copyright permission requests on the second edition.
- *Susan Fehl, Joe Monaco, Dennis Mankin, Chuck Harpham*, and *Carol Panza,* who gave their time for interviews and shared their stories about their careers and HPI project experiences.

Preface

Managers continue to demand results from training departments and from other people-related functions of organizations as never before. Gone are the days when training efforts—and other HR activities—were undertaken vaguely for the sake of improving morale. The goal in today's dynamic organizations is *achieving results*—and thereby *improving performance*. The more demonstrable and measurable those changes are, the better.

Human performance improvement (HPI) is a means to the end of achieving improved results. HPI is also focused on identifying opportunities for improvement and on taking proactive steps for continuous improvement. While many models and approaches to HPI exist, they share several assumptions:

- Training is only one means of achieving improved performance and is often the strategy of last resort because rigorous, results-oriented training is time-consuming and expensive to produce.
- Most problems in workplaces stem from the environment in which workers perform rather than in the individuals who perform the work. While training may "fix" a lack of individual knowledge, skill, or appropriate attitude, it will not fix problems that stem from the environment in which workers must carry out their work.
- The root causes of performance problems must be identified and addressed, though it is easy for managers and others in organizations to be misled into focusing their attention on the *consequences* of problems rather than on their *causes*.

Since HPI is focused on solving problems or even avoiding problems before they arise, it is a powerful tool for achieving any or all goals, such as building intellectual capital, establishing and maintaining a high-performance workplace, enhancing profitability, and encouraging productivity—as well as achieving such other worthwhile goals as increased return on equity and improved safety.

HPI is implemented through *human performance improvement interventions,* which are also sometimes called *performance improvement strategies.* A *performance improvement intervention* (or *performance improvement strategy*) is any effort designed to achieve better results in productivity, profitability, safety, or other measures of success. An intervention is not a quick fix; rather, it implies a long-term action plan to improve performance by addressing the root causes of performance problems or seizing upon possibilities to achieve quantum leaps in productivity improvement. An intervention may be applied with a surgeon's precision to solve a specific problem. Alternatively, many interventions may be applied in combination to address the causes of multiple problems.

Almost anyone can apply HPI. HPI is not a tool reserved exclusively for training and development practitioners, human resource specialists, or external consultants. While HPI can be used effectively by members of these groups, HPI can also be applied just as easily by managers, supervisors, and even employees. Indeed, the most powerful applications of HPI are often undertaken by members of the latter groups. Consequently, a key assumption of HPI is that everyone has a stake in improving organizational, work group, and individual performance.

Familiarity with HPI is thus increasingly important to practicing managers and HR professionals alike.

In the future, you can either focus your attention on activities—such as training, daily supervision, or management—or you can help your organization improve human performance. In this book are many tools, techniques, and models that can prove useful if you choose to focus on improving human performance. We also describe key trends that will affect organizations in the future, and give you some concrete ideas about how to transform a traditional training department into an HPI department, as well as the means for assessing and building your own practitioner competence in HPI. The rest, however, is up to you. We wish you great success and many accomplishments.

William J. Rothwell
University Park, Pennsylvania

Carolyn Hohne
Lumberton, New Jersey

Stephen B. King
Laurel, Maryland

Introduction

This book introduces the concepts of human performance improvement (HPI). It is written for a broad audience that may include trainers, human resources (HR) practitioners, line managers, workers, college students who are being introduced to HPI, and anyone else who is interested in improving how well and how much people perform in organizational settings. *Improving Human Performance* is thus intended for a multifaceted audience, and serves a twofold purpose. The first purpose is to introduce HPI by defining what it is, what people must know to carry it out, and what tools and techniques are fundamental to its practice. The second purpose is to show how HPI is applied in organizations. HPI is intended, pure and simple, to improve the bottom-line, measurable results of organizations, work groups, or individuals.

Chapter 1, aptly entitled "Laying the Foundation," opens with a case study to demonstrate how HPI can be applied in practice. This chapter also defines such key terms as *performance* and *human performance improvement. Performance*, it should be emphasized here, refers to the results or outcomes of work. *Human performance improvement* (HPI) is "a systematic process of discovering and analyzing important human performance gaps, planning for future improvements in human performance, designing and developing cost-effective and ethically justifiable interventions to close performance gaps, implementing the interventions, and evaluating the financial and nonfinancial results" (Rothwell, 2000).

The roles of the HPI practitioner are the focus of Chapters 2 through 5. Their intent is to describe—and build reader competence with—the roles of those who apply HPI as those roles were defined in *ASTD Models for Human Performance Improvement* (Rothwell, 2000), an important research-based competency study of the HPI field. As described by Rothwell, a *role* is "a part enacted" and should not be confused with job titles or position descriptions. In this sense, then, a role is akin to the part played by an actor or actress in a theatrical production. Anyone can play a role.

Chapter 2 is entitled "The Role of Analyst." The *analyst* identifies performance problems or improvement opportunities by pinpointing gaps between actual and desired results. This chapter addresses such important questions as:

- What is the role of the analyst?
- What are some models of analysis?
- How is the role of the analyst enacted?

Perhaps the most important contribution of this chapter is its emphasis on discovering the underlying causes of performance problems and underscoring opportunities for performance improvement.

Chapter 3 centers on the role of *intervention specialist.* Once the cause of a performance problem or gap is identified by the analyst, an intervention specialist selects the best (or most appropriate) intervention to solve the problem or narrow the gap. This chapter describes the role of the intervention specialist, supplies models to use in selecting appropriate HPI interventions, and describes what intervention specialists do.

Chapter 4 focuses on the role of the *change manager,* defined by *ASTD Models for Human Performance Improvement* as the role that "ensures that interventions are implemented in ways consistent with desired results and that they help individuals and groups achieve results" (Rothwell, 2000). In other words, the change manager guides individuals or groups through the implementation of a performance improvement strategy. This chapter defines the change manager's role, describes some approaches for managing change, and provides suggestions for carrying out this role.

Chapter 5 reviews the role of the *evaluator,* defined by *ASTD Models for Human Performance Improvement* as the role that "assesses the impact of interventions and follows up on changes made, actions taken, and results achieved in order to provide participants and stakeholders with information about how well interventions are being implemented" (Rothwell, 2000). The evaluator, then, helps ensure that performance improvement strategies are measurable and that stakeholder groups receive feedback on results.

Chapters 6, 7, and 8 provide a broader frame of reference that clarifies what has led up to HPI, where HPI is likely to be headed in the future, and how you can prepare to become an HPI practitioner. Chapter 6 is entitled "Trends and

Their Implications for HPI." It describes important changes affecting corporations, the workforce, and the human resource function that make "improving performance" a daunting challenge that requires some "leading of the target." After all, performance is not static; rather, performance requirements are driven by changing external environmental and competitive conditions. This chapter provides a broad context for HPI practitioners to reflect on those changing conditions and to identify their implications for the field of HPI.

Chapter 7, entitled "Transforming the Training Department into an HPI Function," provides the authors' suggestions—based on their consulting experience—for helping traditional training organizations make the shift from "doing training" to "improving performance." This chapter is written for human resource development or workplace learning and performance practitioners—and for anyone else who depends on the training department to provide support or leadership in HPI.

Chapter 8 is entitled "Building Your Competence as an HPI Practitioner." It helps traditional trainers ponder why and how to make the transition from "trainer" to "HPI practitioner." It naturally leads into Chapter 9, entitled "From Theory to Practice: Real-World HPI Projects," which is all new in the book's second edition. Appendix I provides a self-assessment instrument for individuals to compare themselves—and/or invite others to help them compare themselves—to the competencies required for success as an HPI practitioner. Appendix II gives HPI practitioners an opportunity to plan for their competency-building efforts in HPI.

Chapters 8, 9, and Appendixes I and II also provide the basis for Appendix III, which is a resource guide written for anyone who wishes to improve his or her competence in HPI. It lists the competencies of the HPI practitioner, as they have been identified in *ASTD Models for Human Performance Improvement* (Rothwell, 2000), and offers resources targeted to help individuals build their competence in each competency area linked to the roles of the HPI practitioner.

If you should need to supplement this book, it works particularly well with Rothwell, W. (2000) *ASTD Models for Human Performance Improvement*, 2nd ed. Alexandria, VA: The American Society for Training and Development. Also useful is *In Action: Improving Human Performance: Eleven Case Studies from the Real World of Training.* Alexandria, VA: The American Society for Training and Development; and Deterline, W., and Rosenberg, M. (Eds.) (1992) *Workplace Productivity Performance Technology Success Stories.* Washington, DC: International Society for Performance Improvement. These works provide real-world case examples of efforts to apply HPI in organizations.

Laying the Foundation

Human Performance Improvement (HPI)

Performance

Performance can be an elusive concept. It deals with the outcomes, results, and accomplishments achieved by a person, group, or organization. Too often, the term *performance* is confused with *behavior*. In human performance improvement (HPI), there is a clear distinction between these terms. A simple way to distinguish them is to view performance as the end result and behavior as a means to that end. Behaviors are thus the actions that can contribute to accomplishments, but they are not in themselves accomplishments. Stated another way, behaviors are what people take with them and accomplishments are what they leave behind.

As an example, Bruce has worked at Futurescape, Inc., a software development firm, for over 10 years. His car is generally parked in the first space in the lot, evidence that he is one of the first employees to arrive at work each day. He frequently works late into the evening, and often comes in on weekends. During a typical day, Bruce appears to be serious and highly productive. He can be seen busily typing away at his computer, working through lunch, speaking with customers on the phone, and hustling from place to place through the office. He often carries a large bundle of file folders, reports, and other documents.

Then there's Stacey. Stacey has less experience than Bruce and has been with Futurescape for a little more than a year. She shows up to work each day promptly, but not a minute before starting time. Stacey works normal hours and only works evenings or weekends when deadlines must be met or when work backs up. She always takes her full lunch hour and on pleasant days takes a brisk walk through the downtown area with several colleagues. Stacey enjoys the people she works with and can often be seen socializing with them about a variety of work- and nonwork-related topics.

Consider these two vignettes. What opinions did you form about Bruce and Stacey? For the most part, these brief depictions described behaviors or actions that these people exhibited. Little was said, however, about their performance. Would you be surprised to learn that Stacey consistently outperforms Bruce in virtually all areas? Too often people are judged and rewarded or punished based on the behaviors they display. For example, in many companies, the people who work long hours or appear to be busy are rewarded with promotions and bonuses, even though others who might not demonstrate these behaviors actually produce more and with higher-quality results. Organizations and managers, in many cases, place higher value on behaviors and outward appearances that people exhibit rather than on the results they produce. This is especially true in jobs and work environments where the results may be less tangible and visible, but no less important. For example, it is clearly easier to recognize the results of a salesperson in comparison to a financial analyst.

The ultimate focus of HPI is on performance, results, outcomes, and accomplishments, with secondary emphasis on behaviors, efforts, and activities. This is not to say that behaviors should be ignored. Since behaviors are contributors to performance, they represent factors that can either positively or adversely impact performance. Further, positive and focused behaviors enable and lead to successful performance. In the next section, readers will learn that a variety of factors contribute to performance. Figure 1-1 shows some of those key influences on performance that will be explained in more depth later.

Another way to understand the difference between performance and behavior is to examine their grammatical usage. Performance is typically stated as a noun, whereas behaviors are actions that generally contain a verb plus a subject. Figure 1-2 shows the differences between statements of performance and statements of behavior.

Consider several examples drawn from nonbusiness life that further illustrate the differences between behavior and performance. During a typical game of golf, a player exhibits a number of observable and nonobservable behaviors. Lining up a shot, estimating the distance to the target, selecting a club, assuming a proper stance, taking a practice swing, and hitting the ball all represent behaviors. None of these, however, necessarily equates to performance. Taken together, they contribute to and enable successful performance, but do not portray accomplishments.

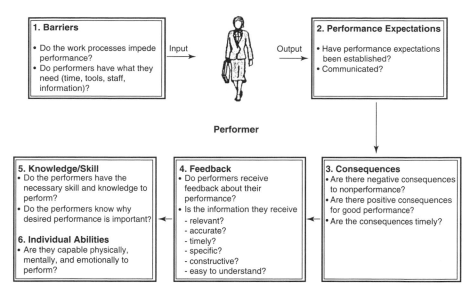

Figure 1-1 Factors that may influence performance. After: Rummler, G. (1999). Transforming Organizations Through Human Performance Technology. In H. Stolovich and E. Keeps (eds.), *Handbook of Human Performance Technology: A Comprehensive Guide for Analyzing and Solving Performance Problems in Organizations*. San Francisco: Jossey-Bass. Copyright 1988. The Rummler-Brache Group.

Examples of Behaviors or Actions	Examples of Performances, Outcomes, or Results
Create table	Hole in one
Open the discussion	House under contract
Turn wrench	Machine ready for operation
Take a practice swing	Productive employee
Document incident	Problem solved
Provide feedback on performance	Delicious meal
Determine proper gauge setting	House ready for move-in
Season to taste	College diploma
Read blueprint	Clean bedroom
Push blue button on press	Profits
Schedule meeting	Healthy patient
Attend class	Correct answer to problem
Demonstrate product features	Repeat customer
Deliver pizza to customer's home	Functional vehicle

Figure 1-2 Statements of behavior and statements of performance.

One representation of performance in the golf scenario is the score that is achieved. For example, the golfer may shoot one-under par, even par, one-over par, two-over par, or some other score on a particular hole. The score attained for a hole represents the performance because it is the quantifiable end result, accomplishment, or final outcome achieved by the golfer. Each behavior that the golfer demonstrates, such as lining up the shot and estimating the distance to the target, contributes to the end result, but is not equivalent to it.

The score, usually written on the scorecard, is what the golfer takes away with him or her after the round. The behaviors are all left behind. When golfers talk with colleagues after the round, they do not speak much about how well shots were lined up, the great practice swings they took, or how hard they tried to hit the ball properly. Instead, golfers cut to the chase and talk about their final scores. Of course, there may be a variety of feelings and emotions associated with one's performance on a round of golf, from disgust to jubilation.

Think about another nonbusiness example that demonstrates the difference between behavior and performance. When preparing a meal, a gourmet chef selects ingredients, mixes, stirs, sautés, adjusts the cooking temperatures, seasons to taste, and serves the meal. As with the golf example, each activity is linked to behavior. A delicious meal, served at the proper temperature and in a timely manner, is the accomplishment or performance that the chef attempts to produce. These outcomes are what the customers value, and this may vary. One customer may accept a longer waiting time if the meal is hot and tasty. Another person, on a tight schedule, may give lower overall performance marks to a high-quality meal that takes too long to arrive.

Since the context of HPI for this book is primarily organizations, the reader should be able to distinguish between behaviors and performance in organizational settings as well. An administrative assistant, for instance, engages in a number of behaviors. Examples of these might include typing memos and letters, scheduling meetings, coordinating activities, and responding to customer requests. Examples of performances, or final results, produced by the secretary might include error-free memos or satisfied repeat customers.

Factors Affecting Performance

Many factors can influence performance. This section will explore some of these in greater depth. Several authors have defined broad classifications for such variables. The descriptions of factors described extensively by Rummler and Brache (1990) and Gilbert (1978) are presented in this section. Readers should be aware that there is some overlap between these two authors, but there are differences as well.

A Basic Systems Model: The Work of Rummler and Brache

Rummler and Brache (1990) pinpointed six variables that affect job performance. Figure 1-1, discussed earlier, shows the influences of performance specifications, task interference, consequences, feedback, knowledge/skill, and individual capacity.

At the core of Figure 1-1 is the individual, who is the central figure in the human performance system. The basic systems model, comprised of input, output, consequences, and feedback, is also depicted. The roots of behavioral psychology are clear in the HPI field. Behavioral terminology, such as stimulus, response, consequences, and feedback, are, in some cases, used to describe HPI. Note that the six variables in Figure 1-1 affect different elements of the system. Some performance variables influence the performer directly. Other variables, though, affect performers only indirectly through the environment that surrounds performers as they carry out their work. Organizational culture is an example of a less direct, but sometimes powerful, influence on performance.

Performance expectations, as seen in Figure 1-1, are linked with outputs because they relate to standards, goals, and expectations regarding output. Barriers, on the other hand, are linked with the inputs to performance. Included in this category are signals to perform, along with conflicting tasks or actions, and resources, such as tools, equipment, finances, and information. Consequences, for obvious reasons, are linked with the outcomes of performance, and may be positive or negative in nature. A performance bonus, team luncheon, and individual recognition are examples of consequences.

Similar to consequences, feedback relates to information that the people obtain regarding their performance. It lets performers know how they are doing. Some feedback may be provided by the person's manager or supervisor, while others may be built into the job itself, thus allowing the performer to know without external feedback whether performance was adequate or in need of correction. A monthly budget report represents this type of feedback because it is a high-level indicator of how the department is doing from a financial perspective.

The last two variables—knowledge/skill and individual capacity—are the two that reside within the performer. They relate to the individual's knowledge, skill, and capability with respect to the job and task, as well as his or her ability to perform.

The Behavior Engineering Model (BEM) of Thomas Gilbert

The Behavior Engineering Model (BEM), which will be discussed in the next chapter as a comprehensive analysis model, identifies six factors affecting performance (Gilbert, 1978). As mentioned, these variables correlate strongly to those listed by Rummler and Brache and include the following:

- Data and information
- Resources, tools, and environmental supports
- Consequences, incentives, and rewards
- Skills and knowledge
- Individual capacity
- Motives

These items can be divided into two general categories. The first three variables are environmental variables that influence performance because they are external to the individual performer. Generally speaking, it is the responsibility of the organization or management to provide performers with what they need to be successful. Likewise, it is the manager's job to remove barriers to performance. The last three—skills and knowledge, individual capacity, and motives—are internal to the person. These variables also strongly affect performance but reside within the individual. Each is described in the following paragraphs.

Data and information are important influences on performance. Included in this category are the expectations that are conveyed to the person about the job and the desired performance. Also, job standards, desired outputs, or goals are information that can, when provided, help drive a person to high performance. When standards or goals are nonexistent or have not been properly communicated, then substandard performance may result. Feedback is another aspect of data and information, and it is information that a performer receives about both positive and negative performance. Timely, specific, and useful feedback helps a person to correct poor performance, as well as maintain or enhance effective performance. More research today emphasizes the importance of focusing on strengths, rather than deficiencies, when providing feedback to facilitate successful performance (Buckingham and Coffman, 1999; Buckingham and Clifton, 2001).

Resources include financial resources, tools, equipment, time, and other environmental supports. It is management's responsibility to supply sufficient resources to performers to enable them to achieve optimal performance. When such resources are absent—or when wrong or inappropriate resources are supplied to performers—the result is often lower levels of performance. For example, a cellular phone might be a standard tool used by a sales force. If one salesperson was not provided with a cell phone or had one that did not function properly, then the result could be substandard performance compared with salespeople who possessed this important tool.

Consequences, incentives, and rewards serve to stimulate employees to perform. Consequences can be positive or negative. When a person receives a negative consequence following a particular behavior or performance, then it is likely that this action will not be repeated. The opposite is true with positive consequences. Incentives and rewards have a similar affect on performance. Consequences, incentives, and rewards can take many forms, from a verbal "tongue lashing" to formal recognition at the company's annual honors and awards banquet.

Skills and knowledge are the first items on the list of performance variables that are internal to an individual performer. People obtain skills and knowledge through a variety of sources, including formal education and training programs, on-the-job training, and various other formal and informal sources. Consider the resources shown in Chapter 8, which point HPI practitioners to resources for developing key skills and competencies. When knowledge or skills are lacking, the result can be poor performance due to quality problems, time needed to perform, and inaccuracy.

Capacity has to do with talents or with the capability to perform. Some people simply do not possess the capabilities required to perform effectively. These issues can be classified under the label of insufficient capacity. Capabilities may be limited for many reasons, including individual physical or mental limitations. For example, a particular job might require the incumbents to lift 30-pound propane tanks for eight hours per day. This job duty might not be physically possible for some people. When a lack of capacity is identified as a problem, a solution that is often applied is to provide a better match between the person and the job requirements. That can be accomplished by changing the job (by making a reasonable accommodation, for instance) or by moving the person to another job for which he or she is better suited.

Motives are deeply embedded characteristics possessed by people that can affect performance. Motives include the reasons that people do what they do, how people view themselves, their needs, desires, hopes, fears, and a variety of other internal personality traits. While they can strongly influence performance, motives can be extremely difficult for HPI practitioners to alter. For example, if a candidate for the position of supervisor possesses low self-esteem, it may be difficult for this person to coach employees effectively. Attempting to improve that person's self-esteem, even by a nominal amount, might involve years of coaching, training, and require counseling or therapy. In many cases, the time and expense involved in such an effort become prohibitive. In fact, it may be necessary to review motives during the selection process, since it may not be a cost-effective or timely process to alter them after the individual is hired.

\ After reading through the list of variables, you might consider the impact each has on your own performance. Consider a challenge you are experiencing in your current role. It has been said that 80 percent of all performance problems that exist in organizations can be attributed to a lack of expectations, standards, and feedback—the first category in the list of variables above. Is that true in your situation? In addition, ponder the ease by which each of the variables could be influenced by an HPI practitioner. A rule of thumb is that, as you progress through the list of variables displayed above, it becomes increasingly difficult, time consuming, and expensive to influence or change the variable.

For example, it is considerably easier to provide a person with feedback on performance, which falls under the Data and Information category in Gilbert's model, than it is to change a person's self-esteem, which falls under the Motives category. Gilbert's Behavior Engineering Model, which will be described in Chapter 2, is a model for analyzing performance problems. Following the logic discussed above from a diagnostic standpoint, the analysis process begins with an examination of the environmental factors, such as data and information, and then progresses through the factors that are more difficult and costly to influence.

Defining Human Performance Improvement

There are many characterizations, definitions, and models associated with human performance improvement (HPI). In addition to HPI (Rothwell, 2000), some of the more common labels include:

- Human Performance Technology (Pershing, 2006)
- Performance Engineering (Gilbert, 1978; Dean, 1994)
- Human Performance Enhancement (Rothwell, 2005)
- Performance Consulting (Robinson and Robinson, 1995a)

For the most part, these labels are synonymous, while the precise definitions or focus may vary slightly (Rothwell, 1995).

Several definitions of HPI that have been gleaned from the performance improvement literature are shown in Figure 1-3. Note that not all authors use the label *human performance improvement* when describing and defining the field. For example, Joe Harless uses *human performance technology* for the definition he provides.

We can also look to professional associations focused on human performance improvement for definitions they have adopted and advocate. The American Society for Training and Development (ASTD) and the International Society for Performance Improvement (ISPI) are two such associations. ASTD, as sponsor for the HPI study (Rothwell, 2000), has adopted the definition presented in the ASTD Models study. ISPI uses the term *human performance technology* and defines it as "a systematic approach to improving productivity and competence, uses a set of methods and procedures—and a strategy for solving problems—for realizing opportunities related to the performance of people" (ISPI, 2006). ISPI continues the definition by stating, "More specific, it is a process of selection, analysis, design, development, implementation, and evaluation of programs to most cost-effectively influence human behavior and accomplishment. It is a systematic combination of three fundamental processes: performance analysis, cause analysis, and intervention selection, and can be applied to individuals, small groups, and large organizations" (ISPI, 2006).

There are both common elements and differences found in these definitions. In an attempt to sort out the numerous definitions in the field, Stolovitch and Keeps (1999) categorize authors into those whose definitions focus on processes and methods, such as Rosenberg, and those who focus on final outcomes, such as Gilbert. While definitions vary widely, Stolovitch and Keeps (1999) contend that "consensus as to its critical attributes appears to have formed." They list the following characteristics associated with human performance technology:

- HPT is systematic.
- HPT is systemic.
- HPT is grounded in scientifically derived theories and the best empirical evidence available.
- HPT is open to all means, methods, and media.
- HPT is focused on achievements that human performers and the system value.

Author and Year	Definition of HPI
ASTD (1992)	"A systemic approach to analyzing, improving, and managing performance in the workplace through the use of appropriate and varied interventions."
Gilbert (1978)	"The purpose of [human] performance [technology] ... is to increase human capital, which can be defined as the product of time and opportunity ... technology is an orderly and sensible set of procedures for converting potential into capital."
Harless (1992)	"The process of analysis, design, development, testing, implementation, and evaluation of relevant and cost-effective interventions on worthy human performance."
Pershing (2006)	"Human performance technology is the study and ethical practice of improving productivity in organizations by designing and developing effective interventions that are results-oriented, comprehensive, and systemic."
Rosenberg (1990)	"A set of methods and processes for sloving problems— or realizing opportunities—related to the performance of people."
Rothwell (1996)	"A systematic process of discovering and analyzing important human performance gaps, planning for future improvements in human performance, designing and developing cost-effective and ethically justifiable interventions to close performance gaps, implementing the interventions, and evaluating the financial and nonfinancial results."
Stolovitch and Keeps (1999)	"An engineering approach to attaining desired accomplishments from human performaers. HP technologies are those who adopt a systems view of performance gaps, systematically analyze both gap and system, and design cost-effective and efficient interventions that are based on analysis data, scientific knowledge, and documented precedents, in order to close the gap in the most desirable manner."
Van Tiem, Moseley, and Dessinger (2004)	"The systematic process of linking business goals and strategies with the workforce responsible for achieving goals. Moreover, performance technology practitioners study and design processes that bring about increased performance in the workplace using a common methodology to understand, inspire, and improve. And finally, performance technology systematically analyzes performance problems and their underlying causes and describes exemplary performance."

Figure 1-3 Selected definitions of human performance improvement.

These characteristics emphasize the important aspects of the field of human performance improvement. It is systematic in nature because a structured approach to performance improvement is favored above a random, unplanned, "gut feel" approach. A number of step-by-step and dynamic models will be presented throughout this text that demonstrate the systematic nature of HPI.

Human performance improvement is also systemic because it accounts for the interconnectedness of organizational systems. The phrase "You can't pick up one end of the stick without picking up the other" applies to the HPI approach. This creates in the practitioner an awareness that interventions applied in one area of an organization are likely to have immediate and longer-term, direct and indirect, consequences and results in other areas. This phenomenon has been likened to a spiderweb, where force applied to one part tends to echo, resound, and reverberate throughout the web.

Another unique feature of the human performance improvement field is that it is data-driven. The phrase "In God we trust, all others bring data" (a phrase many people attribute to quality guru Edward Deming) certainly applies to HPI because the focus is always on issues of cost, quality, quantity, productivity, sales, profit, number of grievances or complaints, as well as other bottom-line, results-based measures. It should be noted that qualitative measures are also important. For example, grievances filed represent quantitative, as well as qualitative, data that an HPI practitioner might find useful. The number of grievances (quantitative) could be tracked, along with the content or nature (qualitative) of the grievances. Data can be culled from many other sources—including exit interviews, performance appraisals, financial databases and reports (sales, cost, profitability), production/quality reports, information from customers (satisfaction, on-time delivery, service), employees, executives, supervisors, absentee, and benchmarking studies.

Donald Kirkpatrick (1994) developed a four-level framework for evaluating training programs. This will be discussed at length in Chapter 5, which covers the role of the HPI evaluator. Level Four in Kirkpatrick's model focuses on impact or bottom-line results. This is the primary area of focus for human performance improvement efforts. Some HPI practitioners believe that Kirkpatrick's Levels One (reaction), Two (learning), and Three (behavior change) should be de-emphasized and that greatest attention should be devoted to Level Four (results) and Level Five (Return on Investment), which were added later by Jack Phillips (Phillips, 2003). Many HPI practitioners are also of the opinion that if producing measurable results is the focus from the start, then Levels One through Three become far less important than Levels Four and Five. It is this results-orientation that drives performance improvement efforts focused on achieving organizational accomplishments. We believe, as we shall describe in Chapter 5, that all evaluation levels provide important perspective and that all should be used.

HPI practitioners are not bound to the same solution for all problems. They go beyond relying on one preferred solution and are open to any potential solution(s). In that important respect, they differ from stereotypical, traditional trainers, who have been accused of relying on one preferred solution—training. If morale is low, then people need motivational training. If the workers in two departments are not cooperating, they need a teambuilding exercise. If quality is low, quality improvement workshops are the answer.

Human performance improvement, on the other hand, are heavily steeped in analysis and attempts to obtain a firm grasp on what is happening compared with what should be happening. There are no preconceived notions about what the solution ought to be. This open-ended approach, based on analysis and data, allows the appropriate intervention to rise to the surface so that it can be brought to bear on the problem or goal at hand.

Jacobs (1987) also identified eight characteristics associated with HPI (which he refers to as HPT, for Human Performance Technology) that are consistent with those presented by Stolovitch and Keeps. These include the following:*

- HPT distinguishes between human performance and behavior.
- HPT determines worthy performance as a function of the value of the accomplishment and the costs to achieve it.
- HPT applies systems approaches to five components of human performance-technology systems—the job, the person, responses, consequences, and feedback.
- HPT focuses on engineering competent human performance.
- HPT emphasizes analysis of performance problems, needs, and goals.
- HPT emphasizes the role of exemplary—that is, exceptional—performance.
- HPT focuses on identifying and addressing causes of human performance problems.

---

* *Source:* Ronald R. Jacobs, *Human Performance Technology: A Systems-Based Field for the Training and Development Profession* (Columbus, Ohio: Center on Education and Training for Employment [formerly NCRVE], Ohio State University). Copyright 1987, used with permission.

According to Jacobs, HPT tends to favor the application of five classes of performance-improvement strategies to problems. They are training, job performance aids, feedback systems, employee selection, and organizational redesign.

Stolovitch and Keeps (1999) conclude their discussion of human performance improvement characteristics by providing a definition, which is also displayed in Figure 1-3.

In 1996, the American Society for Training and Development (ASTD) sponsored research to identify the roles, competencies, and outputs associated with human performance improvement work. The result was *ASTD Models for Human Performance Improvement* (Rothwell, 2000), which represents a formal attempt to identify competencies associated with human performance improvement work. *Human performance improvement* is the label used by Rothwell (2000) in the *ASTD Models* study.

Since *ASTD Models* provides the basis for this text, the term *human performance improvement* (HPI) will be used. The definition developed by Rothwell is displayed as an item in Figure 1-3. HPI is "a systematic process of discovering and analyzing important human performance gaps, planning for future improvements in human performance, designing and developing cost-effective and ethically justifiable interventions to close performance gaps, implementing the interventions, and evaluating the financial and nonfinancial results" (Rothwell, 2000).

This definition contains the key elements found in definitions proposed by other authors. Also, note that this definition encompasses many characteristics of human performance improvement that have already been covered, in that it emphasizes the systematic nature of HPI and its focus on results or accomplishments. The core of the definition contains the primary steps of the HPI process model, including analysis, intervention selection, implementation, and evaluation. These basic steps will be expanded on and discussed further in the next section.

Anyone can perform human performance improvement work. In fact, it could be argued that everyone should be involved in HPI and that everyone really is, or could be, an HPI practitioner. The difference is that managers and employees alike go about improving performance through trial and error, overreliance on past experience, or random activities, instead of the approach we advocate here. The focus of this book is primarily trainers who are transitioning away from their traditional role of emphasizing instructional solutions and moving toward solutions designed to address the root causes of performance problems. We firmly believe, however, that other organizational members at all levels can incorporate the methods, models, and tools described in this book to improve performance. Employees, first-line supervisors, middle- and upper-level managers, individual contributors, and teams can all benefit from applying the methods and competencies associated with HPI.

The Six-Step Human Performance Improvement Process Model

Human performance improvement is a field of practice that has produced many models. A model is, of course, "a simplified representation of an object, process, or phenomenon" (Rothwell and Sredl, 2000). Stolovitch and Keeps (1999) contend that "the HPI field has not developed its own widely accepted model." Some models focus on the entire HPI process and usually follow some version of the general systems process model that is sometimes referred to as the "ADDIE" model. ADDIE is an acronym for Analysis, Design, Development, Implementation, and Evaluation (Stolovitch and Keeps, 1992).

Examples of such comprehensive human performance improvement models include conceptual frameworks by Deterline and Rosenberg (1992), Robinson and Robinson (1995a), and Rothwell (2000). Other schemas isolate and describe a particular component of HPI, such as those that focus only on analysis (Rossett, 1999; Swanson, 1996) or on interventions (Langdon, Whiteside, and McKenna, 1999) or on evaluation (Brinkerhoff, 2006). A number of HPI models will be covered in detail in subsequent chapters of this book, especially Chapter 2, which focuses on performance and cause analysis.

ASTD Models for Human Performance Improvement includes a six-step HPI process model, which was derived from many sources and confirmed through an expert-based research study. These six steps are depicted in Figure 1-4.

This HPI process model contains the primary components that are found in most comprehensive performance improvement frameworks. This process model

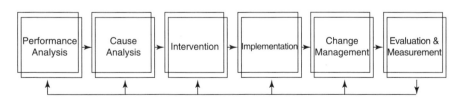

Figure 1-4 ASTD human performance improvement process model. Source: Rothwell, W. (2000). *ASTD Models for Human Performance Improvement: Roles, Competencies, and Outputs.* Alexandria, VA: The American Society for Training and Development. Used by permission of the American Society for Training and Development.

has six steps, which include "performance analysis, cause analysis, intervention, implementation, change management, and evaluation" (Rothwell, 2000). In explaining the first step, performance analysis, Rothwell (2000) notes that "at this point, people who do human performance improvement work identify and describe past, present, and future human performance gaps." The second step, cause analysis, involves determining the root cause or causes of the gaps identified in the first step.

Rothwell states that in the third step—selection of appropriate interventions—"people who do human performance work consider possible ways to close past, present, or possible future performance gaps by addressing their root cause(s)." In the fourth step, implementation, "people who do human performance improvement work help the organization prepare to install an intervention." In the fifth step, change management, they monitor the implementation of the intervention. Finally, in the sixth step, evaluation and measurement, they "take stock of the results achieved by the intervention."

The Roles of the HPI Practitioner

Four roles are directly linked to the six steps of the human performance improvement process model described in *ASTD Models for Human Performance Improvement*. A role is defined as "a part played by a person involved in human performance improvement work" (Rothwell, 2000). Specifically, these include the four roles of the analyst, intervention specialist, change manager, and evaluator. Figure 1-5 shows the relationship between the roles and each of the steps

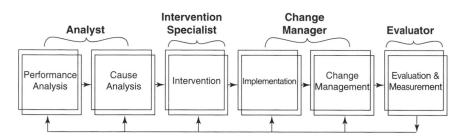

Figure 1-5 Relationship between the human performance improvement process and roles. Source: Adapted from Rothwell, W. (2000). *ASTD Models for Human Performance Improvement: Roles, Competencies, and Outputs*, 2nd ed. Alexandria VA: The American Society for Training and Development. Used by permission of the American Society for Training and Development.

in the HPI process. Note that several roles are aligned to multiple steps in the process model. The Analyst, for example, is associated with the two process steps of performance analysis and cause analysis.

Each role will be described in detail in the next four chapters. A brief overview of the roles is provided here. The role of the human performance improvement analyst, considered by many to be the most important, involves performance analysis and cause analysis. The analyst "conducts troubleshooting to isolate the cause(s) of human performance gaps or identifies areas in which human performance can be improved" (Rothwell, 2000). The process of analysis helps the HPI practitioner to accurately and thoroughly diagnose the problem or situation prior to recommending and implementing the appropriate solution system. This role will be covered in detail in Chapter 2.

Many performance improvement interventions or strategies can be selected by the HPI practitioner and may involve training, as well as management (non-training) solutions. Appropriate intervention selection is the responsibility of the role of the intervention specialist and will be covered extensively in Chapter 3. The person in this role "selects appropriate interventions to address the root cause(s) of performance gaps" (Rothwell, 2000). The selection of interventions is a natural extension of the analysis work that was conducted in the previous steps.

Implementation of the intervention that was chosen involves engaging in short- and long-term change management. For this reason, the third human performance improvement role is that of the change manager. The change manager "ensures that interventions are implemented in ways consistent with desired results and that they help individuals and groups achieve results" (Rothwell, 2000). Chapter 4 focuses on this role, and the change management process, in depth.

The evaluator role is the fourth and final role of the HPI practitioner. Evaluation and measurement, the focus of Chapter 5, are important to performance improvement efforts to ensure that the intended results of the intervention were achieved. The focus of evaluation is on the original performance problem or opportunity identified in the analysis phase. In other words, the stage for evaluation is set during analysis. The evaluator "assesses the impact of interventions and follows up on changes made, actions taken, and results achieved in order to provide participants and stakeholders with information about how well interventions are being implemented" (Rothwell, 2000).

The Dynamic Nature of Human Performance Improvement

It is not necessary for one person to become an expert in all four roles, but a certain degree of competence is expected, especially if a single person is functioning in all roles. Since roles do not equate to job titles, a common issue relates to the separation of the roles. It is acknowledged that each role is unique, possessing distinctive competencies and outputs. For discussion purposes, it is useful to separate them.

In cases where one person serves in multiple roles during performance improvement efforts, though, the roles may blur together. Further, when a team or group of people engage in HPI, the process is much more fluid and dynamic than the step-by-step process model may imply. When you examine Figure 1-4, you might assume that HPI work progresses in linear fashion from performance analysis to cause analysis, and then from cause analysis to intervention selection. Similarly, this sequential model makes it seem as if the HPI practitioner starts in the role of analyst and only later adopts the roles of intervention specialist, change manager, and evaluator.

This assumption of a linear, sequential flow is simply not accurate or realistic. During an HPI project, the HPI practitioner may assume each role simultaneously. It may be true that a particular role may play a larger part at a particular point in the performance improvement efforts. In reality, however, and due to the dynamic nature of HPI, all roles should be kept in the forefront of the practitioner's mind. In other words, when HPI practitioners are involved in implementation and change management (the role of change manager), they should be considering the other three roles.

For example, during implementation, the results of the analysis (the role of analyst) are taken into account to ensure that progress toward solving the underlying cause of the performance problem is being made. The reasons for the intervention and the criteria by which it was selected (the role of intervention specialist) should be weighed as well, to convey to key stakeholders what is happening and why this approach is being taken. Finally, during implementation, HPI practitioners should continually monitor progress and make midcourse corrections as necessary (the role of evaluator). Another example is the role of change manager. Many of the competencies associated with change management can, and should, be demonstrated throughout the HPI process as a way to build buy-in and commitment to the performance improvement effort.

HPI Competencies and Outputs

One of the most important research-based contributions of *ASTD Models for Human Performance Improvement* was the identification of the competencies and outputs associated with human performance improvement work. Figure 1-6 displays the complete listing of competencies and their definitions.

Competencies are "internal capabilities that people bring to their jobs. They may be expressed in a broad, even infinite, array of on-the-job behaviors" (McLagan, 1989). The competencies in Figure 1-6 are organized according to the four roles with which they are linked. Note that the first sixteen competencies are considered core competencies because they are "essential to all roles and across all steps in the human performance improvement process" (Rothwell, 2000). Each role—analyst, intervention specialist, change manager, and evaluator—has six role competencies associated with it.

One way in which competencies can be broadly classified is to distinguish between those that are technical and those that are nontechnical. Technical competencies, on the one hand, are specific to certain roles, such as the role of the analyst. Nontechnical competencies, on the other hand, are competencies that are more generic in nature and apply across the complete terrain of HPI activities. Nontechnical competencies are sometimes referred to as core competencies. An example of a core competency is "industry awareness." It cannot be isolated and linked to one of the four roles. *ASTD Models for Human Performance Improvement*, however, revealed that industry awareness was of importance to HPI work and that it applies to all of the HPI roles. The next section will take a closer look at the core competencies for HPI and how each is applied in this field.

Core Competencies

This section provides a brief overview of each of the sixteen core competencies. These competencies are fundamental to the success of HPI practitioners. Unlike the role competencies, which are specific to the roles assumed by practitioners, core competencies cut across all activities and are essential to successful performance in HPI.

Industry Awareness: HPI practitioners, especially those working as external consultants, must possess a broad understanding of the industry in which the client organization exists. Internal HPI practitioners, new to an industry, must

Core Competencies

1. **Industry Awareness:** Understanding the vision, strategy, goals, and culture of an industry; linking human performance improvement interventions to organizational goals.
2. **Leadership Skills:** Knowing how to lead or influence others positively to achieve desired work results.
3. **Interpersonal Relationship Skills:** Working effectively with others to achieve common goals and exercising effective interpersonal influence.
4. **Technological Awareness and Understanding:** Using existing or new technology and different types of software and hardware; understanding performance support systems and applying them as appropriate.
5. **Problem-Solving Skills:** Detecting performance gaps and helping other people discover ways to close the performance gaps in the present and future; closing performance gaps between actual and ideal performance.
6. **Systems Thinking and Understanding:** Identifying inputs, throughputs, and outputs of a subsystem, system, or suprasystem and applying that information to improve human performance; realizing the implications of interventions on many parts of an organization, process, or individual and taking steps to address any side effects of human performance improvement interventions.
7. **Performance Understanding:** Distinguishing between activities and results; recognizing implications, outcomes, and consequences.
8. **Knowledge of Interventions:** Demonstrating an understanding of the many ways that human performance can be improved in organizational settings; showing how to apply specific human performance improvement interventions to close existing or anticipated performance gaps.
9. **Business Understanding:** Demonstrating awareness of the inner workings of business functions and how business decisions affect financial or nonfinancial work results (McLagan, 1989).
10. **Organization Understanding:** Seeing organizations as dynamic, political, economic, and social systems that have multiple goals; using this larger perspective as a framework for understanding and influencing events and change (McLagan, 1989).
11. **Negotiating/Contracting Skills:** Organizing, preparing, overseeing, and evaluating work performed by vendors, contingent workers, or outsourcing agents.
12. **Buy-in/Advocacy Skills:** Building ownership or support for change among affected individuals, groups, and other stakeholders.
13. **Coping Skills:** Knowing how to deal with ambiguity and how to handle the stress resulting from change and from multiple meanings or possibilities.
14. **Ability to See "Big Picture":** Looking beyond details to see overarching goals and results.
15. **Consulting Skills:** Understanding the results that stakeholders desire from a process and providing insight into how efficiently and effectively those results can be achieved.
16. **Project Management Skills:** Planning, costing, organizing, resourcing, and managing complex projects.

Figure 1-6 Competencies associated with the HPI roles. Source: Adapted from Rothwell, W. (2000). *ASTD Models for Human Performance Improvement: Roles, Competencies, and Outputs.* 2nd ed. Alexandria VA: The American Society for Training and Development. Used by permission of the American Society for Training and Development.

Analyst	Intervention Specialist
1. **Performance Analysis Skills (Front-end Analysis):** The process of comparing actual and ideal performance in order to identify gaps or opportunities.	1. **Performance Information Interpretation Skills:** Finding useful meaning from the results of performance analysis and helping performers, performers' managers, process owners, and other stakeholder to do so.
2. **Needs Analysis Survey Design and Development Skills (Open-ended and Structured):** Preparing written (mail), oral (phone), or electronic (e-mail) surveys using open-ended (essay) and closed (scaled) questions in order to identify human performance improvement needs.	2. **Intervention Selection Skills:** Selecting human performance improvement interventions that address the root cause(s) of performance gaps rather than symptoms or side effects.
3. **Competency Identification Skills:** Identifying the knowledge and skillrequirements of teams, jobs, tasks, roles, and work (McLagan, 1989).	3. **Performance Change Interpretation Skills:** Forecasting and analyzing the effects of interventions and their consequences.
4. **Questioning Skills:** Gathering pertinent information to stimulate insight in individuals and groups through use of interviews and other probing methods (McLagan, 1989).	4. **Ability to Assess Relationship Among Interventions:** Examining the effects of multiple human performance improvement interventions on parts of an organization, its interactions with customers, suppliers, distributors, and workers.
5. **Analytical Skills (Synthesis):** Breaking down the components of a larger whole and reassembling them to achieve improved human performance.	5. **Ability to Identify Critical Business Issues and Changes:** Determining key business issues and applying that information during the implementation of a human performance improvement intervention.
6. **Work Environment Analytical Skills:** Examining work environments for issues or characteristics affecting human performance.	6. **Goal Interpretation Skills:** Ensuring that goals are converted effectively into actions to close existing or pending performance gaps; getting results despite conflicting priorities, lack of resources, or ambiguity.

Figure 1-6 *Continued*

rapidly develop an awareness of the industry in order to develop context and be able to interact with, and have credibility with, their clients and executives. This industry awareness creates a recognition of the trends that are shaping it. This understanding helps practitioners to link analysis and intervention efforts to organizational goals that, in turn, take into account the external industry environment. Note that this competency focuses on awareness, implying that although an HPI practitioner need not become an industry expert, the more awareness of the issues, the better.

Leadership Skills: While people involved in performance improvement work may not possess formal leadership positions, they must constantly exert leader-

Change Manager	Evaluator
1. **Change Implementation Skills:** Understanding the nature of individual and organizational change and applying that knowledge to effectively lead organizations successfully through change.	1. **Groups Dynamics Process Understanding Performance Gap Evaluation Skills:** Measuring or helping others to measure the difference between actual perfomance and ideal performance.
2. **Change Impetus Skills:** Determining what the organization should do to address the cause(s) of a human performance gap at present and in the future.	2. **Ability to Evaluate Results Against Organizational Goals:** Assessing how well the results of a human performance improvement intervention match intentions.
3. **Communication Channel, Informal Network, and Alliance Understaning:** Knowing how communication moves through an organization by various channels, networks, and alliances; building such channels, networks, and alliances to achieve improvements in productivity and performance.	3. **Standard Setting Skills:** Measuring desired results of organizations, processes, or individuals; helping others to establish and measure work expectations.
4. **Groups Dynamics Process Understanding:** Understanding how groups function; influencing people so that group, work, and individual needs are addressed (McLagan, 1989).	4. **Ability to Assess Impact on Culture:** Examining the effects of human performance gaps and human performance improvement interventions on shared beliefs and assumptions about "right" and "wrong" ways of behaving and acting in one organizational setting.
5. **Process Consultation Skills:** Observing individuals and groups for their interactions and the effects of their interactions with others.	5. **Human Performance Improvement Intervention Reviewing Skills:** Finding ways to evaluate and continuously improve human performance improvement interventions before and during implementation.
6. **Facilitation Skills:** Helping performers, performers' managers, process owners, and stakeholders to discover new insights.	6. **Feedback Skills:** Collecting information about performance and feeding it back clearly, specifically, and on a timely basis to affected individuals or groups (McLagan, 1989).

Figure 1-6 *Continued*

ship behaviors. Effective leaders are able to create a sense of direction, rally people to action, and move toward the desired goals or the realization of a vision. While countless volumes have been written about the topic of leadership, Chevalier (2006) notes that very little has been written about leadership skills related to performance improvement, and he presents some useful strategies and tactics.

Interpersonal Relationship Skills: HPI practitioners must interface with many people in an organization during a typical performance improvement project. They may come into contact with representatives from top management, purchasing, finance, scheduling, front-line employees, supervisors, administrators, and virtually any other person inside, as well as outside, the organization. For this reason, the ability to work effectively with diverse groups in order to obtain information, communicate results, and build trust is paramount to success. Countless stories exist of people with superior technical skills who "derailed" in their job, role, or even career as a result of poor interpersonal skills. Thus, sound interpersonal relationship skills are essential to an HPI practitioner's success.

Technological Awareness and Understanding: Many interventions that are brought to bear on performance problems contain technological elements. While in-depth expertise in computer hardware and software may not be required, an awareness of the options available and the impact on performance is necessary. Practitioners may find themselves working on a project where technical specialists must be called upon. The ability to understand how technology will be used and its implications on performance is important. Further, a certain level of technical awareness enables an HPI practitioner to identify experts who must be called upon for a particular project or task.

Problem-Solving Skills: Human performance improvement is all about problem solving. The focus, however, is on human performance problems. The ability to engage in a systematic process to determine performance gaps, their causes, and workable solutions is the goal of HPI practitioners.

Systems Thinking and Understanding: An organization is a system within which are countless interconnected subsystems. In order to be successful, HPI practitioners must be able to view organizations as systems. During the analysis phase, it is important to examine the inputs, the processes, and the outputs that are being produced to pinpoint deficiencies. During the intervention selection and implementation planning phases, it is critical to take into account the inter-relationships among various system components to ensure that direct and indirect negative side effects are prevented.

Performance Understanding: The differences between activities and results have been covered in this chapter. Many who are unfamiliar with HPI mistake behaviors for accomplishments. This is quite easy to do because behaviors are often more visible and easy to label. Human performance improvement practitioners have this understanding of performance at the forefront of their thinking. When engaging in analysis, they focus on results and carefully select and implement interventions that will influence performance and achieve results.

Knowledge of Interventions: Chapter 3 is dedicated to the topics of interventions, often called "solutions," and intervention selection. A multitude of potential interventions exist that can be used to solve performance problems. While it is impossible to be an expert in all interventions, knowledge of options available is important. The more wide-ranging this knowledge of potential interventions, the more likely it will be that the appropriate one will be chosen and implemented. Also, as will be discussed in Chapter 3, it is important for HPI practitioners to be able to tap into people with expertise in various interventions.

Business Understanding: Often the client of the HPI practitioner is a line manager or other businessperson. Understanding the fundamental functions of a business and the interrelationships between functions is important. Such business understanding allows those engaged in performance improvement to speak the language of business leaders. This ability to communicate in business terms helps to build the credibility of HPI practitioners and facilitates understanding between business leaders and practitioners.

Organization Understanding: Similar to having business understanding, HPI practitioners must recognize how organizations function, in general, and specifically how their own organization operates. This competency relates also to systems thinking because it highlights the need for HPI practitioners to view the political, economic, and social components of organizations. These organization elements must be constantly monitored due to their changing nature.

Negotiating/Contracting Skills: During a given performance improvement project, a variety of external resources may be required. These include internal resources, such as other departments, as well as external resources, such as independent consultants, consulting firms, and other external vendors of products or services. For this reason, it is important that the HPI practitioner be able to negotiate and contract with such vendors. The contracting process may be less formal with internal groups, but is no less important to ensure expectations are met. Then, once a supplier is secured, it becomes necessary to monitor, evaluate, and manage work that is carried out so that the project stays on track and the desired results are attained. Internal as well as external suppliers become partners in the performance improvement process and are often an extension of the HPI practitioner and project team.

Buy-in/Advocacy Skills: Throughout the life cycle of a performance improvement project, practitioners must work to build support and commitment for the effort. They must facilitate the momentum building process that helps to get a project off the ground and through to completion. This applies not only to the implementation and change management phases of HPI, but also to the analysis and evaluation phases. The importance of analysis and evaluation must often be sold to management because of the propensity of many to jump to solutions. As with interpersonal relationship skills, which were mentioned earlier in this section, buy-in must be sought among a wide variety of constituents.

Coping Skills: Although systematic and structured in nature, many aspects of the human performance improvement process may be vague and unclear. There are many questions that remain unanswered and issues that are left unresolved. Further, scarce resources, limited budgets, political dynamics, level of support, and tight timelines add to the pressure and stress that is often experienced. HPI practitioners often feel as though they are flying by the seat of their pants while trying to shoot at a moving target. For this reason, coping skills are essential for seeing a project through to completion. Coping skills involve patience, persistence, and recognizing the dynamics of personal change and transition (Bridges, 2003), to which HPI practitioners are not exempt.

Ability to See the "Big Picture": There is a balance that HPI practitioners must strike between concentrating on the details while always maintaining a focus on the big picture. This competency relates to the ability to step back from the details and keep the larger issues and overall project in mind. This strategic perspective helps practitioners to ensure that project goals and purposes are being achieved, and that there are no disconnects between interrelated elements of organization.

Consulting Skills: HPI practitioners may be internal or external consultants. Regardless of their relationship to the organization, they must possess strong consulting skills. Consulting involves contracting, obtaining a firm grasp on the needs and desired results of the client and the client organization, making recommendations on how to best meet those needs, gaining buy-in, and many other related activities (Schaffer, 2002). This is best accomplished through forging a close, mutual partnership with the client. The role of the consultant is to facilitate self-discovery on the part of the client. It often involves the transference of the HPI skills and knowledge to the client so that dependence on the consultant is reduced and the client's capacity to engage in HPI is developed. Trust-based relationships are at the center of effective consulting engagements (Block, 2000).

Project Management Skills: Most human performance improvement projects have a discrete beginning and end. Further, many principles and techniques associated with basic project management can be applied to HPI activities. Such skills help in the establishment of goals, task items, milestones, and timelines as well as resource allocation, monitoring, and budgeting. Many software-based project management tools can also be incorporated into human performance improvement efforts to facilitate project management. Project management has become a more developed profession with standards created through the Project Management Institute, known as the Project Management Body of Knowledge (PMBOK) (PMI, 2006a). Project managers can also become certified and achieve a credential such as the Project Management Professional (PMP) (PMI, 2006b).

Outputs

A number of outputs are produced through the enactment of the competencies. An output is "a product or service that an individual or group delivers to others, especially to colleagues, customers, or clients" (McLagan, 1989). Figure 1-7 displays some outputs, or products or services, associated with each competency linked to HPI.

There are two primary types of outputs. A terminal output is "a final outcome directly associated with a particular role" (Rothwell, 2000). For example, a terminal output associated with the role of the analyst is "persuasive reports to stakeholders about past, present, and future performance gaps and their cause(s)" (Rothwell, 2000). An enabling output is "a specific output associated with the demonstration of a particular competency" (Rothwell, 2000). As the name implies, enabling outputs contribute to the delivery of the terminal output. For example, one of the enabling outputs linked with an analyst competency includes "statistical summaries of needs analysis results" (Rothwell, 2000).

HPI Competencies and Associated Output	
Core Competency	**Outputs**
Industry Awareness: Understanding the vision, strategy, goals, and culture of an industry or organization; linking human performance improvement interventions to organizational goals.	■ Descriptions of industry/organizational status
Leadership Skills: Knowing how to lead or influence others positively to achieve desired work results.	■ Positive influence on others exhibited
Interpersonal Relationship Skills: Working effectively with others to achieve common goals; exercising effective interpersonal influence	■ Positive relationships established and maintained with clients, stakeholders, and decision makers
Technological Awareness and Understanding: Using existing or new technology, different types of software and hardware and understanding performance support systems and applying them as appropriate.	■ Facility in using technology
Problem-Solving Skills: Detecting performance gaps and helping other people discover ways to close performance gaps in the present and future; closing performance gaps between actual and ideal performance.	■ Strategies for groups, teams, or individuals to discover present or anticipated performance gaps ■ Application of quality tools to identify special and general causes (histograms, trend charts, etc.). Written and oral briefings to performers, performers' managers, process owners and other stakeholders about performance gaps ■ Problem-solving activities to lead performers, performers' managers, process owners, and other stakeholders to discover/forecast the likely impact of multiple interventions on processes, individuals, or the organization
Systems Thinking and Understanding: Identifying inputs, throughputs, and outputs of a subsystem, system or suprasystem and applying that information to improve human performance; realizing the implications of interventions on many parts of an organization, process or individual; taking steps to address side effects of human performance improvement interventions.	■ Systems flowcharts showing the impact of interventions on processes, individuals, or the organization

Figure 1-7 HPI competencies and associated outputs. Source: Adapted from Rothwell, W. (2000). *ASTD Models for Human Performance Improvement: Roles, Competencies, and Outputs.* 2nd ed. Alexandria VA: The American Society for Training and Development. Used by permission of the American Society for Training and Development.

Core Competency	Outputs
Performance Understanding: Distinguishing between activities and results; recognizing consequences.	■ Written and oral descriptions of performance ■ Visual charts or other aids to show performance
Knowledge of Interventions: Demonstrating an understanding of the many ways that human performance can be improved in organizational settings; showing an understanding of how to apply specific human performance improvement interventions to close existing or anticipated performance gaps.	■ Employee recruitment programs ■ Employee orientation programs ■ Employee training programs using systematic approaches ■ Establishing learning organizations ■ Employee performance appraisal practices and programs ■ Career development programs ■ Organization development interventions ■ Compensation, reward, and incentive programs ■ Employee feedback programs ■ Employee discipline programs ■ Employee counseling and wellness programs ■ Safety programs ■ Improved tools and equipment ■ Improved on-the-job training ■ Improved on-the-job learning ■ Job aids ■ Organizational design ■ Job design ■ Task design ■ Ergonomic Improvements ■ Improved employee staff planning and forecasting programs ■ Other human performance improvement strategies/interventions
Business Understanding: Demonstrating awareness of the inner workings of business functions and how business decisions affect financial or nonfinancial work results (McLagan, 1989).	■ Flowcharts of work processes ■ Flowcharts of organizational operations/networks ■ Flowcharts of interactions with customers and other stakeholders ■ Cash flow statements ■ Budget documents ■ Income sheets and balance statements

Figure 1-7 *Continued*

Core Competency	Outputs
Organization Understanding: Seeing organizations as dynamic, political, economic, and social systems which have multiple goals; using this larger perspective as a framework for understanding and influencing events and change (McLagan, 1989).	■ Stories about organizational culture/ history and experiences ■ Descriptions of the likely impact of changes on different parts of an organization, work processes, or individuals
Negotiating/Contracting Skills: Organizing, preparing, overseeing and evaluating work performed by vendors, other contingent workers or outsourcing agents.	■ Requests for proposals ■ Written or oral proposals to management or to clients ■ Written and oral agreements ■ Management plans for oversight of vendors, contingent workers, or outsourcing agents
Buy-in/Advocacy Skill: Building ownership or support for change among affected individuals, groups, and other stakeholders.	■ Action plans ■ Agreements for action ■ Support for change voiced by performers, performers' managers, process owners and/or stakeholders
Coping Skill: Knowing how to deal with ambiguity and how to handle the stress resulting from change and from multiple meanings or possibilities.	■ Strategies for managing stress and ambiguity ■ Strategies for helping others manage stress and ambiguity ■ Strategies for addressing resistance to change
Ability to see the "Big Picture": Looking beyond details to see overarching goals and results.	■ Descriptions of the impact of human performance improvement strategy on organizational plans, work processes, and individuals
Consulting Skills: Understanding the results that stakeholders desire from a process and providing insight into how efficiently and effectively those results can be achieved.	■ Flowcharts ■ Policy and procedure preparation ■ Written policies ■ Written procedures ■ Preparation of work standards/expectations
Project Management Skills:** Planning, costing, organizing, resourcing, and managing complex projects.	■ Performance contracts ■ Project goals ■ Project task items ■ Project milestones ■ Project timelines ■ Project resource requirements ■ Resource management ■ Project budget

Figure 1-7 *Continued*

Analyst Role	Terminal Output
Conducts troubleshooting to isolate the cause(s) of human performance gaps or one who identifies areas in which human performance can be improved.	■ Persuasive reports to stakeholders about past, present, and future performance gaps and their cause(s)

Analyst Competencies	Enabling Outputs
1. **Performance Analysis Skills (Front-End Analysis):** The process of comparing actual and ideal performance in order to identify performance gaps or opportunities.	■ Models and plans to guide trouble-shooting of human performance gaps ■ Work plans to guide performance analysis ■ Information on trends affecting existing or possible future performance gaps ■ Task analysis ■ Job analysis ■ Observations
2. **Needs Analysis Survey Design and Development Skills (Open-Ended and Structured):** Preparing written (mail), oral (phone) or electronic (e-mail) surveys using open-ended (essay) and closed (scaled) questions to identify human performance improvement needs.	■ Written (mail) surveys ■ Oral (phone) surveys ■ Electronic (e-mail) surveys ■ Survey administration plans ■ Research designs ■ Data analysis and interpretation plans ■ Reports of needs analysis surveys ■ Statistical summaries of needs analysis results ■ Content analysis summaries of needs analysis results
3. **Competency Identification Skill:** Identifying the knowledge and skill requirements of teams, jobs, tasks, roles, and work (McLagen, 1989).	■ Work portfolios ■ Job descriptions ■ Behavioral events interview guides ■ Written critical incident survey questionnaires ■ Competency models by function, process, organization or work category ■ 360-degree assessments
4. **Questioning Skill:** Gathering information to stimulate insight in individuals and groups through use of interviews and other probing methods (McLagen, 1989).	■ Interview guides ■ Interview administration plans ■ Content analyses of interview results ■ Team meeting agendas and plans ■ Focus groups* ■ Interviews*
5. **Analytical Skill (Synthesis):** Breaking down the components of a larger whole and reassembling them to achieve improved human performance.	■ Strategies for analyzing the root cause(s) of performance gaps ■ Fishbone diagrams ■ Storyboards of problem events

Figure 1-7 *Continued*

Outputs Associated with the roles and Competencies of Human Performance Improvement Work	
Analyst Competencies	**Enabling Outputs**
6. **Work Environment Analytical Skill:** Examining work environments for issues or characteristics affecting human performance.	■ Environmental scans ■ Business/organization plans ■ Team/group plans ■ Process improvement strategies/plans
Intervention Specialist Role	**Terminal Output**
Selects appropriate interventions to address the root cause(s) of performance gaps.	■ Persuasive reports to stakeholders about the appropriate intervention(s) to close past, present or future performance gap(s)
Intervention Specialist Competencies	**Enabling Outputs**
1. **Performance Information Interpretation Skills:** Finding useful meaning from the results of performance analysis and helping performers, performers' managers, process owners, and other stakeholders to do so.	■ Written or oral briefings to performers, performers' managers, process owners, or other stakeholders about the results of performance analysis or cause analysis ■ Useful information drawn from performance or cause analysis
2. **Intervention Selection Skills:** Selecting human performance improvement interventions that address the root cause(s) of performance gaps, rather than symptoms or side effects.	■ Approaches for choosing appropriate human performance improvement strategies to close performance gaps
3. **Performance Change Interpretation Skill:** Forecasting and analyzing the effects of interventions and their side effects.	■ Written and oral briefings to performers, performers' managers, process owners, and other stakeholders about the likely impact of change or of a human performance improvement intervention on processes, individuals, or the organization ■ Problem-solving activities to lead performers, performers' managers, process owners and other stakeholders to discover/forecast the impact of an intervention's implementation on processes, individuals or the organization
4. **Ability to Assess Relationship Among Interventions:** Examining the effects of multiple human performance improvement interventions on parts of an organization, its interactions with customers, suppliers and distributors, and workers.	■ Written and oral briefings to performers, performers' managers, process owners, and other stakeholders about the likely impact of multiple interventions on processes, individuals or the organization ■ Problem-solving activities to lead performers, performers' managers, process owners, and other stakeholders to discover/forecast the likely impact of multiple interventions on processes, individuals, or the organization

Figure 1-7 *Continued*

Intervention Specialist Competencies	Enabling Outputs
5. **Ability to Identify Critical Business Issues and Changes:** Determining key business issues and applying that information during the implementation of a human prformance improvement intervention.	■ Organizational analyses ■ Process analyses ■ Individual assessments ■ White papers on improvement strategies ■ Oral and written briefings to performers, performers' managers, process owners or stakeholders about possible improvement strategies Customer satisfaction information/survey results
6. **Goal Interpretation Skills:** Ensuring that goals are converted effectively into actions to close existing or pending performance gaps; getting results despite conflicting priorities, lack of resources, or ambiguity.	■ Written or oral goals for human performance improvement ■ Performance objectives for interventions ■ Facilitated performance objectives

Change Manager Role	Terminal Outputs
Ensures that interventions are implemented in ways consistent with desired results and that they help individuals and groups achieve results.	■ Performance improvement interventions effectively monitored with participants and stakeholders ■ Effective interpersonal interactions among participants and stakeholder of interventions ■ Tracking systems to compare actual and ideal performance and progress toward narrowing or closing performance gaps, or realizing performance opportunities as the intervention is implemented ■ Oral and/or written agreements among most or all stakeholders about the results desired from the intervention ■ Measurable financial or nonfinancial objectives to be achieved during and after implementation of the intervention(s)

Figure 1-7 *Continued*

Change Manager Competencies	Enabling Outputs
1. **Change Implementation Skills:**** Understanding the nature of individual and organizational change and applying that knowledge to effectively lead organizations successfully through change.	■ Plans for managing the change ■ Effect involvement of stakeholders ■ Individual and organizational needs in balance ■ Conflict resolution utilized to resolve differences ■ Process for surfacing issues ■ Management understanding the dynamics of change
2. **Change Impetus Skills:** Determining what the organization should do to address the cause(s) of a human performance gap at present and in the future.	■ A convincing case made for the need for change ■ Organizational sponsorship identified and secured ■ Evidence of support obtained through commitment of resources ■ Designs/action plans for introducing and consolidating interventions ■ Designs/plans for reducing resistance to interventions ■ Recommendations to management about management's role in introducing and consolidating change ■ Recommendations to workers about their role in introducing and consolidating change
3. **Communication Channel, Informal Network, and Alliance Understanding:** Knowing how communication moves through an organization by various channels, networks, and alliances; building such channels, networks, and alliances to achieve improvements in productivity and performance.	■ Communication plans established to keep participants in change and stakeholders of change informed about the progress of the human performance improvement intervention
4. **Groups Dynamics Process Understanding:** Understanding how groups function; influencing people so that group, work, and individual needs are addressed (McLagan, 1989).	■ Groups successfully observed ■ Plans for influencing groups based on knowledge of small group development theory
5. **Process Consultation Skills:** Observing individuals and groups for their interactions and the effects of their interactions with others.	■ Group process observation forms ■ Descriptions to group members and individuals about the effects of their behavior on a group or on individuals
6. **Facilitation Skills:** Helping performers, performers' managers, process owners, and stakeholders to discover new insights.	■ Plans for facilitating group discussions ■ Plans for facilitating individual or group decision making and problem solving

Figure 1-7 *Continued*

Evaluator Role	Terminal Outputs
Assesses the impact of interventions and follows up on changes made, actions taken, and result achieved in order to provide participants and stakeholders with information about how well interventions are being implemented.	■ Written and oral reports to participants and stakeholders about the progress of an intervention ■ Written or oral reports to the organization about performance ■ Written or oral reports to the organization about progress of interventions ■ Written or oral reports to work groups or teams about their performance ■ Written or oral reports to work groups or teams about the progress of interventions ■ Written or oral reports to management about performance ■ Written or oral reports to management about interventions

Evaluator Competencies	Enabling Outputs
1. **Performance Gap Evaluation Skills:** Measuring or helping others to measure the difference between actual performance and ideal performance.	■ Human performance improvement evaluation objectives ■ Human performance improvement evaluation designs and plans ■ Human performance improvement evaluation instruments ■ Pre- and post-measures of worker performance ■ Evaluation findings, conclusions, and recommendations ■ Reports to management and workers on the outcomes of human performance improvement strategies
2. **Ability to Evaluate Results Against Organizational Goals:** Assessing how well the results of a human performance improvement intervention match intentions.	■ Linkage of human performance improvement interventions to other change efforts of the organization ■ Linkage of each human performance improvement intervention with other interventions ■ Linkage of human performance improvement interventions to organizational plans, goals and objectives ■ Linkage of human performance improvement interventions to organizational/business needs

Figure 1-7 *Continued*

Evaluator Competencies	Enabling Outputs
3. **Standard Setting Skills:** Measuring desired results of organizations, processes, or individuals; helping others to establish and measure work expectations.	■ Work standards/expectations established ■ Work standards/expectations communicated
4. **Ability to Assess Impact on Culture:** Examining the effects of human performance gaps and human performance improvement interventions as well as shared beliefs and assumptions about "right" and "wrong" ways of behaving and acting in one organizational setting.	■ Linkage of human performance improvement interventions to organizational culture
5. **Human Performance Improvement Intervention Reviewing Skills:** Finding ways to evaluate and continuously improve human performance improvement interventions before and during implementation.	■ Written and oral reports to stakeholders and participants about the progress of an intervention
6. **Feedback Skills:** Collecting information about performance and feeding it back clearly, specifically, and on a timely basis to affected individuals or group (McLagan, 1989).	■ Feedback to the organization about performance ■ Feedback to organization about progress of interventions ■ Feedback to work groups or teams about performance ■ Feedback to work groups or teams about progress of interventions ■ Feedback to management about performance ■ Feedback to management about interventions

*Additional outputs identified by King, S. B. (1998). *Practitioner Verification of the Human Performance Improvement Analyst Competencies and Outputs*. Doctoral dissertation. University Park, PA.

**Additional competencies identified by the authors.

Figure 1-7 *Continued*

The Growing Importance of Human Performance Improvement

In recent years, many workplace learning and performance professionals have attempted to broaden their perspective from providing training alone to engaging in human performance improvement work (Rothwell, 2000). The American Society for Training and Development (ASTD) in its annual State of the Industry report showed that best practice learning organizations in 2005 allocated 40 percent of their resources to nonlearning efforts and activities (Sugrue and

Rivera, 2005). Some training professionals began several years ago to reinvent themselves to become HPI practitioners, labeling themselves performance consultants or performance technologists (Robinson and Robinson, 1995a). In discussing this trend, Rothwell (2000) describes several points that capture the essence of the transformation toward human performance improvement and that still stand today:

> (1) A paradigm shift is underway in the training field that requires training professionals to shift their focus from such traditional development inputs as classes and hours to such outputs as performance at the individual, team, and organizational levels; (2) The shift from training to performance is beginning to manifest itself in changing titles, changing perceptions, and changing skill requirements for trainers; (3) The shift to human performance improvement holds great potential for transforming training in companies and increasing its value to the organization.

In addition to professionals who completely reinvent their roles, many trainers expand their focus to emphasize training for the purpose of impact or performance improvement versus training for the sake of training, sometimes referred to as activity-based training (Robinson and Robinson, 1989). Hequet (1995) notes that many training "gurus" have always advocated this performance perspective, but he later states that many organizations and individuals are only recently starting to hear the message.

Increasing emphasis is being placed on performance improvement as training professionals move away from training as the primary solution to all problems and situations and toward HPI, where analysis is paramount and a portfolio of potential solutions are possible. Countless books, articles, college courses, conference presentations, and workshops bear witness to this trend.

Many training professionals are expanding their perspective to emphasize results-based training. They have come to realize that thick course catalogs are poor measures of training effectiveness. Survey research conducted by the American Society for Training and Development (ASTD, 1994) discusses the shift to performance improvement as one of the primary trends in the training field.

"The emphasis in business on high-performance work will shift training content away from isolated skill building and information transfer to performance improvement and support" (ASTD, 1994). Trainers must "think performance. Accept that better performance is the only thing that matters in a competitive organization—and that if you can help make better performance happen, you will add real value. Don't limit your choice of methods to training."

The time is now to broaden your thinking from that of a traditional trainer to an HPI practitioner. The remainder of this book is designed to help you identify and develop the competence to do just that.

Summary

This chapter set the initial framework for performance and the practice of human performance improvement (HPI). The term *performance* was defined and a clear distinction was made between performance and behaviors. Performance refers to accomplishments, outcomes, and results that individuals, groups, and organizations achieve. Next, some of the key factors that influence performance were presented and discussed. This led to a description of key definitions and characteristics. Human performance improvement was defined as "a systematic process of discovering and analyzing important human performance gaps, planning for future improvements in human performance, designing and developing cost-effective and ethically justifiable interventions to close performance gaps, implementing the interventions, and evaluating the financial and nonfinancial results" (Rothwell, 2000).

A six-step human performance improvement process model, from the research-based competency study *ASTD Models for Human Performance Improvement*, was also introduced. The roles, competencies, and outputs associated with human performance improvement were introduced. Finally, the growing importance of HPI was explored.

References

Allerton, H. (1996). Hot! New Job Titles for Trainers (and Others). *Training & Development, 50*(7), 20–23.

American Society for Training and Development. (1994). Trends That Will Influence Workplace Learning and Performance in the Next Five Years. *Training & Development, 48*(5), S29–S35.

Block, P. (2000). *Flawless Consulting.* San Francisco: Jossey-Bass Pfeiffer.

Bridges, W. (2003). *Managing Transitions: Making the Most of Change.* Cambridge, MA: Da Capo Press.

Brinkerhoff, R.O. (2006). Using Evaluation to Measure and Improve the Effectiveness of Human Performance Technology Initiatives. In J.A. Pershing (Ed.) *Handbook of Human Performance Technology: Principles, Practices, Potential,* 287–311. San Francisco: Pfeiffer.

Buckingham, M., and Coffman, C. (1999). *First, Break all the Rules: What the World's Greatest Managers Do Differently.* New York: Simon & Schuster.

Buckingham, M., and Clifton, D.O. (2001). *Now, Discover Your Strengths.* New York: The Free Press.

Chevalier, R. (2006). Leadership in Performance Consulting. In J.A. Pershing (Ed.) *Handbook of Human Performance Technology: Principles, Practices, Potential,* 964–985. San Francisco: Pfeiffer.

Cram, D.D. (1992). If I Were King (Reflections on How I'd Set Up Training in My Corporation). *Training, 29*(4), 55–59.

Dean, P.J. (1994). *Performance Engineering at Work.* Batavia, IL: International Board of Standards for Training, Performance and Instruction.

Deterline, W.A., and Rosenberg, M.J. (Eds.). (1992). *Workplace Productivity: Performance Technology Success Stories.* Washington, DC: International Society for Performance Improvement.

Filipczak, B. (1994). The Training Manager in the '90s. *Training, 31*(6), 31–35.

Gilbert, T.F. (1978). *Human Competence: Engineering Worthy Performance.* New York: McGraw-Hill.

Harless, J. (1992). Whither Performance Technology? *Performance & Instruction, 31*(2), 4–8.

Harless, J. (1995). Performance Technology Skills in Business: Implications for Preparation. *Performance Improvement Quarterly, 8*(4), 75–88.

Hequet, M. (1995). The New Trainer. *Training, 32*(12), 23–29.

International Society for Performance Improvement. (2006). What Is HPT? Retrieved April 30, 2006, from www.ispi.org.

Jacobs, R.L. (1987). *Human Performance Technology: A Systems-Based Field for the Training and Development Profession.* Columbus, OH: ERIC Clearinghouse on Adult, Career, and Vocational Education, National Center for Research in Vocational Education, Ohio State University.

King, S.B. (1998). Practitioner Verification of the Human Performance Improvement Analyst Competencies and Outputs. Doctoral Dissertation. University Park, PA.

Kirkpatrick, D.L. (1994). *Evaluating Training Programs: The Four Levels.* San Francisco: Berrett-Koehler.

Langdon, D.G., Whiteside, K.S., and McKenna, M.M. (Eds.) (1999). *Intervention Resource Guide: 50 Performance Improvement Tools.* San Francisco: Jossey-Bass/Pfeiffer.

McLagan, P. (1989). *Models for HRD Practice.* Alexandria, VA: The American Society for Training and Development.

Pershing, J.A. (Ed.) (2006). *Handbook of Human Performance Technology: Principles, Practices, Potential.* San Francisco: Pfeiffer.

Phillips, J.J. (2003). *Return on Investment in Performance Improvement Programs,* 2nd ed. Woburn, MA: Butterworth–Heineman.

Project Management Institute. (2006a). *A Guide to the Project Management Body of Knowledge,* 3rd ed. Newtown Square, PA: Project Management Institute, Inc.

Project Management Institute. (2006b). PMI Certification Program. Retrieved April 30, 2006, from www.pmi.org.

Robinson, D.G., and Robinson, J.C. (1989). *Training for Impact: How to Link Training to Business Needs and Measure the Results.* San Francisco: Jossey-Bass.

Robinson, D.G., and Robinson, J.C. (1995a). *Performance Consulting: Moving Beyond Training.* San Francisco: Berrett-Koehler.

Robinson, J.C., and Robinson, D.G. (1995b). Performance Takes Training to New Heights. *Training & Development, 49*(9), 21–24.

Rossett, A. (1999). *First Things Fast: A Handbook for Performance Analysis.* San Francisco: Jossey-Bass/Pfeiffer.

Rothwell, W. (2005). *Beyond Training and Developing: The Groundbreaking Classic,* 2nd ed. New York: Amacom.

Rothwell, W.J. (1995). Beyond Training and Development. Unpublished research study. University Park, PA: The Pennsylvania State University.

Rothwell, W.J. (2000). *ASTD Models for Human Performance Improvement: Roles, Competencies, and Outputs,* 2nd ed. Alexandria, VA: The American Society for Training and Development.

Rothwell, W.J., and Sredl, H.J. (2000). *The ASTD Reference Guide to Workplace Learning and Performance: Present and Future Roles,* 3rd ed. 2 vols. Amherst, MA: HRD Press.

Rummler, G.A., and Brache, A.P. (1990). *Improving Performance: How to Manage the White Space on the Organization Chart.* San Francisco: Jossey-Bass.

Schaffer, R.H. (2002). *High Impact Consulting: How Clients and Consultants Can Work Together to Achieve Extraordinary Results,* 2nd ed. San Francisco: Jossey-Bass.

Smalley, K.A., and DeJong, M.J. (1995). Strategic Planning: From Training to Performance Technology Within Three Years. *Performance Improvement Quarterly, 8*(2), 114–124.

Sorohan, E.G. (1996). The Performance Consultant at Work. *Training & Development, 50,* 34–38.

Stolovitch, H.D., and Keeps, E. (Eds.) (1999). *Handbook of Human Performance Technology: A Comprehensive Guide for Analyzing and Solving Performance Problems in Organizations.* San Francisco: Jossey-Bass.

Sugrue, B., and Rivera, R.J. (2005). *2005 State of the Industry: ASTD's Annual Review of Trends in Workplace Learning and Performance.* Alexandria, VA: American Society for Training and Development.

Swanson, R.A. (1996). *Analysis for Improving Performance: Tools for Diagnosing Organizations & Documenting Workplace Expertise.* San Francisco: Berrett-Koehler Publishers Inc.

Van Tiem, D.M., Moseley, J.L., and Desssinger, J.C. (2004). *Fundamentals of Performance Technology.* Washington, DC: International Society for Performance Improvement.

The Role of Analyst

Chapter 1 set the stage for human performance improvement by defining foundational terms and by emphasizing the importance of HPI. The HPI process model was presented as a systematic way to approach performance improvement efforts in organizations. The first chapter provided a broad overview of HPI. This chapter descends from that high-level perspective and zeroes in on the first role associated with HPI—that is, the analyst role. This role, as well as the six key competencies and associated outputs, is defined and described in this chapter. An important goal is to introduce readers to some key analytical tools and models used by HPI practitioners as they analyze human performance problems and improvement opportunities. The chapter details practical strategies for enacting the analyst role and opens with a case to dramatize the importance of analysis and the role of the analyst.

A Case Study

As your read the following case study, think about the role played by the people in the case.

The Setting*

The San Diego Unified School District, the nation's eighth largest school district, provides an array of programs for which transportation services are provided.

Source: This case is used by permission of the International Society for Performance Improvement. The source is Deterline, W., and Rosenberg, M. (1992). San Diego Unified School District: The Power of Performance Analysis. In W. Deterline and M. Rosenberg (Ed.), *Workplace Productivity Performance Technology: Success Stories.* Washington, DC: International Society for Performance and Instruction, Suite 1250, 1300 L. Street, N.W., Washington, DC 20005.

For these programs, the district's transportation department buses nearly 16,000 students each school day. Smooth operations depend on a cooperative relationship between transportation staffers (particularly dispatchers and clerks) and school staff personnel.

The principal at each school selects a transportation site liaison each school year. The liaison assignment is a duty in addition to regular responsibilities and assignments. The duties of the site liaisons include:

- Being an advocate on behalf of students and parents
- Promoting resident school programs, especially those supported by the transportation service
- Implementing, supporting, and explaining relevant district and transportation department policies and decisions

The Problem/Opportunity

Both the coordinator of one of the district's major desegregation programs and the assistant director of Transportation Services were being deluged by complaints about poor transportation services, especially when those services were seen to impact the district's desegregation programs. The district first sought to design a new manual to provide better guidelines for the site liaisons. The nature of the complaints suggested that the problems might require more than a simple training solution. Some of the complaints identified problems that were beyond the control of the site liaisons, no matter how well-trained they might be. Other complaints, however, suggested that some of the problems seemed to originate outside the scope of the site liaison's responsibilities.

The Performance Technology Solution

An extensive performance analysis was conducted, including:

- An examination of relevant transportation and related records
- Interviews with program administrators, transportation staff members, school personnel, and parents
- Reviews of existing school bulletins and directives
- A review of the existing manual for site liaisons

The findings of the performance analysis pointed to several situations and conditions. In addition to the need for formal training of site liaisons:

- Liaison duties varied from one school site to another, depending, in part, on the liaison's paid position;
- Problem resolution was impacted by an outdated phone system;
- No one at the transportation department was assigned responsibility for resolving chronic service problems;
- Liaisons expressed frustration over defending transportation department decisions in which they had played no role.

Results

As a result of these findings, recommendations were made and implemented, such as:

- The transportation department now provides biannual formal training of site liaisons;
- A new *Transportation Site Liaison Handbook* has been developed;
- The transportation department's vision and mission statements stress customer satisfaction as well as bus routes and schedules;
- Transportation staffers regularly visit school sites to advise and better understand the environments in which liaisons work;
- Liaisons can air concerns in a special column added to the transportation department newsletter;
- Principals have been given district-provided selection criteria;
- A new phone system has been installed to improve accessibility.

The number of complaints regarding transportation service has dropped dramatically. The site liaisons have a clearer view of their responsibilities and authorities. The new phone system has greatly facilitated problem resolution, and transportation staffers and site liaisons report improved working and personal relationships.

Thus, the first step in the performance technology process, analysis, proved instrumental in uncovering the real causes of the problems of the transportation department, thus assuring that the recommended solutions would achieve the desired results: better performance and fewer complaints.

Defining Analysis

Analysis serves a vital purpose in performance improvement efforts conducted in organizational settings. Various methods were employed in the case study to accurately identify and define the problem. As shall be seen, many have argued that analysis is the most important aspect in the entire HPI process. The purpose of analysis in performance improvement efforts is comparable to the diagnostic process undertaken by physicians. Before a physician prescribes a treatment for an ailing patient, the patient is systematically diagnosed. Through this careful analysis, in which various tools and mental models are utilized, the physician identifies the problem's source, determines possible causes, isolates the most acute cause(s), and makes an accurate diagnosis that sets in motion therapeutic treatment. The treatment is akin to the focus of the next chapter, which will deal with intervention selection.

The parallels with analysis in human performance improvement are close. HPI practitioners sometimes use the doctor-patient approach. Through the diagnostic phase of human performance analysis, the HPI practitioner can troubleshoot the cause(s) of the problem and then select appropriate human performance improvement intervention(s)—that is, the "cures" or the "solutions"—to address those causes. The purpose of analysis, then, is to accurately diagnose the problem or situation and set the stage so that the appropriate intervention(s) can be selected, implemented, and evaluated to achieve positive performance results and outcomes. It should be noted that many practitioners have assumed a less-directive stance and attempt to facilitate HPI efforts among others in the organization. This, however, in no way diminishes the emphasis placed on analysis. In fact, the partnership or collaborative approach to performance analysis is clearly an approach that can help to build not only the trust and confidence of the client but also the buy-in and commitment to the eventual solution that arises from the analysis efforts.

Thomas Gilbert (1982), a pioneer of the performance improvement field, provided another excellent context for viewing analysis and its position and purpose in human performance improvement work. He wrote:

> To cope with the explosion of thoughts and answers, we need some framework—some sets of questions—to help us keep an eye on what we are trying to accomplish and to sort out, in some logical way, the useful means for accomplishing it. Performance analysis provides such a structure. It is an attempt at a method of disciplining ourselves as we seek to delineate our problems before we rush into a solution.

The Importance of Analysis

Many people who have written about HPI tout the importance of analysis. HPI practitioners must "diagnose situations before implementing solutions"

(Rummler and Brache, 1995). To cite a few other examples of authors who have emphasized the importance of analysis, consider the following memorable quotes:

- "Because the analysis phase defines, frames, and directs the remaining steps, it is considered the most critical" (Swanson, 1994).
- "The foundation of the HPT model is the analysis of human performance" (Elliot, 1996).
- "Without analysis, there is no Human Performance Technology (HPT). Analysis provides the foundation for HPT, a profession and a perspective that demands study before recommendations, data before decisions, and involvement before actions" (Rossett, 1999a).
- "The most important human performance improvement role is that of analyst" (Kirrane, 1997).

Many other practitioners and researchers have echoed the importance of analysis (see Spitzer, 1988; Hutchison, 1990; Robinson and Robinson, 1995; Marker, 1995; Harless, 1995; Rossett and Czech, 1995; and Medsker, Stepich, and Rowland, 1995). The number of quotations and references is ample testimony to the importance of analysis. We agree to the criticality of analysis, and our intent for the remainder of this chapter is to introduce readers to key definitions as well as to practical models and tools for carrying out analysis activities.

Definitions of Analysis

As a process, analysis wears many labels. Recall that the definition for the role of the analyst was presented earlier in this chapter. Analysis has a number of names, including all of the following:

- Front-end analysis (Harless, 1973)
- Performance analysis (Gilbert, 1978; Sleezer, 1992)
- Performance assessment (Robinson and Robinson, 1995)
- Performance audit (Rothwell, 1989)
- Performance diagnosis (Ruona and Lyford-Nojima, 1997)
- Training needs assessment (Rossett, 1987)
- Needs analysis (Kaufman, 1986)

While there is some conceptual overlap among the meanings of these terms, there is also much inconsistency. Some authors, for instance, have expressed disdain over the term "training needs assessment" (Watkins and Kaufman, 1996). They argue that attaching the word *training* to *needs assessment* represents an erroneous assumption that training is the appropriate solution before knowing if a problem exists and (if it does) what causes it.

While a wide variety of terms, definitions, and perspectives exists, it is critical to convey the definitions and assumptions that will be used in this context. Analysis, for the purpose of this book, is an assessment and analysis of human performance rather than of training or other prescriptive purposes. Anyone who undertakes analysis concentrates on identifying problems or opportunities in these areas and surfacing the cause(s) so that one or more appropriate interventions can be recommended that will lead to improvement.

There are two steps in the HPI process model that are linked with the role of the analyst. These are performance analysis and cause analysis. Both are described below.

Performance Analysis

Performance analysis is "the process of identifying the organization's performance requirements and comparing them to its objectives and capabilities" (Rothwell, 2000). It involves the identification of gaps, or discrepancies, in performance. A discrepancy can be thought of as the difference between current and desired performance levels. Allison Rossett (1999b) uses the terms "optimals" and "actuals." For example, if a customer care center's desired performance (optimals) is a 30-second wait time and the current performance level is a 55-second wait (actuals), then the discrepancy—the performance gap—is 25 seconds. Twenty-five seconds may not seem like a huge gap at first glance, but if translated into a dollar value, it could be worth millions. Through this simple example it probably becomes readily apparent how performance analysis begins to set the stage for evaluation—the last stage of the HPI process. The description of a discrepancy shown in Figure 2-1 is frequently cited as a simple formula:

Desired Performance – Current Performance = Performance Gap or Discrepancy.

In addition to defining the gap in performance, part of the performance analysis process involves assessing (or at least estimating) the impact, results, or consequences of the discrepancy.

Another way of viewing the impact of the discrepancy is to ascertain how much "pain" is being felt by organizational stakeholders as a result of the gap.

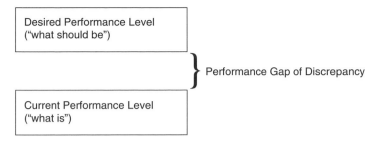

Figure 2-1 Performance gap or discrepancy.

There are direct costs, such as poor quality resulting in products that cannot be sold, downtime, or other tangible costs to the organization. Then there are opportunity costs that are not quite as easy to measure but that have a direct impact on the bottom line, such as missed sales and less-than-optimum productivity. Finally, there are intangible costs, such as employees' morale and customer confidence. While these are difficult to assign an actual cost to, they are critical factors in determining the true "pain" an organization is experiencing due to a performance problem.

Why is determining the impact so important? One reason is to ensure that the cost of minimizing or eliminating the problem does not exceed the cost of the problem in the first place, thus resulting in a negative return on investment (ROI). In most cases, the true cost of a performance discrepancy is far greater than management realizes. Therefore, calculating this cost, and sharing it with management at the onset of a performance improvement effort, will help you generate management support for your work.

In addition to assessing problems, performance analysis can involve assessing opportunities for new performance as well. For example, if new technology is to be introduced into an organization, then desired performance levels can be determined and analyzed void of any immediate problems. The notion of focusing on what could be in an ideal world has received much attention in recent years. Much of this popularity can be indirectly linked to the work of David Cooperider in the area of appreciative inquiry, which focuses not on fixing problems but on finding possibilities, often drawing upon people's most positive experiences to envision success (Cooperrider et al, 2000; Cooperrider and Whitney, 2005). The outcome of performance analysis, according to *ASTD Models for Human Performance Improvement*, "should be a clear description of existing and desired conditions surrounding performance" (Rothwell, 2000).

Cause Analysis

The second part of analysis is cause analysis. Cause analysis is defined as "the process of determining the root cause(s) of past, present, or future performance gaps. It follows, but is integrally related to, performance analysis" (Rothwell, 2000). Cause analysis involves examining the discrepancies identified through performance analysis and determining their root cause(s). In other words, cause analysis attempts to determine the reason for the discrepancy. Returning to our customer care center example, the performance analyst, upon defining the gap of 25 seconds in wait time (current wait time of 55 seconds minus a desired wait time of 30 seconds), would now begin determining the reason(s) for this discrepancy. Perhaps the gap is due to understaffing, perhaps some call center reps are on a slower technology than others, perhaps there are spikes in call volumes during certain times of the day, perhaps no one has ever informed the reps of the goal of 30 seconds, perhaps reps have never received feedback on their current performance—perhaps, perhaps, perhaps. As you have gathered, the reasons for a gap in performance are limitless, and thus, the purpose of cause analysis is to figure out what factors are truly affecting performance.

Many tools and models exist that can be applied to determining the cause(s) of performance problems. Some are described later in this chapter. The outcome of cause analysis "should be a clear description of the cause(s) of the performance gaps" (Rothwell, 2000).

Levels of Analysis

Performance can be viewed from several vantage points, including the organizational level, the work or process level, and the individual performer level (Rummler and Brache, 1990). Describing performance according to these levels helps those who conduct analysis to more clearly delineate the scope of what they are investigating, while also establishing an understanding of the interrelationships among the levels.

Moving from highest to lowest, the organizational level of analysis focuses on the ability of the organization to meet customer needs, compete in the marketplace, carry out strategies, and achieve goals, such as sales, profitability, safety, and market share. Analysts will sometimes find themselves explaining performance issues at this higher, more strategic level. They may also begin analysis efforts at this level and "drill down" to isolate key variables at the other levels.

The work or process level deals with the internal systems and processes that are in place to achieve the goals of the organization. Many organizations have been experimenting with process improvement strategies, such as continuous improvement programs, Six Sigma efforts, and other similar initiatives, and those are clearly focused on this level of analysis.

Finally, the individual performer level of analysis relates to the people carrying out work activities in the organization. Taken collectively, these individual performers produce results through the organizational processes that contribute to the overall performance of the organization. Various models and tools, which are introduced later in this chapter, can be helpful in analyzing performance at each level.

The Analyst's Role

According to *ASTD Models for Human Performance Improvement* (Rothwell, 2000), the analyst is the role that "conducts troubleshooting to isolate the cause(s) of human performance gaps or identifies areas in which human performance can be improved." The role is linked directly to performance analysis and cause analysis in the HPI process model appearing in *Models*.

Competencies Associated with the Role of Analyst

ASTD Models for Human Performance Improvement identified six key competencies that are associated with the role of the analyst. They represent the important characteristics that contribute to exemplary performance and success in the role. Chapter 8 also discusses a self-assessment tool that can be used to calculate individual development needs. In addition, Appendix III provides a comprehensive list of resources, current at the time this book went to press, for building competence in each competency area. The six competencies linked to the analyst role are (Rothwell, 2000):

- **Performance analysis skills (front-end analysis):** Comparing actual and ideal performance in order to identify performance gaps or opportunities
- **Needs analysis survey design and development skills (open-ended and structured):** Preparing written (mail), oral (phone), or electronic (e-mail) surveys using open-ended (essay) and closed (scaled) questions in order to identify human performance needs

- **Competency identification skills:** Identifying the knowledge and skill requirements of teams, jobs, tasks, roles, and work
- **Questioning skills:** Gathering pertinent information to stimulate insight in individuals and groups through the use of interviews and other probing methods
- **Analytical skills (synthesis):** Breaking down the components of a larger whole and reassembling them to achieve improved human performance
- **Work environment analytical skills:** Examining work environments for issues or characteristics affecting human performance

Outputs Linked to the Role

Each competency of the analyst role is linked to a number of outputs that generally represent the tangible outcomes or results that are produced when someone enacts the competencies. Figure 2-2 lists the outputs related to each of the six analyst competencies.

As you read through the list, you may wish to compare some of the outputs you currently produce—if you are employed and have an opportunity to apply HPI—with those shown in Figure 2-2. Are there outputs that you do not produce in your job? Are there outputs that you currently produce that are not shown?

What It All Means

Taken together, the role, competencies, and work outputs of the analyst are the foundation upon which the HPI model can stand. HPI is data driven; therefore, the role of analyst is the most critical factor in the entire process. The outputs of this role are the basis for all decisions forthcoming in the performance improvement efforts. If the mark is missed at this stage, tremendous amounts of time, effort, and financial resources may be squandered on activity that does not solve the problem or achieve the goal.

Analysts may apply their competencies as illustrated by the following examples:

- With performance analysis skills (front-end analysis), analysts may:
  - ☐ Identify the best sources of data to identify existing gaps or expected gaps due to anticipated changes in the work processes or environment
  - ☐ Work with job holders, their managers, exemplary (star) performers, and possibly their customers to complete job and task analyses

Analyst Role	Terminal Output
Conducts troubleshooting to isolate the cause(s) of human performance gaps or one who identifies areas in which human performance can be improved.	■ Persuasive reports to stakeholders about past, present and future performance gaps and their cause(s)

Analyst Competencies	Enabling Outputs
1. **Performance Analysis Skills (Front-End Analysis):** The process of comparing actual and ideal performance in order to identify performance gaps or opportunities.	■ Models and plans to guide troubleshooting of human performance gaps ■ Work plans to guide performance analysis ■ Information on trends affecting existing or possible future performance gaps ■ Task analysis ■ Job analysis ■ Observations*
2. **Needs Analysis Survey Design and Development Skills (Open-Ended and Structured):** Preparing written (mail), oral (phone) or electronic (e-mail) surveys using open-ended (essay) and closed (scaled) questions to identify human performance improvement needs.	■ Written (mail) surveys ■ Oral (phone) surveys ■ Electronic (e-mail) surveys ■ Survey administration plans ■ Research designs ■ Data analysis and interpretation plans ■ Reports of needs analysis surveys ■ Statistical summaries of needs analysis results ■ Content analysis summaries of needs analysis results
3. **Competency Identification Skill:** Identifying the knowledge and skill requirements of teams, jobs, tasks, roles, and work (McLagen,1989).	■ Work portfolios ■ Job descriptions ■ Behavioral events interview guides ■ Written critical incident survey questionnaires ■ Competency models by function, process, organization or work category ■ 360-degree assessments
4. **Questioning Skill:** Gathering information to stimulate insight in individuals and groups through use of interviews and other probing methods (McLagen, 1989).	■ Interview guides ■ Interview administration plans ■ Content analyses of interview results ■ Team meeting agendas and plans ■ Focus groups*

Additional outputs identified by King, S. B. (1998). Practitioner Verification of the Human Performance Improvement Analyst Competencies and Outputs. Doctoral Dissertation. University Park, PA.

Figure 2-2 Analyst competencies and associated outputs. Source: Rothwell, W. (2000). *ASTD Models for Human Performance Improvement: Roles, Competencies, and Outputs.* 2nd ed. Alexandria, VA: The American Society for Training and Development. Used by permission of the American Society for Training and Development.

Analyst Competencies	Enabling Outputs
5. **Analytical Skill (Synthesis):** Breaking down the components of a larger whole and reassembling them to achieve improved human performance.	■ Strategies for analyzing the root cause(s) of performance gaps ■ Fishbone diagrams ■ Storyboards of problem events
6. **Work Environment Analytical Skill:** Examining work environments for issues or characteristics affecting human performance.	■ Environmental scans ■ Business/organization plans ■ Team/group plans ■ Process improvement strategies/plans

Figure 2-2   *Continued*

■ With needs analysis survey design and development skills (open-ended and structured), analysts may:
  □ Develop surveys to gather information on what is currently happening in the organization
  □ Work with management to help identify pertinent demographic information that should be gathered to report data in a meaningful way
■ With competency identification skills, analysts may:
  □ Utilize job and task analysis data to identify core and role-specific competencies for jobs and job families
  □ Create job descriptions for use in selection and hiring, job evaluation, and employee development
  □ Create 360-degree assessment tools
■ With questioning skills, analysts may:
  □ Interview key stakeholders who can provide essential input to determine the root cause(s) of a performance gap
  □ Prepare hiring and selection interview protocols
  □ Lead stakeholders through a process of discovery
■ With analytical skills (synthesis), analysts may:
  □ Utilize the data gathered from a survey or other data collection method and decipher the pertinent information that provides insight into the root cause(s) of a performance problem
  □ Interpret qualitative data and identify themes that provide insight into the cause(s) of performance gaps
■ With work environment analytical skills, analysts may:
  □ Study the physical layout of the work area and identify features that are impacting, enhancing, or impeding performance

- ☐ Investigate the channels of communication to determine if any barriers to information exist
- ☐ Determine an opportune way to achieve business results given the barriers and constraints in a given situation

Being able to identify the performance gap(s) that exist in an organization and then determine the root cause(s) of those gaps are the most critical skills of the analyst. Thus, perhaps performance analysis skills are the most critical to success in this role.

Models and Tools

Basic analytical tools must be mastered by all HPI practitioners for them to be successful (Carr and Totzke, 1995). The practice of HPI is replete with models and tools. A model is essentially a representation of some real-world phenomenon that is used for descriptive purposes. A city street map is an example of a common model because it represents an actual physical place. A map is useful for providing directions to someone who is seeking a destination, landmarks, and other points of interest. A model that may be used for HPI purposes serves a similar purpose in that it represents a way in which problems can be framed or activities can be described. Similar to models, tools help HPI practitioners conduct analysis. They give some degree of structure to an otherwise fluid process. While some distinguish between models and tools, they are discussed together here in order to introduce readers to practical approaches to conducting analysis.

Models and tools provide an analyst with organized and systematic methods for examining human performance problems and performance improvement opportunities. Similar to a hammer or a saw for a carpenter, analytical models and processes are contained in the toolbox of HPI practitioners to help them conduct their work efficiently and effectively. They provide the methods by which to examine performance problems and opportunities, and they provide the foundation by which subsequent improvement and evaluation efforts are organized and implemented.

The analytical models used by HPI practitioners can be categorized in a number of ways. Some models are comprehensive and thus assume a high-level, holistic focus, such as analysis at the organizational level. In contrast, other models are considered situational because they focus on a specific problem or situation. Another way to think of models is that some are most useful for describing current conditions, while others are most useful for exploring the root cause(s) of problems. This section reviews sources of data and then some of the more commonly used models and tools of HPI practitioners.

Sources of Data

Since HPI is data driven, the important topic of sources of data should be discussed. The focus is often on quantitative (numeric) performance measures concerning issues of quality, productivity, cost, timeliness, profitability, and so on. Equally important are qualitative (nonnumeric) data that exist. A number of potential sources of data can be drawn upon to gain insight and information to drive an analyst's performance improvement efforts (see Figure 2-3). As can be seen in this chart, data can come from various human or nonhuman sources. During HPI efforts, an analyst may be working with existing data (referred to as *extant data*), such as production or quality reports, or may be involved with generating new data, such as gathering data by conducting a survey.

Human Sources	Nonhuman Sources
Employees	Work records
Supervisors	Exit interviews
Executives	Help desk logs
Clients/customers	Absentee reports
Vendors/suppliers	Performance appraisal data
Star performers	Financial reports
Subject experts	Sales logs
	Survey data
	Benchmarking results
	Quality reports

Figure 2-3 Potential sources of data for analysts.

The diverse nature of the data sources that can be used by HPI analysts, along with the various functions that they perform, indicate that it is often necessary to interact with many people throughout the organization. The finance and accounting department, for instance, may be the owner of financial performance measures. Other members of the organization, such as engineers, operations managers, quality specialists, information systems, or human resource professionals, can supply analysts with other relevant data—such as productivity or efficiency metrics, quality records, operating reports, or exit interview data, to name a few. Since the analyst must interact with so many people during data gathering, it comes as no surprise that communication and interaction skills are important nontechnical competencies for HPI work.

One caveat should be mentioned concerning data sources, however: In many organizations, no tracking systems or data infrastructure is in place to gather, document, and monitor performance. In other cases, sources exist, but the data they provide are inadequate for analytical purposes. Still other problems exist when data are collected but are not used for performance monitoring and improvement efforts. For example, operating reports may be generated on a daily basis, but they may only be entered into a computer database for record-keeping purposes and then placed in a filing cabinet for storage.

When such situations are encountered, HPI analysts can pursue one of several possible strategies. One is to create a data collection system and establish a baseline to make it easier to carry out analysis. (Remember it will take time to accumulate enough data for valid analysis.) At other times, establishing a measurement system may actually become part of the recommended performance improvement intervention, especially when lack of information, expectations, or feedback regarding performance is identified as a root cause of, or contributor to, poor performance. In cases where data are collected, but not for the purpose of improving performance, the analyst may need to roll up his or her sleeves and pore over reams of paper files to dig up the data, organize it, and analyze it in a way that makes it meaningful. This is certainly one of the less glamorous activities in which analysts engage, but for some it is energizing.

Models and Tools for the Analyst's Role

The HPI process model, described in Chapter 1, is an example of a process model. The first two steps of this model—performance analysis and cause analysis—apply to the analyst's role. Detailed descriptions of how to carry out those steps were not provided previously. For this reason, the models described in this section attempt to provide readers with useful methods to carry out analysis in organizational or workplace settings.

The Rummler and Brache Model

In their book *Improving Performance* (1995), Rummler and Brache present a framework for viewing organizational performance systems (see Figure 2-4).

One axis of the model consists of three levels of performance—the organizational, process, and individual levels—that can be equated to the three organizational levels that were described earlier. The other axis is comprised of three performance needs—goals, design, and management. These three performance needs and three performance levels intersect to form a grid pattern with nine variables. This matrix provides the analyst with a structured way to examine human performance in dynamic organizational settings.

A clear strength of the Rummler and Brache model is that it is based on a systems perspective of the organization and illustrates the relationships between the three performance levels and needs. Of key importance is the assumption that organizations should be aligned in these areas. For example, in the area of goals, it is important for an organization to have a clear strategy and accompanying goals for making the strategy operational. At the process level of performance, the goals of the process should be congruent with the goals and strategies articulated at the organizational level. At the job/performer level of analysis, the

The Three Levels of Performance	The Three Performance Needs		
	Goals	Design	Management
Organization Level	Organization Goals	Organization Design	Organization Management
Process Level	Process Goals	Process Design	Process Management
Job/Performer Level	Job/Performer Goals	Job Design	Job/Performer Management

Figure 2-4 Nine performance variables. Source: Rummler, G.A., and Brache, A.P. (1995). *Improving Performance: How to Manage the White Space on the Organization Chart.* San Francisco: Jossey-Bass. Used by permission of the publisher.

goals, objectives, and standards for individuals should be aligned to those at the process level.

In this respect, there is consistency among the three levels such that performance at the job level contributes to process level outcomes, which (in turn) result in organizational accomplishments. Analysis may uncover a lack of congruence or alignment among these levels. When that is the case, a potential intervention to remedy this problem may include strategies to achieve goal alignment or cascading goals. Further, communication of these interrelationships can be a key vehicle for creating "line of sight" so that individuals can see how their efforts and accomplishments contribute to the results of the organization, which can be highly motivating in itself. The "balanced scorecard" (Kaplan and Norton, 1996, 2006) represents a common and powerful strategy used by organizations to create alignment around, and visibility into, a balanced set of metrics, including financial, customer, process, and learning.

Analysis may also result in the identification of problems or inefficiencies within the matrix. Various interventions may be recommended to bridge performance gaps. Intervention selection will be discussed at length in Chapter 3.

Regardless of the focus, with the Rummler and Brache model, the analyst can enter the organization and ask a series of probing questions to diagnose the current state of affairs. Figure 2-5 provides some general questions that analysts can pose to surface discrepancies or problem areas, as well as new performance opportunities.

Gilbert's Three Stages of Analysis

Thomas Gilbert is considered by many to be a key founder of the human performance improvement field. In his landmark text *Human Competence: Engineering Worthy Performance*, first published in 1978, Gilbert introduced a number of concepts, models, and tools of performance improvement. Many have become commonly accepted methods still used by HPI practitioners today. Further, many variations on Gilbert's themes and philosophies are evident in the tools and techniques of others.

To understand the performance matrix analytical framework that follows, it is important to first recognize how Gilbert views the analytical process. His three-stage process model is shown in Figure 2-6.

Stage One, labeled "models of accomplishment," is the starting point for the performance analysis process. In this step, the analyst attempts to create a model of exemplary performance. A model of performance begins by attempting to

Performance Needs

Perf. Levels	Goals	Design	Management
Organization	**ORGANIZATION GOALS** ■ Has the organization's strategy/direction been articulated and communicated? ■ Does this strategy make sense, in terms of the external threats and opportunities and the internal strengths and weaknesses? ■ Given this strategy, have the required outputs of the organization and the level of performance expected from each output been determined and communicated?	**ORGANIZATION DESIGN** ■ Are all relevant functions in place? ■ Are all functions necessary? ■ Is the current flow of inputs and outputs between functions appropriate? ■ Does the formal organization structure support the strategy and enhance the efficiency of the system?	**ORGANIZATION MGT** ■ Have appropriate function goals been set? ■ Is relevant performance measured? ■ Are resources appropriately allocated? ■ Are the interfaces between functions being managed?
Process	**PROCESS GOALS** ■ Are goals for key processes linked to customer/ organization requirements?	**PROCESS DESIGN** ■ Is this the most efficient/effective process for accomplishing the process goals?	**PROCESS MANAGEMENT** ■ Have appropriate process subgoals been set? ■ Is process performance managed? ■ Are sufficient resources allocated to each process? ■ Are the interfaces between process steps being managed?

	JOB GOALS	JOB DESIGN	JOB MANAGEMENT
Job/Performer	■ Are job outputs and standards linked to process requirements (which are, in turn, linked to customer and organization requirements)?	■ Are process requirements reflected in the appropriate jobs? ■ Are job steps in a logical sequence? ■ Have supportive policies and procedures beer developed? ■ Is the job environment ergonomically scund?	■ Do the performers understand the job goals (outputs they are expected to produce and standards they are expected to meet)? ■ Do the performers have sufficient resources, clear signals and priorities, and a logical job design? ■ Are the performers rewarded for achieving the job goals? ■ Do the performers know if they are meeting the job goals? ■ Do the performers have the necessary knowledge/skill to achieve the job goals? ■ If the performers were in an environment in which the five questions listed above were answered "yes," would they have the physical, mental, and emotional capacity to achieve the job goals?

Figure 2-5 The nine performance variables with questions. Source: Rummler, G.A., and Brache, A.P. (1995). *Improving Performance: How to Manage the White Space on the Organization Chart.* San Francisco: Jossey-Bass. Used by permission.

Figure 2-6   Gilbert's three stages of analysis. Source: Gilbert, T.F. (1996). *Human Competence: Engineering Worthy Performance.* Washington, DC: International Society for Performance Improvement (ISPI).

identify the key accomplishments or performance results, goals, or outcomes to be achieved. The focus is on top performance as it occurs at the organization, group, or individual level. The source of exemplary performance is typically a select set of "star performers"—those who consistently outperform the average or typical performer in that particular role or job category. In the sales world, the star performers might be the top 5 percent of revenue generators. A model of accomplishment attempts to describe the desired performance—in other words, what should be happening. It entails uncovering the key factors that separate the results achieved by the stars from the other performers. What are the factors that most contribute to the success of the top 5 percent of the sales force?

Stage Two is labeled "measures of deficiency" because the focus is on determining the current level of individual, group, or organizational performance. Whereas the desired level of performance focused on what should be happening, the current level concentrates on what is happening. When information about the current performance level is gathered, it can then be compared with the desired performance level (from Stage One).

The difference between current and desired performance forms the performance gap or performance discrepancy. In addition to defining the performance gap, the analyst must also determine why the gap exists—a process Gilbert called causal analysis.

Finally, Stage Three, labeled "methods of improvement," involves proposing solutions designed to close the gap between current and desired performance. It is equivalent to intervention selection, which will be the focus of Chapter 3. As Chapter 3 will demonstrate, literally hundreds of potential solutions can be applied to close performance gaps.

Gilbert's Performance Matrix

Gilbert's simplified performance matrix is displayed in Figure 2-7 and has as its foundation the three stages of analysis discussed earlier.

Levels	STAGES		
	A Accomplishment Models	B Measures of Opportunity	C Methods of Improvement
I Policy (Institutional Systems)	Organization models 1. Cultural goal of the organization 2. Major missions 3. Requirements and units 4. Exemplary standards	Stakes analysis 1. Performance measures 2. Potential for Improving Performance (PIPs) 3. Stakes 4. Critical roles	Programs and policies 1. Environmental programs (data/tools/incentives) 2. People programs (knowledge/ selection/recruiting) 3. Management programs (organization/resources/standards)
II Strategy (Job Systems)	Job models 1. Mission of job 2. Major responsibilities 3. Requirements and units 4. Exemplary standards	Job assessment 1. Performance measures 2. Potential for Improving Performance (PIPs) 3. Critical responsibilities	Job strategies 1. Data systems 2. Training designs 3. Incentive schedules 4. Human factors 5. Selection systems 6. Recruitment systems
III Tactics (Task System)	Task models 1. Responsibilities of tasks 2. Major duties 3. Requirements and units 4. Exemplary standards	Task analysis 1. Performance measures or observations 2. Potential for Improving Performance (PIPs) 3. Specific deficiencies 4. Cost of programs	Tactical instruments 1. Feedback 2. Guidance 3. Training 4. Reinforcement 5. Selection

Figure 2-7 Gilbert's simplified performance matrix. Source: Gilbert, T.F. (1996). *Human Competence: Engineering Worthy Performance*. Washington, DC: International Society for Performance Improvement (ISPI). Used by permission.

This framework merges the three stages of analysis with the three levels of policy, strategy, and tactics. The result is a comprehensive way to analyze performance problems and pinpoint possible solutions. The performance matrix expands on the three stages of analysis by introducing three vantage points represented by the three levels. With each level, the matrix is meant to be worked from left to right.

First, an accomplishment model is created that describes desired performance. Next, the actual performance is identified and compared with desired performance to articulate the gap or discrepancy. It is important to identify the causes of the gap through some means of root cause analysis. Some useful strategies for cause analysis will be described later in this chapter.

Finally, the far right-hand column lists potential methods of improvement based on the identified root cause. Use of Gilbert's performance matrix can guide an analyst's diagnostic efforts. It can thus help to surface and isolate areas in which problems or opportunities exist. Another value is that it points toward potential solutions based on the level of analysis and the problem situation.

Gilbert's Behavior Engineering Model

Another performance analysis model, developed by Thomas Gilbert (1978) and described in *Human Competence*, is the behavior engineering model (BEM). The BEM is shown in Figure 2-8.

The behavior engineering model is comprehensive. It provides a wide perspective to diagnoses of performance problems. When examining a particular job, for instance, if all the aspects listed in the model were in place, then the likelihood of competence and successful performance would be high. When they are missing or inadequate, the result is decreased performance. The BEM consists of two levels or dimensions. The environmental supports represent those influences that exist in the work environment that affect performance. Performance standards is an example of an environmental support. The second dimension, the person's repertory of behavior, indicates those factors possessed by the individual performer that affect performance. A person's knowledge and skill in project management is an example.

The items listed across the top of the BEM framework represent stimuli, response, and consequences. These make explicit the behavioral psychology roots upon which much of Gilbert's work rest. These translate into the elements of information, instrumentation, and motivation.

	Information	Instrumentation	Motivation
Environmental supports	*Data* 1. Relevant and frequent feedback about the adequacy of performance 2. Descriptions of what is expected of performance 3. Clear and relevant guide to adequate performance	*Instruments* 1. Tools and materials of work designed scientifically to match human factors	*Incentives* 1. Adequate financial incentives made contingent upon performance 2. Nonmonetary incentives made available 3. Career-development opportunities
Person's repertory of behavior	*Knowledge* 1. Scientifically designed training that matches the requirements of exemplary performance 2. Placement	*Capacity* 1. Flexible scheduling of performance to match peak capacity 2. Prosthesis 3. Physical shaping 4. Adaptation 5. Selection	*Motives* 1. Assessment of people's motives to work 2. Recruitement of people to match the realities of the situation

Figure 2-8 The behavior engineering model. Source: Gilbert, T. F. (1996). *Human Competence: Engineering Worthy Performance*. Washington, DC: International Society for Performance Improvement (ISPI). Used by permission.

When examining performance, an analyst is advised to begin at the box in the upper left section of the model, where the focus is information at the environmental level. The troubleshooting process should proceed from left to right, beginning at the work environment level and then at the individual performer level, as shown in Figure 2-9.

In workplace settings today, there seems to be a great propensity among managers and others to approach problems in a manner that is exactly opposite to this. Many point to the person and blame poor performance on a lack of knowledge, capacity, or motivation. Some managers jump to the conclusion that "these people just aren't motivated" or "he's just not smart enough." This attitude underscores a tendency among some managers to blame people—or even specific individuals—for poor performance rather than to examine all elements related to their performance for contributory causes, including turning the mirror inward to look at their own role in the situation.

Gilbert's behavior engineering model assumes that most people want to do a good job and are generally capable. This assumption shifts the focus to aspects of the environment that can become obstacles to high performance. Sometimes managers resist this approach because they are often responsible for erecting these barriers. The focus, however, is not on placing blame or pointing fingers. Rather, the goal is to examine all variables influencing performance—both in

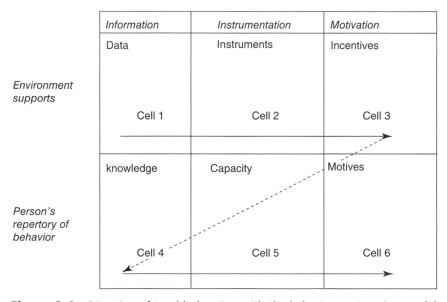

Figure 2-9 Direction of troubleshooting with the behavior engineering model.

the work environment and at the individual performer level—and structure them so that the desired performance is achieved.

A large number of performance problems relate to lack of information. Some believe that up to 80 percent of performance problems can be traced to this cause. For example, looking at the first cell of the BEM, information in the work environment level can be broadly classified as data. Such data may be represented as expectations, role clarity, feedback, or performance standards. As mentioned earlier, these environmental elements generally should be provided by managers. Many analysts have discovered that the major causes of poor performance are that standards have never been established, expectations about desired performance have never been communicated, people are unclear about their roles, and they do not receive clear, specific, relevant, or timely feedback about how well they are performing.

The value of the BEM is that, if aspects of the work environment are missing, they are often relatively easy to fix. It is much easier and less expensive, for instance, to establish standards (cell one), give people the tools they need (cell two), and recognize positive performance (cell three) than it is to increase their competence (cell four), their ability (cell five), or their motivations (cell six). One critique of the behavior engineering model is that it does not provide a comprehensive list of factors within each cell. Also, it does not explicitly direct the analyst toward specific solutions.

Mager and Pipe's Model

Unlike a comprehensive analysis framework, some models are more situation specific. A classic model that falls within this category is the troubleshooting model formulated by Robert Mager and Peter Pipe (1984) and described in their book *Analyzing Performance Problems, or You Really Oughta Wanna*. The Mager and Pipe model, as it is commonly called, is displayed in Figure 2-10.

As can be gathered by the manner in which the Mager and Pipe model is structured, it is designed as a flowchart with alternative branches, decision points, and, unlike Gilbert's BEM, suggested action steps. The process begins with the identification of a specific problem, perhaps through the application of one of the comprehensive analysis models described earlier. Alternatively, a specific problem may be identified when a customer, manager, or worker complains about something or when they request action (such as training) to solve a problem. If possible, the problem should be described in measurable,

PERFORMANCE ANALYSIS FLOWCHART

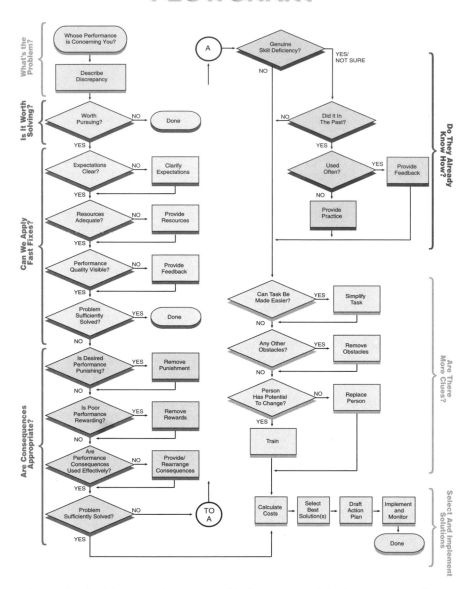

Figure 2-10 Mager and Pipe troubleshooting model. © 1997, "Analyzing Performance Problems". The Center for Effective Performance, Inc., 1100 Johnson Ferry Road, Suite 150, Atlanta, GA 30342. www.cepworldwide.com. 800-558-4237. Reprinted with permission. All rights reserved. No portion of these materials may be reproduced in any manner without the express written consent from The Center for Effective Performance, Inc.

observable, performance-based terms. It is thus worthwhile to describe the problem as a gap or discrepancy between current and desired performance.

Once the problem has been defined as precisely as possible, the analyst or others involved in the performance improvement process answer specific questions about the problem. For example, the first question after the performance discrepancy has been described is to decide whether the problem is important. This question requires the analyst, with the input of clients or other stakeholders, to place a value judgement on the discrepancy to determine the importance or the stakes associated with either solving the problem or ignoring it.

One view of this issue is to gauge how much "pain" the discrepancy is causing the various stakeholders who are affected by it. If, on one hand, the problem is considered unimportant, then the model suggests that it should be ignored—and attention focused on other problems where the payoff for action is higher. On the other hand, if the problem is judged to be important, then the next step is to determine if it involves a deficiency in skill. The model progresses in various directions depending on the response provided to that question.

One criticism of the Mager and Pipe troubleshooting model is that it tends to be too simplistic, especially considering the complex nature of most organizational problems. It is also difficult to answer questions about organizations with a simple "yes" or "no" response. Many problems encountered by analysts involve complex, ill-defined problems with multiple causes that call for multifaceted solutions. This is not to suggest that this HPI model is not powerful and useful to analysts. Indeed, the Mager and Pipe process provides a systematic means for addressing performance and has been used with great success by HPI practitioners and managers alike. When using any model, analysts should be keenly aware of the assumptions on which decisions were based and the weaknesses inherent in them.

Cause Analysis: Determining Root Causes

Analysts must be able to determine the root causes of performance problems they encounter. Too often, the symptoms or visible manifestations of problems are the focus of HPI, while the true cause remains unaddressed. These symptoms are called *presenting problems*. They are the consequences or results of another cause—not the cause itself. Managers and workers alike, however, may confuse the presenting problem with the cause.

A brief example is in order here. If a patient goes to the doctor and complains of a pain in the side, the doctor is made aware of a presenting problem (the complaint about the pain). The complaint should prompt the physician to seek underlying causes. In other words, why is the patient's side hurting?

The same principle applies to cause analysis. Suppose an organization is experiencing what the managers believe to be higher-than-normal turnover. Managers complain to others about it and might say something like this: "Our turnover is too high, so let's do something about it" or "We are spending too much time finding replacements." Of course, these complaints are akin to the patient's complaint to the doctor. High turnover—assuming that it is high, since that begs the question "compared to what?"—is only a presenting problem. The cause is not apparent. Similarly, the time spent on finding replacements is a consequence (side effect) of the problem rather than the problem itself. Surprisingly, a common response to such a situation is to try to reduce the time spent to secure replacements. A project team may even be formed to find ways to decrease the time to replace people. A great deal of time, money, and effort could be expended here rather than on the true cause. In reality, of course, there are many possible causes of turnover, and so a multipronged strategy may have to be discovered to uncover and attack those causes.

The danger for analysts is confusing the presenting problem or the consequence of the problem with the problem's root cause (the underlying reason for the problem). If that happens, analysts will tend to misdirect their attention rather than address underlying causes. This can be extremely costly in terms of time, money, and other resources. For this reason, analysts must be able to uncover root cause(s). The root cause is the underlying reason(s) for a problem. The onion, with its many layers, has become a common metaphor for how problems can be viewed (see Figure 2-11).

The layers of the onion represent the symptoms of the problem. The onion's core is the true root cause. Analysts must therefore invest the time, patience, and

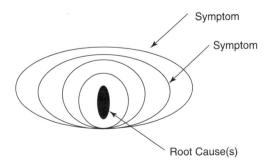

Figure 2-11 Symptoms versus root causes of problems.

persistence required to peel the onion until root causes are discovered. (They must also resist the temptation to believe that problems have only one root cause.) Fortunately, a number of tools and techniques exist to help analysts uncover the root cause of the problem.

Brainstorming

Brainstorming is generally used in group problem solving to generate a large number of ideas or suggestions. This technique can also be used effectively by analysts when working with members of a human performance improvement team. It can be used to generate a list of potential causes of a problem or gap between current and desired states. Brainstorming is helpful because it can help to surface many creative ideas in a relatively short time period. It also encourages the involvement and active participation of everyone in the group.

Brainstorming, as a causal analysis methodology, begins with a question or problem to be explored. The problem should be stated in measurable or observable terms whenever possible to provide clarity and facilitate common understanding. For example, "During the month of January, production in the kiln department was 8,500 tons of brick. The target was 10,000 tons, equating to a gap of 1,500 tons." Using a flipchart or white board helps to provide a common visual focus. If group brainstorming is being used, everyone should have a clear understanding and agreement on the problem before proceeding.

There is typically a set of basic ground rules, or guidelines, that are introduced when brainstorming sessions are conducted. A sample set of rules is shown in Figure 2-12.

While brainstorming is an effective technique for generating a list of possible causes for problems, the results should not be taken as absolute truth. The causes identified through the brainstorming process represent possible reasons only. It

---

- No discussion of ideas.
- No criticism of ideas.
- All ideas are valuable.
- Think "outside the box"—be creative.
- Focus on quantity versus quality of ideas.
- Piggyback on others' ideas.

Figure 2-12   Basic rules of brainstorming.

is strongly recommended that HPI practitioners or teams—such as action learning teams (Rothwell, 1999)—collect data to either support or refute the causes listed in the session. In other words, brainstorming is not an effective substitute for data, and the causes generated from a brainstorming session or focus group must be substantiated through further investigation.

Brainstorming sessions can be conducted in structured or unstructured formats. Unstructured brainstorming typically involves a free flow of ideas with comments being voiced by any participant at any time. Ideas are called out immediately as they come to mind. Structured brainstorming, though, most often involves each person in turn either stating an idea or electing to "pass." Ideas are generally captured on a flipchart or white board. Once an adequate list of causes has been generated, other members may subsequently evaluate the ideas by open or facilitated discussion, multivoting, or some other means.

Sometimes groupthink develops during brainstorming sessions. Groupthink, as its name applies, occurs when the participants become focused on a single train of thought. Overt or covert peer pressure is placed on people who express creative ideas or ideas that fall outside the group's line of thinking. In addition to establishing ground rules, another way to overcome groupthink is to use a technique called the "trigger method" of brainstorming. Before the brainstorming session begins, people are given an opportunity to write their ideas on a sheet of paper. Doing this gives people a chance to consider the topic before brainstorming begins. In addition, when ideas have been documented, it often becomes easier for people to express them. There is a greater likelihood of divergent thoughts, which can help to prevent the onset of groupthink.

Groupware is the generic name for software programs that can be used to conduct electronic brainstorming, plus a number of other activities, such as categorizing information, voting, evaluating options, and making decisions. A groupware session would typically entail a room, often set up in a horseshoe shape, of networked computers at which participants sit. A brainstorming question or topic is introduced and participants type in their responses or ideas, which are collected anonymously via the software. This data is then used to foster discussion, evaluation of ideas, and decision making. The technology is a means to level the playing field because responses are anonymous. Thus, it helps to prevent groupthink from occurring. It is recommended, however, that groupware software not be a substitute for group discussion, dialog, and debate, but rather as a means to avoid negative group dynamics, generate and capture ideas, and expedite the process.

Cause-and-Effect Analysis

Cause-and-effect analysis, as its name implies, identifies and organizes potential causes of performance problems. The primary strength of this tool is that it visually organizes information and shows the linkages between the problem and its possible causes. Arguably the most popular cause-and-effect tool developed by Kaoru Ishikawa is known as the Ishikawa diagram or the fishbone diagram, named for the shape it takes. Another version of the cause-and-effect methodology is known as a tree diagram because it displays potential causes in a branch-like format. A fishbone diagram is shown in Figure 2-13.

As is shown, the problem statement, or effect, is posted in the box at the far right of the diagram. Next, cause categories are determined and written in the appropriate boxes. A rule of thumb is that three to six cause categories should be used. Examples of a set of categories that could be used include people, methods, materials, measurements, and machines. Another set of categories that might be useful in administrative areas are the four P's—policies, procedures, people, and plant. Yet another might be customers, employees, materials, policies/procedures, and environment. A more generic example is to simply ask such simple questions as these: Who? What? Where? When? How? and Why?

As might be suspected, developing categories and identifying possible causes within each is a primary benefit of the fishbone diagram. The specific causes are then listed under the appropriate category branch. These are obtained by asking the question, "Why does this happen?" Brainstorming, which was covered earlier, is a useful technique that can be used at this juncture. Of course, categories can be moved, edited, added, or dropped based on relevance to the problem and situation. The analyst should attempt to generate as many causes as possible for each category. These causes should be related to the problem statement, which is written in the box at the far right of the diagram. As with brainstorming, it is critical to narrow the list and collect data, whenever necessary, so as to verify and validate the causes that might be generated.

The Five Why's Technique

The five why's technique is a variation on the cause-and-effect analysis method. It can complement traditional methods, such as the fishbone diagram, or it can be used by itself. The intent of the five why's approach is to exhaust the list of potential causes, many of which may, in reality, be only symptoms, until the root

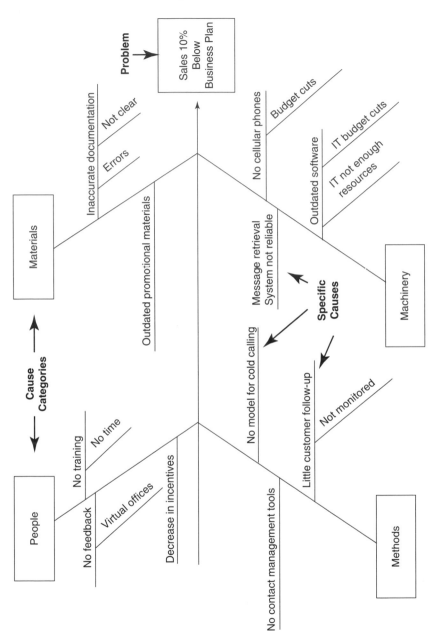

Figure 2-13   Fishbone diagram.

Statements/Responses	"Why" Questions	
"I have a bad headache this morning."	"Really, why do you have a headache?"	1st Why
"I only got four hours of sleep last night."	"Why did you only get four hours of sleep last night?"	2nd Why
"I was up working until 3:00 a.m."	"Why did you work until 3:00 a.m.?"	3rd Why
"I was late meeting an important deadline."	"Why were you late meeting a deadline?"	4th Why
"I procrastinated and put off doing the work until the last minute."	"Why did you procrastinate?"	5th Why
"I'm bored with my work."	"Why are you bored with your work?"	6th Why
Additional Statements	Additional Why Questions	

Figure 2-14   Example of the five why's technique of causal analysis.

cause is all that remains. This technique is simple yet powerful, because it forces the analyst to think through potential causes and to drill down to deeper levels that are more representative of the root cause. A simple example of the five why's method is shown in Figure 2-14.

The initial problem statement in this scenario was that the person had a headache. A simple solution or remedy, such as "take an aspirin," probably could have been applied at this point. This approach, however, would only address the visible symptom of the problem rather than its root cause. This quick fix approach is too shallow and only masks the true problem, which is likely to persist. By continuing to ask "why?" for each symptom that is identified, the analyst digs closer to the root cause.

The example in Figure 2-14 actually asked why six times and still may not have surfaced the root cause of the problem. Upon digging through six layers of symptoms, though, the analyst is much closer to the root than at the beginning of the process. By addressing the boredom with work issue, a longer-term solution that actually removes this problem is much more likely than by the shallow solution of taking aspirin.

Other Analytical Tools

In addition to the performance and cause analysis processes that have been discussed, there are a number of tools that are helpful to the analyst. This section discusses two such methods—system modeling and flowcharting. The next section covers some common methods and tools for data presentation, which are often used in conjunction with analytical methodologies.

System Modeling

The world is comprised of systems and subsystems. The HPI practitioner must adopt a systems perspective to see the complex interrelationships between various components of an organization. When changes are made to one part of a system through interventions, the result can be negative or positive effects on other parts of the system. A common phenomenon that compounds the issue is that there is often a lag or delay between the intervention and the resultant changes throughout the system (Senge, 1990). This delayed ripple effect highlights the importance of thorough analysis and the selection of appropriate interventions to human performance problems. In addition, viewing parts of the organization as systems and subsystems helps the analyst take a more focused approach because a clear delineation between various components can be made.

The most basic system contains the three components: inputs, processes, and outputs, or I-P-O (see Figure 2-15). Inputs are the resources that feed into the processes. They may be in the form of raw materials, information, human resources, or equipment. Processes are the tasks, activities, methods, and procedures that convert these inputs into outputs. Outputs are the products and/or services produced by the process. Often, the output of one system becomes the input to the next system.

Effects and feedback are other elements that can be added to the basic systems model shown in Figure 2-15. Effects are the changes, impacts, or outcomes resulting from the outputs of the system. Feedback is information regarding the system and its operation.

When systems are modeled by analysts, they are rarely as simple as the I-P-O model depicts. Systems often have many inputs, subsystems, and supporting systems, multiple processes, and numerous outputs. One primary benefit of system modeling is that it helps to isolate and document the multitude of inter-

Figure 2-15   Elements of a basic system.

connected components that exist. Modeling a system reveals the linkages or relationships between each element and the impacts they have on each other. System modeling also provides a big-picture view and helps the analyst pinpoint where to start in identifying problems or their causes.

To engage in system modeling, the analyst must first decide upon which process or system to focus (see Figure 2-16). Processes that have never been modeled or that are experiencing painful problems or symptoms are likely to be candidates for selection. The processes are drawn as boxes and labeled appropriately. They are often depicted as high-level steps or tasks. Next, the analyst should identify the specific outputs that are generated by the process. Sometimes it is useful to determine the effects as well, which may be directly or indirectly related to the outputs.

Whenever possible, each output should be described in observable and measurable terms. Measures of success should also be captured so that the analyst and other stakeholders can determine whether the system is functioning adequately. Each output should be drawn as an individual box and labeled accordingly. Inputs that are necessary to drive the process should be identified and documented, each as a separate box.

Inputs may include people, information, material, and resources. It will sometimes be necessary or useful to identify the support systems that produce these

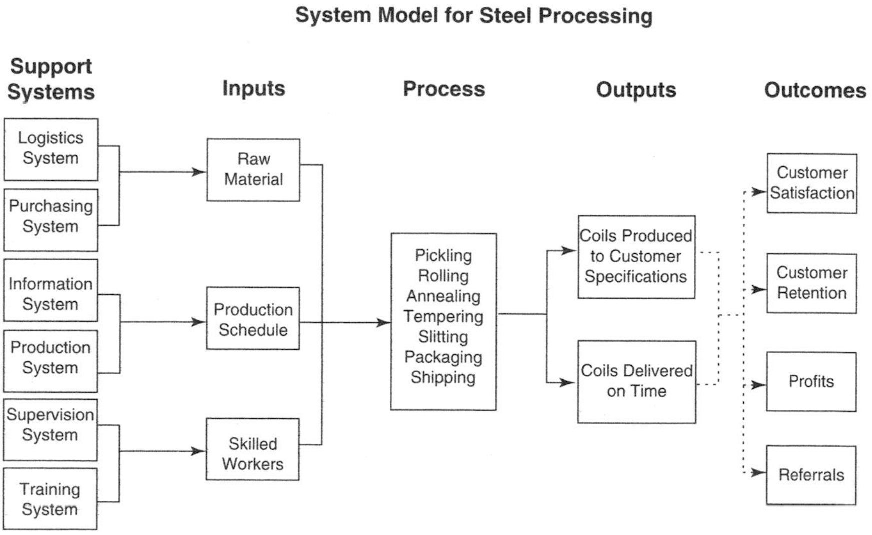

System Model for Steel Processing

Figure 2-16 System modeling.

inputs. An example of a support system is an information system. While it may not be necessary to diagram the entire information support system, it can be helpful to identify and document it in a box that is connected to an input.

Once a system has been diagrammed, the various elements, as well as the big picture, can be reviewed. It is sometimes necessary to establish mechanisms by which to obtain data or measures to determine current and desired performance. Once data are collected or reviewed, inadequate or missing elements of the system can be pinpointed for additional analysis and intervention.

High-Level Flowcharting

A flowchart is a visual representation of a process. It can be used with the system modeling technique described in the previous section or as a separate analysis tool. A flowchart is a way to describe and depict a process. The most basic flowchart consists of a sequence of steps. As with the system model, a flowchart is useful for diagramming the way in which a current process is carried out. It can aid the analyst in isolating missing or inefficient elements and can provide a clear delineation between steps as well as the beginning and ending points of a process. A process flowchart helps the analyst and others involved in performance improvement efforts to describe and discuss a particular process. The visual nature of flowcharting facilitates this endeavor.

While many types of flowcharts exist, the basic high-level variety is shown in Figure 2-17.

Often when analysts create a flowchart to represent a process, they identify the output or outputs, results, or accomplishments that are produced at each step and substep. These results can be thought of as intermediate outputs that contribute to the production of the overall process output. A good place to start is by identifying the external or internal customers as well as suppliers involved in a particular process. While generally meant to capture the external vendors associated with an organization, the notion of "supply chain management," around which an entire profession and body of knowledge has emerged, has relevance inside an organization when the customer and suppliers of processes are analyzed (Hugos, 2003). The general purpose of such a high-level flowchart is to obtain a pictorial representation of the process. This can generally be achieved through drawing three to five steps, which represent those most critical in the process. Then from the critical steps more detailed substeps can be added.

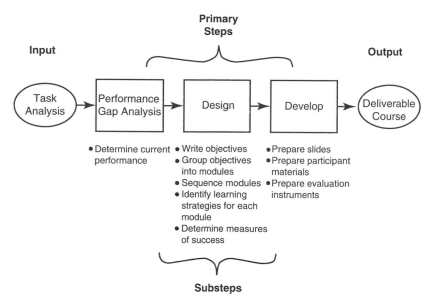

Figure 2-17 High-level flowchart.

Detailed Flowcharting

A detailed flowchart expands on the high-level chart by including additional granularity. Some elements that are commonly found in detailed flowcharts include decision points, delays or bottlenecks, documentation, information into a database, cloudy steps, and feedback loops. Figure 2-18 shows some of the symbols that can be used to represent these parts of a flowchart.

Adding such symbols helps the analyst to more clearly and accurately document what is happening in the process. A detailed flowchart is shown in Figure 2-19.

The type of flowchart that is used by the analyst should depend on the purpose. If the purpose is to gain a basic understanding regarding the primary steps involved in a particular process, then a high-level flowchart may be adequate. If more information is needed and if sufficient time is available, then a detailed flowchart may be required. When developing a flowchart, the analyst should always involve those who are most familiar with the process. These individuals are often referred to as process owners or subject matter experts (SMEs). Several cautions related to working with SMEs are in order. Sometimes, an

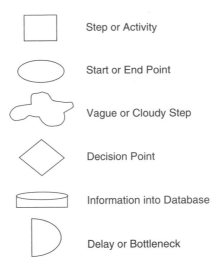

Figure 2-18 Common symbols found in a detailed flowchart.

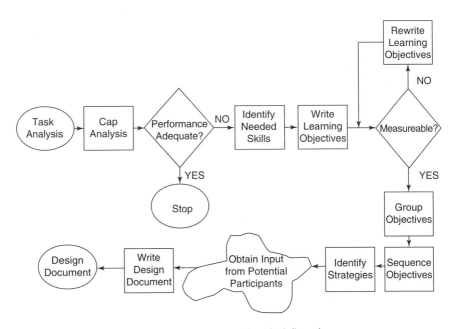

Figure 2-19 Sample detailed flowchart.

expert may feel threatened for a variety of reasons, such as job security, and may be resistant to providing information. For this reason, it is important for the HPI practitioner to first build trust, explain why it is being done, how the results will be used, request the person's support, and generally address any questions and allay any concerns of the expert (Mason, 2002). Another common occurrence when working with SMEs is that because of their expertise, they may overlook steps or make assumptions because they are so familiar with the process. Related to this, it is important to find SMEs who have excellent communication skills so they are able to convey their knowledge and insights in an comprehensible manner. Finally, it can be tempting for the process owner, and sometimes even the HPI practitioner, to diagram a process as it should be (or as the SME would like it to be) rather than as it actually is. This temptation should be avoided, and flowcharts depicting the current state should always reflect the actual rather than the ideal process.

Data Presentation Methods and Tools

Another skill that is important for HPI practitioners is the ability to communicate the results of their analysis to key organizational stakeholders. The importance of being "data driven" has already been discussed. Simply dumping data on people, though, is a recipe for disaster, since many managers and others have little time or patience to wade through reams of facts, figures, or tables. For this reason, it is essential that the analyst present a clear and compelling articulation of the key information so that the decision-making process is facilitated. In addition, analysts must collect, track, and monitor key data so that they can uncover problems and opportunities to improve performance.

Fortunately, a number of methods and tools exist that make it easier to understand data, as well as present it. Many of the tools described below can be created with relative ease using commonly available software packages, such as Microsoft PowerPoint or Excel. This helps analysts to comprehend and convey important information in an understandable manner. One of the foremost authorities on presentation of complex data is Edward Tufte. His text, *The Visual Display of Quantitative Information* (2001), is a classic on the theoretical and practical strategies for converting numeric data into easy-to-interpret charts, graphics, tables, and other visual forms. This section highlights pie graphs, bar graphs, Pareto charts, run charts, histograms, and scatter plots. Each tool provides a visual display of data so that it becomes easier to discern, identify patterns, and make decisions.

Pie and Bar Charts

Pie charts and bar charts are visual representations used to compare quantities, amounts, or proportions. When such charts are used, the results become much more clear, and the differences tend to stand out much more than when displayed as numeric data only. A sample bar chart and pie chart are shown in Figure 2-20. Bar charts are generally used to compare groups or categories, while pie charts typically show the relative percentages making up the whole.

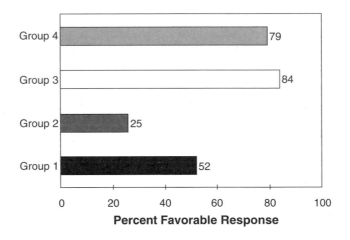

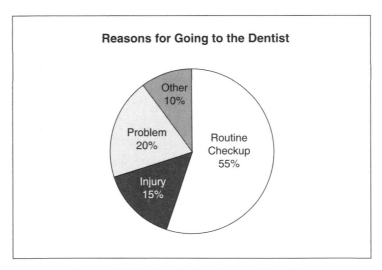

Figure 2-20   Sample bar chart and pie chart.

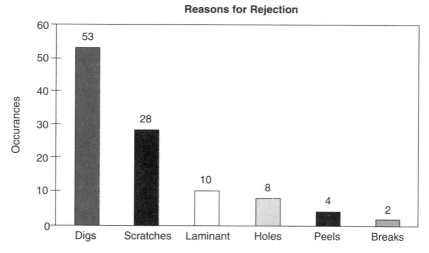

Figure 2-21 Sample Pareto chart.

Pareto Charts

A Pareto chart is a specialized type of bar chart. It follows the Pareto principle, which states that, when there are multiple factors affecting a situation, generally only a small number account for most of the impact. Pareto analysis is useful to the HPI analyst because it helps to determine the causes with the greatest impact. A sample Pareto chart is shown in Figure 2-21.

The Pareto chart organizes the data from highest to lowest (or lowest to highest), based on the problem being investigated. For example, frequency of occurrence or time involved could be diagrammed on a Pareto chart. It makes the primary problems easily visible and powerfully communicates the magnitude and importance of the problem to others. Thus, a Pareto chart is a highly useful way to establish priorities on problems or causes by surfacing and displaying those that are most problematic. Thus, a Pareto chart helps the HPI practitioner to narrow the range of options by surfacing those that are contributing most to the problem or situation.

Line or Run Charts

Line charts or run charts display a series of data points and are useful for showing trends over a period of time. A sample line chart is displayed in Figure 2-22.

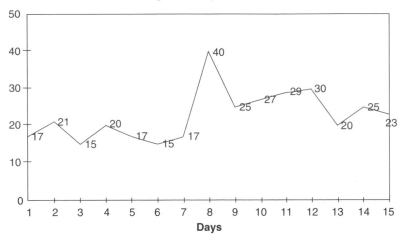

Figure 2-22   Sample line chart.

A wide variety of information, such as volume, cost, or time, can be presented on a line chart. For example, the average time a caller is "on hold" in a customer call center environment or the average die changeover times on a stamping press may be displayed using such a chart. Viewing such data on a line chart can help to detect important trends, such as a spike in customer time on hold on Mondays due, perhaps, to work schedules being released first thing on Monday morning, causing confusion and delay. Data points on a line chart are displayed chronologically.

Summary

This chapter was about the first of the four HPI roles, the role of analyst. Analysis has received much attention, and its pivotal role in the HPI is clear. The role of the analyst was defined as someone who "conducts troubleshooting to isolate the cause(s) of human performance gaps or identifies areas in which human performance can be improved" (Rothwell, 2000). A total of six competencies were identified in *ASTD Models for Human Performance Improvement* as important to the role of analyst. In addition, the outputs linked with the competencies were presented.

Next, the distinction between performance and cause analysis was made. These are the two steps of the HPI process model that are associated with the role of analyst. Performance analysis is "the process of identifying the organization's performance requirements and comparing them to its objectives and capabilities" (Rothwell, 2000), while cause analysis is "the process of determining the root cause(s) of past, present, or future performance gaps. It follows, but is integrally related to, performance analysis." It was also noted that analysis can be carried out at three levels—the organizational, process, and individual levels.

The remainder of the chapter was dedicated to reviewing some important models and tools that can be used by HPI practitioners engaged in performance and cause analysis. Included were models devised by Gilbert, Rummler and Brache, and Mager and Pipe. These models and tools can be used by practitioners as they analyze performance problems. Data presentation tools were also covered as a way to communicate findings.

References

Carr, C., and Totzke, L. (1995). The Long and Winding Path: From Instructional Design to Performance Technology: Installment IV—Two Basic Tools of Human Performance Technology. *Performance & Instruction*, *34*(6), 12–16.

Cooperrider, D.L., Sorensen, P.F., Whitney, D., and Yaeger, T.F. (Eds.) (2000). *Appreciative Inquiry: Rethinking Human Organization Toward a Positive Theory of Change*. Champaign, IL: Stipes Publishing.

Cooperrider, D.L., and Whitney, D. (2005). *Appreciative Inquiry: A Positive Revolution in Change*. San Francisco: Barrett-Khehler.

Deterline, W.A., and Rosenberg, M.J. (Eds.) (1992). San Diego Unified School District: The Power of Performance Analysis. *Workplace Productivity: Performance Technology Success Stories*. Washington, DC: International Society for Performance Improvement, 21–22.

Elliott, P. (1996). Power-Charging People's Performance. *Training & Development*, *50*(12), 46–49.

Gilbert, T.F. (1978). *Human Competence: Engineering Worthy Performance*. New York: McGraw-Hill.

Gilbert, T.F. (1982). A Question of Performance Part I: The PROBE Model. *Training and Development Journal*, *36*(10), 21–30.

Harless, J. (1973). An Analysis of Front-End Analysis. *Improving Human Performance: A Research Quarterly*, *4*, 229–244.

Harless, J. (1995). Performance Technology Skills in Business: Implications for Preparation. *Performance Improvement Quarterly*, *8*(4), 75–88.

Hugos, M.H. (2003). *Essentials of Supply Chain Management.* Hoboken, NJ: John Wiley & Sons.

Hutchison, C.S. (1990). What's a Nice P.T. Like You Doing? *Performance & Instruction, 29*(9), 1–5.

Ishikawa, K. (Lu, D.J. trans.) (1985). *What Is Total Quality Control?* Englewood Cliffs, NJ: Prentice-Hall.

Kaplan, R.S., and Norton, D.P. (1996). *The Balanced Scorecard: Translating Strategy Into Action.* Boston: Harvard Business School Publishing.

Kaplan, R.S., and Norton, D.P. (2006). *Alignment: Using the Balanced Scorecard to Create Corporate Synergies.* Boston: Harvard Business School Publishing.

Kaufman, R. (1986). Obtaining Functional Results: Relating Needs Assessment, Needs Analysis, and Objectives. *Educational Technology, 26*(1), 24–26.

King, S.B. (1998). Practitioner Verification of the Human Performance Improvement Analyst Competencies and Outputs. Doctoral dissertation. University Park, PA.

Kirrane, D. (1997). *The Role of the Performance Needs Analyst.* Alexandria, VA: American Society for Training and Development.

Mager, R.F., and Pipe, P. (1984). *Analyzing Performance Problems, or, You Really Oughta Wanna,* 2nd ed. Belmont, CA: David S. Lake.

Marker, A. (1995). The Harvest of PT: ISPP's Past Presidents' Recommendations for the Preparation of Performance Technologists. *Performance Improvement Quarterly, 8*(4), 22–33.

Mason, C.L. (2002). *Working with Subject Matter Experts: Strategies to Gain Cooperation and Win Respect.* Society for Technical Communication Conference Proceedings.

Medsker, K., Stepich, D., and Rowland, G. (1995). HPT in Academic Curricula: Survey Results. *Performance Improvement Quarterly, 8*(4), 6–21.

Robinson, D.G., and Robinson, J.C. (1995). *Performance Consulting: Moving Beyond Training.* San Francisco: Berrett-Koehler.

Rossett, A. (1987). *Training Needs Assessment.* Englewood Cliffs, NJ: Educational Technology.

Rossett, A. (1999a). Analysis of Human Performance Problems. In H.D. Stolovitch and E. J. Keeps (Eds.), *Handbook of Human Performance Technology: A Comprehensive Guide for Analyzing and Solving Performance Problems in Organizations,* 2nd ed. 139–162. San Francisco, CA: Jossey-Bass.

Rossett, A. (1999b). *First Things Fast: A Handbook for Performance Analysis.* San Francisco: Jossey-Bass/Pfeiffer.

Rossett, A., and Czech, C. (1995). They Really Wanna, But . . . The Aftermath of Professional Preparation in Performance Technology. *Performance Improvement Quarterly*, 8(4), 115–132.

Rothwell, W. (1999). *The Action Learning Guidebook.* San Francisco: Jossey-Bass/Pfeiffer.

Rothwell, W. (2005). *Beyond Training and Developing: The Groundbreaking Classic*, 2nd ed. New York: Amacom.

Rothwell, W.J. (1989). How to Conduct a Real Performance Audit. In C. Lee (Ed.), *Performance Technology: TRAINING Magazine's Best Thinking On: The Art and Science of Performance Technology*, 61–68. Minneapolis, MN: Lakewood Books.

Rothwell, W.J. (2000). *ASTD Models for Human Performance Improvement: Roles, Competencies, and Outputs*, 2nd ed. Alexandria, VA: The American Society for Training and Development.

Rummler, G.A., and Brache, A.P. (1995). *Improving Performance: How to Manage the White Space on the Organization Chart*, 2nd Ed. San Francisco: Jossey-Bass.

Ruona, W.E.A., and Lyford-Nojima, E. (1997). Performance Diagnosis Matrix: A Discussion of Performance Improvement Scholarship. *Performance Improvement Quarterly*, 10(4), 87–118.

Senge, P.M. (1990). *The Fifth Discipline: The Art and Practice of the Learning Organization.* New York: Doubleday Currency.

Sleezer, C.M. (1992). Needs Assessment: Perspectives from the Literature. *Performance Improvement Quarterly*, 5(2), 34–46.

Spitzer, D.R. (1988). Instructional/Performance Technology Competencies. *Performance & Instruction*, 27(7), 11–13.

Swanson, R.A. (1994). *Analysis for Improving Performance: Tools for Diagnosing Organizations & Documenting Workplace Expertise.* San Francisco: Berrett-Koehler.

Tufte, E.R. (2001). *The Visual Display of Quantitative Information*, 2nd ed. Cheshire, CT: Graphics Press.

Watkins, R., and Kaufman, R. (1996). An Update on Relating Needs Assessment and Needs Analysis. *Performance Improvement*, 35(10), 10–13.

3

The Role of Intervention Specialist

Most human performance improvement practitioners, as well as managers and other stakeholders, are eager to find a solution or select a performance improvement intervention. The previous chapter explored the role of the analyst. You learned that one key tenet of HPI work is a strong grounding in performance and cause analysis. In other words, the urge must be resisted to jump to an immediate solution to performance problems. The interventions that are eventually applied to the performance problem or opportunity should result from careful analysis. The reason for this is that careful analysis increases the probability of identifying and choosing the *appropriate* intervention. Without analysis, solutions are unlikely to be effective—and may even make matters worse. Like physicians who are advised to at least "do no harm" in treating their patients, HPI practitioners should avoid causing more problems than they solve. That can happen if the wrong intervention is selected to solve a problem or if it is chosen in haste.

This chapter reviews the role of the intervention specialist. First, the role is defined and the competencies and outputs associated with it are described. Next, a range of possible performance improvement interventions is discussed. This chapter also reviews various techniques for identifying and selecting appropriate human performance improvement strategies. The chapter concludes with some cautions about potential dangers and pitfalls in selecting interventions.

ASTD Models of Human Performance Improvement defines the intervention specialist as the role that "selects appropriate interventions to address the root cause(s) of performance gaps" (Rothwell, 2000). The terminal output related to the role of intervention specialist is "persuasive reports to stakeholders about the appropriate intervention(s) to close past, present, or future performance gap(s)" (Rothwell, 2000). The ultimate objective of the intervention specialist is thus to formulate a solution that will solve the problem by eliminating its cause(s). These causes, you will remember, were surfaced during performance and cause analysis. Choosing and developing a solution is not necessarily an easy task. Often interventions fail—or fall well short of expectations—because they were not adequately and cautiously thought through before implementation, the focus of the next chapter.

Misapplying an intervention can be costly for a number of reasons. A significant amount of time, money, and effort can be expended with a solution that was chosen on "gut feel"—only to find that the problem remains. Such poor decision making leads to loss of credibility of the HPI practitioner with other members of the organization. It may also complicate further efforts to solve the problem by raising the level of skepticism of stakeholders and those involved in the intervention. Some even may take matters into their own hands, drag their feet on moving forward, or sabotage the entire effort.

As an example, consider what happens when training is chosen as a performance improvement strategy when it is not the appropriate solution. Too often, training is chosen as an intervention for the wrong reasons—or for no reason at all. Training may be selected as the solution to low employee morale, quality problems, decreased sales, or a number of other issues. Whenever these issues surface, the quick-fix, knee-jerk approach is to roll out "sheep-dip training" in which everyone is given the same dose of instruction whether they need it, or worse, regardless of whether training will even have a positive impact.

The problem with this familiar scenario is that the desired results are rarely achieved. Low morale persists, quality issues continue, and sales remain sluggish. Then, the blame is placed on the training department for not producing the desired results. With the clarity of hindsight, decision makers realize that training could never have produced the intended results because training was not the correct solution to the problem. The result: wasted resources and negative perceptions of the training department and training in general. For these reasons, the intervention selection phase is not the appropriate time to shoot from the hip for an easy, quick-fix solution. Clearly, the results of the analysis phase must guide and achor the intervention selection phase.

Competencies Associated with the Role of Intervention Specialist

According to *ASTD Models for Human Performance Improvement* (Rothwell, 2000), the following competencies are associated with the role of intervention specialist:

- **Performance information interpretation skills:** Finding useful meaning from the results of performance analysis and helping performers, performers' managers, process owners, and other stakeholders to do so
- **Intervention selection skills:** Selecting human performance improvement interventions that address the root cause(s) of performance gaps rather than symptoms or side effects
- **Performance change interpretation skills:** Forecasting and analyzing the effects of interventions and their consequences
- **Ability to assess relationships among interventions:** Examining the effects of multiple human performance improvement interventions on parts of an organization, as well as the effects on the organization's interactions with customers, suppliers, distributors, and workers
- **Ability to identify critical business issues and changes:** Determining key business issues and applying that information during the implementation of a human performance improvement intervention
- **Goal implementation skills:** Ensuring that goals are converted effectively into actions to close existing or pending performance gaps; getting results despite conflicting priorities, lack of resources, or ambiguity

Outputs Linked to the Role

The outputs associated with the intervention selection competencies are displayed in Figure 3-1.

What It All Means

Taken together, the role, competencies, and work outputs of the intervention specialist are akin to the act of a carpenter selecting tools and material for a building project. The toolbox may be filled to the brim with potential tools that could be utilized for the job at hand. No carpenter, though, would be foolish to simply reach into the box and pull out the first tool he or she touches. Likewise, the carpenter would be foolish to select his or her favorite tool and use it in every situation. Imagine a carpenter using a saw to pound a nail, simply because the saw is the favorite tool! The selection of the appropriate tools and material by the carpenter is based on the analysis the carpenter performed when he or she studied the blueprints, took measurements, analyzed the soil composition, and other analytical activities. Then, and only then, is the proper tool pulled from the box and skillfully used to achieve the desired result.

Intervention Specialist Role	Terminal Output
Selects appropriate interventions to address the root cause(s) of performance gaps.	■ Persuasive reports to stakeholders about the appropriate intervention(s) to close past, preset or future performance gap(s)

Intervention Specialist Competencies	Enabling Outputs
1. **Performance Information Interpretation Skill**: Finding useful meaning from the results of performance analysis and helping performers, performers' man agers, process owners, and other stake holders to do so.	■ Written or oral briefings to performers, performers' managers, process owners, or other stakeholders about the results of performance analysis or cause analysis ■ Useful information drawn from perfor mance or cause analysis
2. **Intervention Selection Skill:** Selecting human performance improvement inter- ventions that address the root cause(s) of performance gaps rather than symptoms or side effects.	■ Approaches for choosing appropriate human performance improvement strategies to close performance gaps
3. **Performance Change Interpretation Skill:** Forecasting and analyzing the effects of interventions and their side effects.	■ Written and oral briefings to performers, performers' managers, process owners, and other stakeholders about the likely impact of change or of a human perfor- mance improvement intervention on processes, individuals or the organization ■ Problem-solving activities to lead perfor- mers, performers' managers, process owners, and other stakeholders to discov- er/forecast the impact of an intervention's implementation on processes, individuals or the organization
4. **Ability to Assess Relationships Among. Interventions:** Examining the effects of multiple human performance improve ment interventions on parts of an organization, its interactions with cus tomers, suppliers and distributors, and workers.	■ Written and oral briefings to performers, performers' managers, process owners, and other stakeholders about the likely impact of multiple interventions on pro- cesses, individuals or the organization ■ Problem-solving activities to lead perfor- mers, performers' managers, process owners, and other stakeholders to discover/forecast the likely impact of multiple interventions on processes, individuals or the organization

Figure 3-1 Outputs associated with the intervention specialist. Source: Rothwell, W. (2000). *ASTD Models for Human Performance Improvement: Roles, Competencies, and Outputs, 2nd ed.* Alexandria, VA: The American Society for Training and Development. Used by permission of the American Society for Training and Development.

Intervention Specialist Competencies	Enabling Outputs
5. **Ability to Identify Critical Business Issues and Changes:** Determining key business issues and applying that information during the implementation of a human performance improvement intervention.	■ Organizational analyses ■ Process analyses ■ Individual assessments ■ White papers on improvement strategies ■ Oral and written briefings to performers, performers' managers, process owners or stakeholders about possible improvement strategies ■ Customer satisfaction information/survey results
6. **Goal Implementation Skills:** Ensuring that goals are converted effectively into actions to close existing or pending performance gaps; getting results despite conflicting priorities, lack of resources, or ambiguity.	■ Written or oral goals for human performance improvement ■ Performance objectives for interventions ■ Facilitated performance objectives

Figure 3-1 *Continued*

The intervention specialist, similarly, reviews the report and other information gathered during analysis regarding the performance gap(s) and their cause(s). Following this examination, decisions are made to determine which solutions should be chosen and applied to the situation. Just as it is imperative for the carpenter to select the correct tools for the building project, the intervention specialist also must select the appropriate interventions so that the desired human performance results will be achieved. In practice, when the analysis stage is performed well, the solutions often seem to surface with relative ease and clarity. For example, if goals and objectives are missing or unclear, the obvious intervention would likely involve establishing or clarifying goals and objectives—certainly not rocket science! However, such potential solutions must still be rigorously vetted through a process such as the one described later in this chapter to ensure the optimal intervention is selected. The other point worth mentioning here is that the rigor and outcomes of the performance and cause analysis steps of the HPI process pay great dividends in the intervention selection phase. Thorough analysis makes intervention selection both easier and more accurate.

Intervention specialists may thus apply their competencies as illustrated by the following examples:

- With performance information interpretation skills, intervention specialists may:
  □ Sift through the key findings contained in the analysis report or other documentation to locate the nuggets representing the key areas to be addressed by the subsequent intervention.
  □ Begin to build a case for change with key stakeholders, such as performers, managers, and process owners. This may involve one-on-one discussions or group briefings to convey the situation, the importance of acting, and the need to select a solution that will address the problem. Influencing skills often come in handy here (Laborde, 2003).
- With intervention selection skills, intervention specialists may:
  □ Consider the wide range of alternative solutions that are available to achieve the purpose of eliminating the root cause of the performance problem or achieving the desired end result. Numerous interventions are possible, and care must be taken so that others do not jump too quickly to a solution.
  □ Explain to others that the most appropriate solution must be chosen. Appropriateness of a solution, which will be discussed later in this chapter, is determined by identifying key criteria, such as its ability to remove the problem, its cost, and the feasibility of implementing it.
  □ Recognize their own strengths and limitations regarding knowledge of potential interventions. It is always good practice to consult with others, sometimes using brainstorming, to generate all possible solutions.
- With performance change interpretation skills, intervention specialists may:
  □ Forecast the effects of interventions. Changes brought about through various interventions may result in both positive and negative effects on individuals, processes, or the overall organization. The intervention specialist must have the ability to forecast these direct and indirect consequences and bring them to the attention of those in the affected areas.
  □ Involve others in attempting to anticipate the impact of the intervention. Discovery of the good and bad aspects of the intervention should be encouraged so that strengths can be capitalized upon and negative ramifications can be minimized or prevented.

- With the ability to assess relationships among interventions, intervention specialists may:
  - ☐ Recognize the systemic nature of organizational reality and attempt to determine how proposed changes to one part of the system will likely affect other parts of the system.
  - ☐ Facilitate the recognition of the effects of interventions on individuals, groups, and the organization by various stakeholders. Tools and techniques from the field of change management, such as stakeholder analysis, can be useful here as well (Change Management Toolbook, 2006).
- With the ability to identify critical business issues and changes, intervention specialists may:
  - ☐ Locate the leverage points or the key business issues that will be impacted by the interventions. Reduction in "pain" felt by various stakeholders as a result of the problem is likely to be welcomed. Much of this information will stem from the analyses conducted in the role of the analyst.
  - ☐ Produce written and oral briefings to key stakeholders about possible strategies for improving human performance. The key business issues and needs driving the change effort must be kept in the forefront of people's thinking so that the link between the findings from the analysis and the selected intervention is clear.
- With goal implementation skills, intervention specialists may:
  - ☐ Establish goals and objectives for the implementation of the intervention(s). Formulating goals helps to drive the project forward because it provides a clear picture of the end result to be achieved through the intervention. This helps the human performance improvement practitioner and others to move ahead despite obstacles, such as insufficient resources, that are bound to be encountered.
  - ☐ Communicate goals with others involved in the performance improvement effort. Keeping all parties informed of the goals, as well as progress toward them, avoids a loss of focus.

Selecting Interventions

Sometimes interventions are selected for inappropriate or incorrect reasons. They may be chosen because they are the least expensive, the most technologically advanced (thus demonstrating "technolust"), or politically correct. While these factors may, in fact, be important in the decision-making process, they should not represent criteria used without thoughtful planning and consideration. Sometimes interventions such as those listed above are selected because the analysis phase was circumvented or shortchanged. When that happens, there is a tendency to make decisions based on what "feels good" at the time (sometimes called "shooting from the hip," just as cowboys used to shoot from the hip without taking careful aim). This is similar to hiring decisions based on the gut feeling of the interviewer versus a structured approach that is more objective and, therefore, has a higher likelihood of leading to the right person for the job.

Decision making based on hunches or intuition can be dangerous because it sets the stage for failure by creating a disconnect between the cause of the actual problem and its proposed solution. It should be noted that the notion of decision making based on immediate reaction or intuition has gained in popularity in recent years (Gladwell, 2005). However, this type of decision making can, and often does, lead to "trash-can decision making" in which problems, solutions, and participants are thrown together, much as trash is thrown together without any order in a can. To avoid this problem, HPI practitioners, while being mindful of what their intuition is saying, should follow a systematic process for selecting interventions. While different scenarios are possible, the following four-step process contains the primary components of solid decision-making systems (see Figure 3-2).

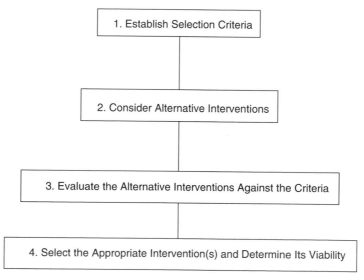

Figure 3-2 Intervention selection process.

This intervention selection process fills a void in the human performance improvement literature. Much has been written about possible interventions. The literature, however, is quite sparse on detailed systematic approaches for intervention selection and decision making. Most processes in the literature approach solution selection by starting with a general category of causes, surfaced through the performance analysis, and suggest a general intervention and, perhaps, some examples (Rossett, 1999; Stolovitch, 2004). The process described here attempts to fill that gap by offering a step-by-step method for choosing solutions. The first task in the process described in this book is to establish selection criteria against which the potential solutions can be judged. Then, a list of potential interventions is generated. Next, this wide array of possible solutions is evaluated against the predetermined criteria until the list is narrowed. From this point, the appropriate solution or solutions (when more than one intervention is appropriate) is selected based on the situation and key factors.

Step 1: Establish Selection Criteria

Criteria are standards or measures by which potential interventions are evaluated or judged, and ultimately chosen, in Step 3, as follows. It is important to determine the criteria in advance because doing so helps the HPI practitioner or team to remain open to all possibilities and more objectively judge the quality of potential interventions. In some cases, such criteria may even be established before or during the analysis phase. Attempting to establish selection criteria after solutions are articulated can introduce bias, which may artificially sway the decision toward that preference. There are many criteria that can be used, but it is up to the HPI practitioner or team to decide which they will incorporate based on their relevance to the situation at hand.

Some criteria are essentially standards that must be met by the proposed intervention. For example, if someone were purchasing a house, he or she may decide beforehand that the house must meet a standard of possessing a basement or must have at least four bedrooms. Certain criteria, though, are considered constraints because they describe limitations or restrictions that exist. A constraint in the house example might be that the house should cost no more than $450,000. These constraints may or may not be negotiable with the client. Keep in mind that criteria do not equate to interventions. Rather, criteria form the basis for evaluating potential interventions. Possible criteria that could be used when considering alternatives include the following:

- The intervention affects the root cause of the problem.
- The intervention is feasible to implement.
- The intervention is affordable to implement.
- The intervention is acceptable to management or other stakeholders (minimal resistance).
- The intervention is efficient.
- The intervention is timely.
- The intervention is (free or relatively free) from negative effects on other areas.

First and foremost, a solution should be able to affect the root cause of the problem or achieve the goal that was identified during the analysis stage. If the solution is unable to eliminate or reduce the cause(s), then perhaps an alternative solution should be sought. Another possibility is that multiple solutions are required to fully deal with the problem. Feasibility to implement focuses on the workability of the potential solution in terms of required resources, such as people, time, money, and effort. Affordability deals with the cost-effectiveness of the intervention relative to budget or cost constraints.

A high-cost intervention applied to a low-cost problem or issue is obviously not advisable. A frequently discovered truth that HPI practitioners realize is that low-cost interventions often have extremely high leverage in dealing with performance issues. Establishing goals or standards for a process is an example of a relatively low-cost intervention that can conceivably result in greater performance gains than hours of costly training.

Acceptability to management or other stakeholders is an important consideration because these people are the decision makers who control the purse strings and other resources, and often make the "go" or "no go" decisions. Politics may enter the picture here, and the HPI practitioner must be adroit at navigating such political waters (Brandon and Seldman, 2004). Interventions should also be efficient and produce a "big bang for the buck."

Timeliness is another possible criterion. It deals with issues such as organizational readiness for the solution and the degree to which the timing matches with other simultaneous initiatives or events that may be occurring throughout the organization. Timeliness also relates to the speed by which the solution can be implemented. The final criterion mentioned above is the effect that the potential solution or intervention might have on other areas. The systemic nature of organizations and organizational changes surfaces the need to examine potential effects that changes in one part of the organization may have on other areas (Senge, 1994).

A number of additional criteria could be added to those listed above, such as safety, legality, urgency, or requirements mandated by external entities like the Environmental Protection Agency or the Occupational Health and Safety Administration. Further, the group brainstorming method is a means by which other potential criteria can be generated for consideration. What is important is that practitioners, in partnership with their clients, carefully choose those criteria that are most relevant and therefore most likely to lead to selection of the appropriate intervention. As was the case in the analysis phase of HPI, involving clients in establishing criteria and ultimately selecting the solution helps to build buy-in and commitment for the subsequent change management activities. John Kotter has written extensively about the importance of, and strategies for building, commitment through involvement (Kotter, 1996; Kotter and Cohen, 2002). In general, the more involvement, the greater chance of commitment. Attempting to impose a solution on a client without input generally does not work. An opportune activity in which to engage the client is in brainstorming criteria or reacting to a draft set of criteria established by the HPI practitioner or team.

A general rule of thumb is to limit the total number of criteria to three to five items. When too many criteria are used, it can become difficult to narrow and focus the list. One means for deciding which criteria options to use is to determine which criteria any intervention absolutely must meet to be considered seriously. Those that do not meet the filter test may have to be dropped. In addition, the intervention specialist should consider which criteria might carry more importance. Such items could then be given more weight when solutions are assessed. These decisions will be determined by the situation at hand. For example, if financial resources are extremely tight, perhaps affordability becomes a criterion that receives additional weight during the selection process. Voting or attempting to reach consensus on which criteria to use (or not use) are other ways to narrow the list of possibilities. Ultimately, it is the client who should decide (or have a serious voice in determining) the major criteria and weighting to be used based on what factors are most important to them.

When selecting an intervention, more than short-term solutions should be considered. In other words, if acceptability to management or feasibility to implement were determined to be criteria, then potential solutions also should be judged according to future acceptability or feasibility. For example, a particular intervention might not be feasible in the short term, but in several months it may be highly feasible. That is particularly true when an intervention is considered on the heels of another, failed, improvement effort or when a crisis confronts the organization that makes the proposal for an intervention particularly opportune. HPI practitioners should factor that information into the decision-making process whenever possible.

Step 2: Consider Alternative Interventions

There are an endless number of interventions that can be used to solve performance problems or to capitalize on performance improvement opportunities. The purpose of Step 2 is to scan the list of potential interventions, generate additional interventions, and weigh the alternatives.

Potential Interventions

Hutchison, Stein, and Carleton (1996) produced a list of approximately 230 potential performance improvement strategies subdivided into 20 classifications (see Figure 3-3).

An excellent text titled *Intervention Resource Guide: 50 Performance Improvement Tools* by Langdon, Whiteside, and McKenna (1999) describes 50 potential interventions. Figure 3-4 shows a matrix of these interventions. Langdon et al. provide useful information in their matrix about these interventions, how they should be used, and strategies for selection. First, they highlight the level at which the intervention can be applied. Similar to the levels of analysis described in Chapter 1, they can be used at the individual, work group, process, or business unit levels.

They also list four types of performance change that can be achieved through the intervention including establishing performance, improving performance, maintaining performance, or extinguishing performance. While the approach may appear to be somewhat simplistic, the authors suggest that the matrix can be used to select interventions by using the results of the performance analysis to match the type of change required with the level of change to yield a list of the potential interventions. This might be an acceptable way to narrow down the choices, but it does not provide for the identification of other interventions (which may or may not be on list). Also, details on how to select from the narrowed list of choices are not offered. Nonetheless, the book provides an excellent first step and describes 50 solid potential interventions.

Career Development Systems

- Action Research Projects
- Affirmative Action Programs
- Assessment Centers
- Career Ladders
- Coaching
- Cross-training
- EEO Programs
- Experiential Learning
- Internet Recruitment Systems
- Job Rotation Systems
- Loaned Executive/Job Exchange
- Mentoring
- Outplacement Systems
- Promotion Systems
- Scholarship Programs
- Structured Practices
- Tuition Reimbursement programs
- Work Assignment Rotation Systems

Communication Systems

- Announcement Systems and Practices
- Computer Networking
- Corporate/Organizational Newsletters and Bulletins
- Electronic Mail
- Electronic Bulletin Boards
- Information Mapping
- Meeting Planning
- Memo Design/Format Systems
- Negotiation Systems
- Social Information Processing
- Suggestion Systems
- Teleconferencing Systems
- Voice Messaging Systems

Cultural Anthropology

- Beliefs and Attitudes
- Ceremonies, Rites, and Rituals
- Cultural Change Programs
- Cultural Diversity Programs
- Cultural Maintenance and Transmission Programs
- Dress and Practices
- Globalization
- Language and Jargon
- Merging Culture Programs
- Myths, Legend, and Heroes

Documentation and Standards

- Articles of Incorporation
- By-Laws
- Contract, Letters of Intent, Letters of Agreement
- Expert Systems
- Formats
- Guidelines
- Partnership Agreements
- Policies
- Procedures
- Quality Assurance Documents (Internal and External Standards, Certification and Licensing)
- Reference Manuals
- Standardization of Materials Equipment

Ergonomics/Human Factors

- Architecture
- Biomechanics
- Color Coding/Accenting
- Controls and Displays
- EEO Compliance (e.g., Handicapped Access)
- Facilities Design/Interior Design
- Fixtures, Furniture, and Equipment Design
- Information Display Systems
- Interior Decoration
- Labeling and Nomenclature
- Man/Machine Interface
- Safety Planning
- Signage and Placement
- Technological Advances
- Tools and Equipment Specification
- Warning Systems
- Work Station Design
- Workload and Fatigue Programs

Feedback Systems

- Benchmarking Systems
- Customer/Client Feedback Mechanisms
- Developmental Practice Sessions
- Graphing and Charting Systems
- Identification and Documentation of Performance Indicators
- Performance Appraisal Systems
- Performance Information Systems
- Performance Management Systems
- "Real Time" Measurement Systems
- Suggestion Systems
- Upward/Peer Appraisal Systems

Financial Systems

- Account and Market Analysis
- Activity Accounting Systems (AAS)
- Bartering Systems

Figure 3-3 Hutchison, Stein, and Carleton's matrix of strategies and tactics. ©1996 International Society for Performance Improvement. Hutchison, C.S., Stein, F., Carleton, J.R. *Potential Strategies and Tactics for Organizational Performance Improvement, Performance and Instruction.* Used with permission of the International Society for Performance Improvement.

- Capital Investment/Spending Systems
- Cash Flow Analysis
- Cost Accounting Systems
- Credit Systems
- Financial Forecasting
- International Exchange Systems
- Pricing Systems (Internal and External)
- Pro Formas

Human Development Systems

- EEO Programs
- Employee Assistance Programs
- Health and Wellness Programs
- Leadership Development Programs
- Literacy Programs
- Personal Networking Systems
- Outplacement Systems
- Psychometric Tests and Measures
- Retirement Planning
- Scholarship Programs
- Support for Professional/ Civic Activities
- Tuition Reimbursement Programs

Industrial Engineering

- Preventive Maintenance Systems
- Process Management Systems
- Process Engineering/ Reengineering
- Product Introduction Systems
- Value Engineering
- Work Methods

Information Systems

- Applicant Tracking
- Artificial Intelligence Systems
- Database Management
- Expert Systems
- File Retrieval Systems
- Human Resources Information Systems (HRIS)
- Information Display/Format Systems
- Information Security Systems
- Management Information Systems (MIS)
- Personal Networking Systems
- Records Management Systems

Instructional Systems

- Computer Managed Instruction (CMI)
- Curriculum Design
- Experiential Learning Programs
- Instructor-led Seminars, Courses, and Programs
- Job Aids
- Learner Controlled/Self- paced Instruction
- Media-based Instruction

Job and Workflow Design/Redesign

- Activity Accounting Systems (AAS)
- Competency Modeling
- Job Classification and Evaluation
- Job Design/Redesign
- Job Enrichment and Enlargement
- Job Instructions
- Materials Handling/ Flow Systems

- Process Engineering/ Reengineering
- Self-managing Work Groups
- Workflow Design/ Redesign
- Work Schedule/Shift Programs

Labor Relations

- Arbitration/Mediation
- Collective Bargaining
- Conflict Management Systems
- Contract Compliance and Documentation
- Grievance Systems

Management Science

- Action Research Projects
- Centralization/ Decentralization
- Distribution Systems
- Forecasting Systems
- Globalization Systems
- Goal Setting Systems
- Marketing Systems
- Matrixing Approaches/ Systems
- Mergers and Alliances
- Operations Planning/ Implementation
- Organizational Structure Design
- Performance Manage- ment Systems
- Problem-Solving and Decision-Making Systems
- Public Relations Systems
- Risk Management/ Legal Review Systems
- Safety Planning/ Implementation
- Self-directed Work Teams
- Strategic Planning/ Implementation

Figure 3-3 *Continued*

- Supervision/Management/ Leadership
- Visioning Systems

Measurement and Evaluation Systems

- Acceptable Quality Levels (AQL)
- Assessment Centers
- Certification/ Accreditation/Licensing Programs
- Competency Testing
- Compliance Monitoring Systems
- Graphing and Charting Systems
- Performance Evaluation Systems
- Performance Measurement
- Performance Standards and Criteria
- Productivity Indicators
- Statistical Process Controls (SPC)

Organizational Design and Development

- Change Management
- Conflict Management
- Cross Functional/ Partnering Systems
- Culture Change Programs
- Customer Focus/Service Systems
- Group Dynamics
- Management Structure Design
- Organizational Impact Studies
- Partnering Programs

- Sociotechnical Systems Design
- Team Building
- Values Clarification

Quality Improvement Standards

- Acceptable Quality Levels (AQL)
- Benchmarking Programs
- Continuous Improvement
- Participative Management Systems
- Quality Assurance Programs
- Quality Auditing
- Quality Committees (Quality Circles, Steering Committees, etc.)
- Quality Process Design
- Quality of Worklife Programs
- Statistical Process Controls (SPC)

Resource Systems

- Benefits Programs
- Budgeting Systems
- Capital Expenditure Planning/Implementation
- Forecasting Systems
- Full Time Equivalent (FTE) Allocation Plans and Ceilings
- Human Resource Planning and Forecasting Systems
- Inventory Control Systems
- Just-in-Time (JIT) Systems
- Manufacturing Systems

- Manufacturing Resources Planning Systems
- Materials Requirement Planning Systems
- Pension Control Systems
- Resource Allocation Systems
- Time-based Competition Systems
- Turnover Control Systems
- Vendor/Supplier Systems and Contracts

Reward/Recognition Systems

- Benefits Programs
- Bonus Systems
- Commission Systems
- Compensation Systems
- Gainsharing/Profit Sharing Systems
- Incentive and Recognition Programs (Tangible/ Intangible, Public/Private)
- Merit Award Systems
- Motivation Programs

Selection Systems

- Internal Recruitment Systems
- Job Postings
- Leadership Development Programs
- Personnel Recruiting & Hiring Systems
- Psychometric Tests and Measures
- Succession Planning Systems

Figure 3-3 *Continued*

	ESTABLISH				IMPROVE				MAINTAIN				EXTINGUISH			
	Business Unit	Process	Work Group	Individual	Business Unit	Process	Work Group	Individual	Business Unit	Process	Work Group	Individual	Business Unit	Process	Work Group	Individual
360-degree feedback				•				•			•					•
Accelerated learning				•				•								
Action learning	•	•	•	•	•	•	•	•								
Assessment centers				•				•			•					•
Automated resume tracking system	•	•	•		•		•		•	•						
Challenge education	•	•	•		•	•	•		•	•	•		•	•	•	
Change style preference models		•				•				•				•		
Cognitive ergonomics	•	•	•	•	•	•	•	•	•	•	•	•	•	•	•	•
Communication		•					•	•	•		•	•	•		•	•
Compensation systems							•	•			•	•				
Competency modeling			•	•			•	•			•	•			•	•
Conflict management			•	•			•	•							•	•
Critical thinking systems		•	•	•		•	•	•								
Cultural change	•		•	•	•		•	•					•		•	•
Customer feedback	•	•	•	•	•	•	•	•	•	•	•	•	•	•	•	•
Electronic performance support system		•	•	•		•	•	•								
Employee orientation				•				•								
Expert systems		•	•	•		•	•	•								
Flowcharts		•		•		•		•		•		•		•		•
Fluency development				•				•								
Human resource information systems	•		•		•		•		•		•		•		•	
Job aids	•		•	•	•		•	•	•		•	•	•		•	•
Leadership development programs				•				•								•
Learner-controlled instruction				•				•								•
Leveraging diversity	•		•	•	•		•	•					•		•	•

Figure 3-4 Langdon, Whiteside, and McKenna's matrix of intervention. Source: Langdon, D., Whiteside, K., and McKenna, M. (Eds.). (1999). *Intervention Resource Guide: 50 Performance Improvement Tools.* San Francisco: Jossey-Bass/Pfeiffer. Used by permission of Jossey-Bass/Pfeiffer.

	ESTABLISH				IMPROVE				MAINTAIN				EXTINGUISH			
	Business Unit	Process	Work Group	Individual	Business Unit	Process	Work Group	Individual	Business Unit	Process	Work Group	Individual	Business Unit	Process	Work Group	Individual
Mentoring/coaching			•					•			•					•
Motivation systems		•	•				•	•		•	•			•	•	
Needs assessment							•	•			•	•			•	•
On-the-job training			•					•			•					•
Organizational development	•	•	•		•	•	•		•							
Organizational scan	•				•											
Outplacement																•
Partnering agreements			•	•			•	•			•	•			•	•
Performance analysis	•	•	•	•	•	•	•	•	•	•	•	•	•	•	•	•
Performance appraisal			•					•			•					•
Performance management			•	•			•	•								
Policies and procedures			•		•	•		•	•	•	•					•
Process mapping		•				•				•			•			
Recognition programs			•	•			•	•			•	•			•	•
Reengineering	•	•	•	•	•	•	•	•					•	•	•	•
Results-based management	•	•	•	•	•	•	•	•	•	•	•	•	•	•	•	•
Safety management								•			•					•
Simulation			•	•			•	•			•	•			•	•
Strategic planning and visioning	•		•		•		•		•		•		•		•	
Structured writing		•	•	•		•	•	•		•	•	•		•	•	•
Team performance			•	•			•	•			•	•			•	•
Teaming	•	•	•	•	•	•	•	•					•	•	•	•
Training			•	•			•	•								
Usability assessments		•	•	•		•	•	•		•	•	•		•	•	•
Work group alignment			•				•				•				•	

Figure 3-4 *Continued*

The listing of interventions in Figures 3-2 and 3-3 can provide you with an idea of the range of possibilities. The array of options available for performance improvement efforts begs the question, "How can one person possibly master them all?" By glancing at the lists of interventions, you will see that there is a simple answer to that question: It is virtually impossible for one person to be competent in all performance improvement strategies or interventions. That is why the HPI practitioner, when enacting the intervention specialist role, merely identifies the strategy but seeks competent professional help to implement and activate the strategy. Of course, the danger always exists that HPI practitioners will select the wrong intervention or will single-handedly undertake to plan and implement interventions for which they are not competent.

Hutchison and Carleton (1991) provide some insight into this dilemma facing HPI practitioners. They suggest that the HPI practitioner should "be expert in 15 to 25 or more tactics across 10 or more of the strategy areas listed. Have working knowledge of 45 to 75 or more tactics across 15 or more strategies." In addition, Hutchison and Carleton propose that the HPI practitioner should "know the basic tenets or principles in half or more of the tactics and be able to recognize expertise in them." HPI practitioners are well advised to develop a network of contacts with expertise in the various interventions. More individuals and organizations are recognizing the importance of building networks and the power of social networks in building personal, professional, and organizational success (Uzzi and Dunlap, 2005; Cross and Parker, 2004; Cross, Liedtka, and Weiss, 2005). They can do this by participating in professional associations, such as local chapters of the International Society for Performance Improvement or the American Society for Training and Development, and/or getting involved with numerous online communities of practice that now exist in cyberspace.

The approach offered by Hutchison and Carleton addresses the issue of developing expertise in many strategy areas. It is important for HPI practitioners to develop in-depth knowledge and expertise in several interventions. The intervention specialist should be able to recognize his or her limitations, as well as know when and how to seek outside expertise and assistance when needed.

This also points to the usefulness of a team approach where, collectively, a group of HPI practitioners—or a broad cross-section of individuals from inside the organization—can team up. You may want to examine the list of potential performance improvement interventions shown in Figures 3-2 and 3-3 and perform a self-assessment. Examine each item and determine your current level of expertise or competence, as well as your knowledge of who you could turn to for assistance if you needed help to select, plan, implement, and evaluate each intervention.

Use Analysis Results to Suggest Interventions: When identifying potential interventions, you need a place to start. Intervention selection can begin at the point where the analysis left off. Proper analysis should have identified the root cause(s) of the performance problem as well as the desired end state or requirements associated with successful performance. The intervention specialist should use this insight as a framework for pinpointing potential interventions to use in isolation or in combination.

Rossett (1999) identifies four broad categories from which performance problems are caused: "lack of skill and/or knowledge, flawed incentives, flawed environment, and lack of motivation." Similarly, Stolovitch (2004) identify three categories of performance gaps: "environmental, skill/knowledge, and emotional/political." These cause categories can point toward certain types of interventions. Figure 3-5 lists these cause categories and suggests potential generic interventions that could be used to address each one. The specific intervention, however, must still be selected.

These cause categorization schemas helps the intervention specialist to rule out certain solutions and concentrate on others. For example, if the cause

Causes	Interventions
Lack of skill and/or knowledge	Trainning Job aids Coaching
Flawed incentives	Revised policies Revised contracts Training for supervisors Incentive and bonus plans
Flawed environment	Work redesign New and/or better tools Better selection/development for jobs
Lack of motivation	Inform workers so they can see benefits, impact, value Link to work challenges Use of role models Early successes to instill confidence

Figure 3-5 Causes and interventions from HPT handbook. Source: Rossett, A. (1999). Analysis of Human Performance Problems. In H.D. Stolovitch and E.J. Keeps (Eds.), *Handbook of Human Performance Technology: A Comprehensive Guide for Analyzing and Solving Performance Problems in Organizations*. San Francisco, CA: Jossey-Bass. Used by permission.

category is determined to be a problem with the environment, such as inadequate lighting, then it is probably safe to rule out training as a potential intervention. Likewise, if a lack of knowledge is the cause category identified through analysis, then it would probably not make sense to focus on goal alignment.

Brainstorm to Generate Additional Interventions: The interventions listed in Figures 3-2 and 3-3 provide a useful foundation for selecting potential interventions. Another technique that can either supplement the initial list or that can be used to generate a list from scratch is to brainstorm. You will recall from Chapter 2 that the brainstorming method is often used in group situations to generate a large volume of ideas or suggestions to identify the causes of performance problems. Brainstorming is helpful because it can help to bring out a large number of creative ideas while encouraging the involvement and active participation of everyone on the performance improvement team.

A sample list of ground rules or guidelines for brainstorming was displayed in the last chapter in Figure 2-12. When applied to selecting potential interventions, this brainstorming method can prove to be highly effective, especially if one of the ground rules prohibits initial judgment of the ideas. This rule can release the creativity of participants and encourage the development of novel intervention ideas. Conducting several rounds of brainstorming may prove to be a fruitful exercise in an effort to exhaust all potential interventions for further investigation and evaluation against the criteria, the focus of the third step.

Groupware technology, which was discussed in Chapter 2, can be applied here to facilitate the brainstorming process. At the same time, groupware can also reduce negative group dynamics, such as one person highjacking the discussion.

Step 3: Evaluate the Alternative Interventions Against the Criteria

Step 3 is the time when each potential intervention (generated in Step 2) is evaluated against the criteria that were established in Step 1. Each potential intervention is evaluated independently in light of the chosen criteria. A useful tool for organizing and facilitating this evaluation process is the criteria matrix.

A *criteria matrix* is a grid that displays the potential interventions on one axis and the criteria along the other. As mentioned previously, a criterion is a standard, measure or guideline by which the potential interventions can be evaluated or judged and ultimately chosen. It is useful when multiple criteria are involved

Potential Interventions	Criterion #1	Criterion #2	Criterion #3	TOTAL
Intervention 1				
Intervention 2				
Intervention 3				
Intervention 4				

Figure 3-6   Blank criteria matrix.

in the decision-making process. In HPI efforts, it is common and also recommended that more than one criterion be used. The result is a grid pattern that allows the HPI practitioner or team to view each alternative and the overall priority ratings for several choices (see Figure 3-6).

The intervention specialist should begin by listing the potential intervention options in the rows on the left side of the matrix. Discussion of and reflection on these options should be undertaken to ensure that everyone involved understands the intervention and can make an informed evaluation based on its merits. The criteria should be displayed as column headers across the top. These, too, should be well understood by everyone before proceeding. Each alternative is then rated according to the criteria items. Whenever possible, the list of interventions, as well as criteria, should be narrowed to minimize the complexity of the matrix. Certain interventions may be eliminated as options, or at least moved into a "parking lot" representing options of last resort. Possible solutions may be eliminated if they are too large to be supported by realistic estimates of the budget, time, or other resources available. Or, if it is determined that the intervention will not effectively eliminate the root cause but rather will only serve as a temporary solution, then a simple "yes" or "no" decision can be made about whether to keep or drop the item.

Once the intervention options and criteria are filled in, a rating scale must be developed. The voting feature embedded in many groupware software platforms can automate this process to improve efficiency. Many options are possible for the scales. It is important to use the same scale for each criteria item to ensure consistency and obtain an accurate overall rating. A simple rating scale is a Likert type system containing five-, seven-, or ten-point increments. For example, if

Criteria: *Feasibility*

5	4	3	2	1
High		Moderate		Low

Criteria: *Cost*

5	4	3	2	1
Low		Moderate		High

Criteria: *Management Support*

5	4	3	2	1
High		Moderate		Low

Figure 3-7   Sample rating scales for criteria.

the intervention specialist were considering the cost of the intervention as one criterion, the rating scale might run from 1 (representing highest cost) to 5 (representing lowest cost). Figure 3-7 displays several rating scales for various criteria that could be used.

Notice in Figure 3-7 that the rating scales are consistent, with 5 representing the positive side and 1 representing the negative side. Also, note that the overall ratings are calculated by adding the scores. The higher the total score, the better the option based on the criteria used. In Figure 3-7, the maximum overall score possible is 15, which would equate to the best option, and the minimum possible score is 3, representing the worst option. The ratings assigned to each intervention and each criterion can be done by a single person or by many people if a team approach is used. In the team-based scenario, each individual member could rate the items separately and an average score could be calculated. Another option is that the individual scores could be added together to reach a total score. Alternatively, the team may decide to discuss each item and attempt to reach consensus on the rating to be assigned. Figure 3-8 shows a completed criteria matrix.

In this example, Intervention 3 had the highest overall rating. Often, when a criteria matrix is completed, several options emerge as viable solutions. In such cases, it may be appropriate to select multiple interventions for implementation. On the other hand, it may be necessary to choose one over another with the knowledge that both are acceptable. In Figure 3-8, in the criteria areas of management support and feasibility, Intervention 3 was the clear "winner." On the

Potential Interventions	Cost	Management Support	Feasibility	TOTAL
Intervention 1	5	1	5	11
Intervention 2	1	1.5	1.5	4
Intervention 3	4	4.5	5	13.5
Intervention 4	3	2	3	8

Figure 3-8   Completed criteria matrix.

Criteria	Total Points	Intervention #1	Intervention #2
Cost	20	5	15
Mgt. Acceptance	30	15	15
Feasibility	50	20	30
Total Score:	100 points	40	60

Figure 3-9   Weighted points method of intervention selection.

cost criterion, however, Intervention 1 was the lowest cost. When certain interventions rate more favorably along selected criteria, these should be explored to ascertain whether elements from that intervention option can be transferred to the desired option to improve upon any weaknesses it may possess.

Option 3 in Figure 3-8 clearly meets all established criteria. This is not always the case, however. Sometimes an intervention may be very strong in several criteria areas but deficient in others (for example, Intervention 1 in Figure 3-8 was rated as having high feasibility and low cost, but low support). In such cases, it may be necessary to reconsider its viability as an intervention and the risks associated with moving forward. At times, the intervention specialist may need to return to the drawing board and revisit the criteria identified in Step 1, the list of potential solutions, and the decision-making process that led to the particular results. While frustrating, this is a better route to follow than to move forward with much uncertainty or minimal stakeholder commitment.

It is possible to use a more sophisticated intervention selection strategy than has been described. Accuracy can be added when weights are assigned to the criteria being used. The various maximum scores (or weights) are then distributed among the intervention options. Figure 3-9 provides a scenario where different criteria are assigned varying degrees of weight, based on importance to the intervention specialist or the HPI team.

Points within each criterion are distributed among the various intervention possibilities. In this manner, greater depth is gained about which intervention is most appropriate, based on the relative importance of certain criteria. The process of reaching clarity and agreement on the weight assigned to criteria can be both important and enlightening. The HPI practitioner may be under the assumption that stakeholder buy-in, for example, is an important criterion, while the client may place much more weight on cost (regardless of the level of buy-in). This discussion can be very helpful to ensure all parties are viewing the decision-making process through a similar lens.

Another way to utilize weighted criteria appears in Figure 3-10. Each criterion is assigned a weight. The total weight equals 1.00.

Step 4: Select the Appropriate Intervention(s) and Determine Its Viability

After the intervention specialist, or team, has carefully considered each potential intervention and the results of the criteria matrix exercise, the appropriate intervention(s) is then selected. Since most performance problems in organizations are usually multifaceted, often, a combination of interventions may be required to effectively deal with the problem or issue. Other situations may call for only one intervention. Identifying potential interventions, done earlier, is commonly highly creative and can be quite fun and engaging. Now it's time to make the tough decisions and select an intervention. This can be less fun and may even be agonizing for the HPI practitioner, especially when stakes are high. Before actually selecting an intervention for implementation, there are several other activities in which the intervention specialist can engage to reduce the

Potential Interventions	Cost (.15)	Management Support (.35)	Feasilbility (.50)	TOTAL
Intervention 1	$5 \times 1.15 = 5.75$	$1 \times 1.35 = 1.35$	$5 \times 1.5 = 7.5$	14.600
Intervention 2	$1 \times 1.15 = 1.15$	$1.5 \times 1.35 = 2.025$	$1.5 \times 1.5 = 2.25$	5.425
Intervention 3	$4 \times 1.15 = 4.6$	$4.5 \times 1.35 = 19.575$	$5 \times 1.5 = 7.5$	31.675
Intervention 4	$3 \times 1.15 = 3.45$	$2 \times 1.35 = 2.7$	$3 \times 1.5 = 4.5$	10.65

Figure 3-10 Another weighted points method for intervention selection.

stress and help ensure that the most appropriate one is ultimately chosen. These activities help further analyze a potential intervention and determine its true viability and likelihood of success. It is not recommended that all techniques described below be used because, similar to the problem of analysis paralysis, "intervention selection paralysis" can be dangerous as well. For this reason, it is suggested that these tools be used when deemed necessary and when time and resources permit. It is recommended that each activity be done with as much engagement of the client as possible to build buy-in and ownership.

Listing and Considering Advantages and Disadvantages: It may be useful to create a list of advantages and disadvantages of the interventions under consideration. This is especially helpful when opinion is divided about what intervention(s) will most effectively address the underlying causes of a performance problem. The intervention specialist or team, working with various stakeholders, can conduct a modified brainstorming session or engage in a discussion to develop an exhaustive list of the pros and cons for the intervention(s). Doing this can shed additional light on the intervention by illuminating its strengths and weaknesses or other realities previously ignored. Sometimes a flash of insight on a previously unconsidered factor may arise that causes the group to either reinforce its preliminary decision or rethink it.

Feasibility Analysis: This exercise involves attempting to forecast the chances of success of the intervention under consideration. According to Kirkey and Benjamin (2005), there are three primary categories to examine—practical considerations, cultural considerations, and political considerations. Practical considerations include elements such as cost, resources needed, time required, timing of the project itself, and bandwidth available. Cultural considerations include workplace climate, organizational values and cultural attributes, and organizational receptivity to change. Finally, political considerations include power dynamics, resistance levels, sensitivities that exist, sponsorship, and stakeholder support.

Force-Field Analysis: A useful tool when selecting interventions is force-field analysis, a technique originated by social psychologist Kurt Lewin (1947). This is a more structured method for determining advantages and disadvantages of a particular intervention by identifying forces that help (driving forces) and forces that may impede (restraining forces) progress toward a goal or desired outcome. Figure 3-11 shows an example of a force-field analysis diagram.

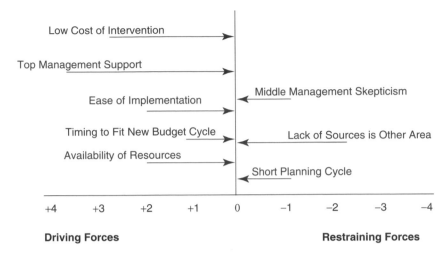

Figure 3-11   Force-field analysis diagram.

Brainstorming can be used again here to develop a list of the driving and restraining forces that are helping or working against a particular intervention under consideration. When forces are generated, they are mapped on the force-field diagram according to whether they work for—or against—the successful adoption of the intervention. In addition to determining on which side of the force-field diagram a particular force falls, an attempt is made to quantify the magnitude or strength of the force.

The diagram in Figure 3-11 uses a scale from 0 to plus or minus 4. When using this scale, a line is drawn to represent the magnitude of the force. The name of the force is written as a label next to the line representing it. The overall number of forces and corresponding magnitudes can be calculated for both drivers and restrainers. This helps to arrive at an overall direction for the intervention based on the difference between the two.

For example, if the sum total of the restraining forces is 21 and the sum total of the driving forces is 12, the difference is 9. This helps to paint a picture of the overall nature of the intervention and conveys that it is an intervention with more forces working against it than working in its favor. This analysis can cause the HPI practitioner to consider the probability of success of the intervention and develop strategies to strengthen the driving forces and/or reduce those that are hindering.

Force-field analysis is useful in further quantifying and getting a better handle on some of the subjective issues associated with choosing an intervention. The current level of employee morale, the prevailing work climate, or the quality of the management team may be forces that are taken into consideration in the analysis diagram and that may help to further delimit and define the merits of a potential intervention. One caution when using force-field analysis is the potential to omit an important force in either direction. This error creates an inaccurate portrayal of the factors surrounding the intervention and can lead to adverse impact on the future change effort. For this reason, care should be taken to ensure that all significant forces are included in the force-field analysis.

Force-field analysis is an enjoyable method that helps to forecast and even dramatize some workplace realities that might accompany alternative intervention selections. It also facilitates a discussion among stakeholders and decision makers about the nature of each—especially those with the largest impact. It helps to consider and develop strategies that can be employed to strengthen the forces that drive the intervention forward and reduce the forces that undermine the success of the intervention.

Ease-Impact Analysis: Another tool that can be used when selecting an intervention is an ease-impact analysis. For this analysis, a four-quadrant grid pattern, with one axis representing ease and the other representing impact, is drawn (see Figure 3-12). Using this diagram, interventions can be evaluated in light of their

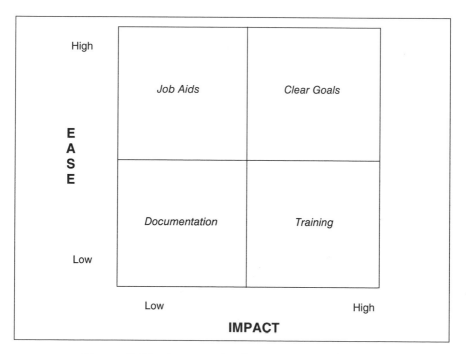

Figure 3-12 An example of an ease-impact diagram.

ease of implementation as well as their potential for impact. Obviously, interventions that are easy to implement and have a high potential for impact are stronger candidates than those with less ease or impact. The desirable quadrant then, in this diagram, is the upper right-hand corner. Other descriptors can be substituted; for example, cost or support could be used. The ease-impact diagram can be used to display a number of potential interventions in a visual manner. Further, a performance improvement team can utilize the ease-impact diagram in combination with voting as a way to visually represent people's view of alternative options.

Principles of Intervention Design

Once an intervention(s) has been selected, the design and development phase can be commenced. Remember that the terminal output related to the role of intervention specialist is "persuasive reports to stakeholders about the appropriate intervention(s) to close past, present, or future performance gap(s)" (Rothwell, 2000). This intervention design and development will lead directly into the implementation and change management effort. Spitzer (1992) presents a list of intervention design principles. These principles should be kept in the forefront of the intervention specialist's thinking—both during the selection process and also when formulating a design and report for stakeholders. Spitzer's principles* follow.

High-impact interventions should:

- Aim at high-leverage performance improvement opportunities
- Be powerful
- Be sustainable
- Be enhanced interventions
- Often start with a small, focused intervention
- Focus on the users
- Involve the right people in the design process
- Have a strong evaluation component
- Be designed with development and implementation in mind
- Be designed with an iterative approach

---

*Source: Spitzer, D.R. (1999). The Design and Development of Effective Interventions. In H.D. Stolovitch and E.J. Keeps (Eds.) *Handbook of Human Performance Technology: A Comprehensive Guide for Analyzing and Solving Performance Problems in Organizations.* San Francisco: Jossey-Bass. Used with permission of Jossey-Bass. All rights reserved.

These items become a litmus test against which potential interventions selected by the intervention specialist can be evaluated.

Bear in mind that you, as the HPI practitioner, may or may not be responsible for the actual implementation of the intervention. Sometimes an integration design and development team may be assembled to work on creating the intervention. The HPI practitioner may have no or very limited involvement or oversight, may be part of a team, or may be fully responsible. The level of subsequent involvement in implementation is often largely governed by the practitioner's depth of expertise in the intervention that is selected.

Dangers, Pitfalls, and Cautions

Many potential problems associated with intervention selection have been discussed in this chapter. It should be clear by now to readers that one trap some people fall into is selecting a solution too quickly. During the analysis phase, discussed in the previous chapter, we stressed the importance of trying to remain as objective as possible and not engaging in analysis with an intervention already in mind. The same caveat applies to this chapter and to this step as well.

Intervention specialists should be wary of rushing to a solution without careful consideration of the criteria, the alternative interventions, and other relevant factors. Another mistake that some make is the opposite of moving too quickly. Similar to analysis paralysis, sometimes intervention specialists consume too much time and are unable to reach decisions. This danger can cause momentum to be lost and people to become frustrated because they see no progress toward rectifying a problem or seizing an improvement opportunity.

Another danger that was alluded to earlier in the chapter is the potential adverse effects of a solution on another area. The interconnected nature of organizational systems gives rise to the ripple effect when changes are introduced. Interventions may represent a change in one area that concurrently creates a negative change in another, sometimes unrelated, part of the organization. For this reason, potential side effects and direct and indirect relationships among variables should be carefully considered before moving forward with an intervention. Sometimes a strategy employed by intervention specialists is to include "lack of negative effects on the organization" as one criterion used in the decision-making process.

Lack of knowledge about available interventions can be dangerous because it may cause intervention specialists to neglect viable solutions in favor of ones that they recognize more easily or are more comfortable using. The intervention that was passed over may have been more appropriate to the situation at hand or it may have been less costly, it may have had more impact on the root cause, or it may have had a higher level of acceptability among stakeholders. This potential problem highlights the importance of drawing others into the process, generating exhaustive lists of possible interventions (both creative and mundane should be included), and using techniques like brainstorming to consider all of the options before a decision is made.

Lack of buy-in or commitment to a solution can create major problems for HPI practitioners as they move into the implementation and change management stages. If an unpopular solution is chosen without stakeholder buy-in, or if the appropriate people are not consulted, then that may give rise to problems. A general principle of change management that applies here is that if commitment is needed, then a high level of involvement should be sought.

When those who are affected by change participate in the analysis, intervention selection, and change management stages they are likely to have a higher level of commitment to the solutions that are chosen. This is not to suggest that everyone who is remotely related to the project must be involved. Including certain people, however, will not only improve commitment to the ideas, but it also will probably improve the quality of those ideas.

Expertise and knowledge of potential pitfalls or barriers can be recognized and the intricate details of the process, people, and work area can be communicated by those most closely involved with it. Other people, such as key managers and those with ancillary involvement, may only need to be briefed occasionally. The importance of a communication plan as a strategy will be discussed later in this section.

Sometimes interventions that are selected to improve a performance problem can be too large or may be out of the control of the HPI practitioner. The stage is set for rejection of the idea or inability to carry through with it if it is approved. There is sometimes a tendency to lean toward ambitious solutions requiring cutting-edge technology because they are the most fun to work on. This highlights the related danger of resorting to familiar interventions. Trainers who are changing their role to that of HPI practitioner sometimes have difficulty letting go of training as the intervention of first choice.

Others encounter a different, but related, problem when they view intervention selection as a chance to experiment with a dazzling intervention that lacks much substance. Some people may become overly enamored with technology-based solutions because they are viewed as "state-of-the-art"—or because they may increase the employability of individuals working on them or the consulting opportunities available to external vendors. This is acceptable if they are, in fact, the appropriate solution. Many find, however, that the low-tech solution that is appropriate for the situation at hand often has more impact on the problem at lower cost. In fact, some have noted that 80 percent of performance problems can be solved through communicating expectations, goals, and standards, and providing people with information they need to perform.

Development of a communication plan, along with the intervention that is chosen, is an important strategy for avoiding problems. HPI efforts take place in a political context, and HPI practitioners must therefore be skilled communicators with organizational and political savvy. The importance of sales and marketing of intervention ideas in order to gain buy-in, commitment, and support of key stakeholders has been mentioned. Among the many items that intervention specialists should be equipped to discuss in great detail are the results of the analysis, the intervention selection process that was used, and details related to the solution that was chosen. A detailed justification should be provided to demonstrate deep understanding and build credibility with others. Doing this also influences the level of buy-in and the commitment discussed earlier in this section.

Summary

Intervention selection is not an easy task. This chapter has covered some steps that an intervention specialist can take to approach the task in a structured manner. There is often a tendency to jump to a solution. Through careful consideration of alternative interventions and sound decision making using relevant criteria, though, the *appropriate* solution is more likely to be selected. When the appropriate intervention is chosen, the probability of success, while not guaranteed, improves dramatically. This chapter also presented some supplemental tools, such as force-field analysis and ease-impact analysis, that can be used to generate additional insight and information about an intervention and its potential for success during the implementation phase, which will be the subject of Chapter 4. In addition to the intervention that is chosen, the information garnered through the selection process itself becomes extremely valuable during the implementation stage in areas such as forecasting potential sources of resistance.

References

Brandon, R., and Seldman, M.B. (2004). *Survival of the Savvy: High Integrity Political Tactics for Career and Company Success.* New York: Free Press.

Change Management Toolbook (2006). *The Theory and Practice of Stakeholder Analysis.* Retrieved May 13, 2006, from www.change-management-toolbook. com.

Cross, R.L., Liedtka, J., and Weiss, L. (2005). A Practical Guide to Social Networks. *Harvard Business Review, 83*(3).

Cross, R.L., and Parker, A. (2004). *The Hidden Power of Social Networks: Understanding How Work Really Gets Done in Organizations.* Boston: Harvard Business School Publishing.

Gladwell, M. (2005). *Blink: The Power of Thinking Without Thinking.* New York: Little, Brown & Co.

Hutchison, C.S., and Carleton, J.R. (1991). Survey Results Regarding Strategies and Tactics for Organizational Performance Improvement. Unpublished working document.

Hutchison, C.S., Stein, F., and Carleton, J.R. (1996). Potential Strategies and Tactics for Organizational Performance Improvement. *Performance & Instruction, 35*(3), 6–9.

Kirkey, D., and Benjamin, C.M. (2005). *Feasibility Analysis: An Instruction and Implementation Reality Check.* Paper presented at the annual meeting of the International Society for Performance Improvement, Vancouver, B.C.

Kotter, J.P. (1996). *Leading Change.* Boston: Harvard Business School Press.

Kotter, J.P., & Cohen, D.S. (2002). *The Heart of Change: Real Life Stories of How People Change Their Organization.* Boston: Harvard Business School Press.

Laborde, G.Z. (2003). *Influence with Integrity: Management Skills for Communication and Negotiations.* Carmorthen, UK: Crown House Publishing.

Landgon, D.G. (1999). Selecting Interventions. In D.G. Langdon, K.S. Whiteside, and M.M. McKenna (Eds.). *Intervention Resource Guide: 50 Performance Improvement Tools.* San Francisco: Jossey-Bass, 15–25.

Langdon, D.G., Whiteside, K.S., and McKenna, M.M. (Eds.) (1999). *Intervention Resource Guide: 50 Performance Improvement Tools.* San Francisco: Jossey-Bass.

Lewin, K. (1947). Frontiers in Group Dynamics: Concept, Method, and Reality in Social Science, Social Equilibria, and Social Change. *Human Relations, 1,* 5–41.

Rossett, A. (1999). Analysis of Human Performance Problems. In H.D. Stolovitch and E.J. Keeps (Eds.), *Handbook of Human Performance Technology: A Comprehensive Guide for Analyzing and Solving Performance Problems in Organizations*, 139–162. San Francisco, CA: Jossey-Bass.

Rossett, A. (1999). *First Things Fast: A Handbook for Performance Analysis.* San Francisco: Pfeiffer.

Rothwell, W.J. (2000). *ASTD Models for Human Performance Improvement: Roles, Competencies, and Outputs*, 2nd ed. Alexandria, VA: The American Society for Training and Development.

Senge, P.M. (1994). *The Fifth Discipline: The Art and Practice of the Learning Organization.* New York: Doubleday Currency.

Spitzer, D.R. (1999). The Design and Development of Effective Interventions. In H.D. Stolovitch and E.J. Keeps (Eds.) *Handbook of Human Performance Technology: A Comprehensive Guide for Analyzing and Solving Performance Problems in Organizations*, 173–180. San Francisco: Jossey-Bass.

Stolovitch, H.D. (2004). *Training Ain't Performance.* Alexandria, VA: American Society for Training & Development.

Uzzi, B., and Dunlap, S. (2005). How to Build Your Network. *Harvard Business Review, 83*(12), 53–60.

4

The Role of Change Manager

To function effectively as an HPI practitioner, you must be able to enact the role of change manager. But what is that role? What competencies and work outputs are associated with it? With what approaches for managing change should the change manager be familiar? How is the role of change manager enacted? This chapter addresses these questions.

According to *ASTD Models for Human Performance Improvement* (Rothwell, 2000), the change manager is the role that "ensures that interventions are implemented in ways consistent with desired results and that they help individuals and groups achieve results." Think of this role as akin to that of a project manager who follows through on performance improvement interventions to ensure that they are implemented in ways intended to achieve the desired results and impact. The change manager's role is thus key to successful implementation. Without effective implementation, of course, grand designs falter in crude procedures.

Competencies Associated with the Role of Change Manager

According to *ASTD Models for Human Performance Improvement* (Rothwell, 2000), the following competencies are linked to the change manager role:

- **Change implementation skills:** Understanding the nature of individual and organizational change and applying that knowledge to effectively lead organizations successfully through change
- **Change impetus skills:** Determining what the organization should do to address the cause(s) of a human performance gap at present and in the future

121

- **Communication channel, informal network, and alliance understanding:** Knowing how communication moves through an organization by various channels, networks, and alliances; building such channels, networks, and alliances to achieve improvements in productivity and performance
- **Group dynamics process understanding:** Understanding how groups function; influencing people so that group, work, and individual needs are addressed (McLagan, 1989)
- **Process consultation skills:** Observing individuals and groups for their interactions and the effects of their interactions with others
- **Facilitation skills:** Helping performers, performers' managers, process owners, and stakeholders to discover new insights

Outputs Linked to the Role

The outputs associated with the competencies are listed in Figure 4-1. Recall that an enabling output is associated with the demonstration of a competency, while a terminal output is the final outcome associated with the role.

What It All Means

Taken together, the role, competencies, and work outputs of the change manager are essentially descriptive of a project manager. Change managers thus facilitate, orchestrate, guide, and gently nudge along performance improvement interventions in much the same manner as a project manager works to achieve project results.

In the words of one practitioner, "a good change manager will do anything it takes—within reason and ethical boundaries—to move a project along in keeping with the objectives established for results."

The operative phrase here is "move a project along." That phrase encapsulates exactly what a good change manager does. Change managers may thus apply their competencies as illustrated by the following examples:

- With change implementation skills, change managers may:
  - Establish a change management plan and then manage its implementation.
  - Prepare the organization for the impending change by soliciting stakeholder involvement.

Change Manager Role	Terminal Outputs
Ensures that interventions are implemented in ways consistent with desired results and that they help individuals and groups achieve results.	■ Performance improvement interventions effectively monitored with participants and stakeholders ■ Effective interpersonal interactions among participants and stakeholders of interventions ■ Tracking systems to compare actual and ideal performance and progress toward narrowing or closing performance gaps, or realizing performance opportunities as the intervention is implemented ■ Oral and/or written agreements among most or all stakeholders about the results desired from the intervention ■ Measurable financial or nonfinancial objective to be achieved during and after implementation of the intervention(s)
Change Manager Competencies	**Enabling Outputs**
1. **Change Implementation Skills****: Understanding the nature of individual and organizational change and applying that knowledge to effectively lead organizations successfully through change.	■ Plans for managing the change ■ Effect involvement of stakeholders ■ Individual and organizational needs in balance ■ Conflict resolution utilized to resolve differences ■ Process for surfacing issues ■ Management understanding the dynamics of change
2. **Change Impetus Skills:** Determining what the organization should do to address the cause(s) of a human performance gap at present and in the future.	■ A convincing case made for the need for change ■ Organizational sponsorship identified and secured ■ Evidence of support obtained through commitment of resources ■ Designs/action plans for introducing and consolidating interventions ■ Designs/plans for reducing resistance to interventions ■ Recommendations to management about management's role in introducing and consolidating change ■ Recommendations to workers about their role in introducing and consolidating change

**Additional competencies identified by the authors.

Figure 4-1 Outputs associated with the change manager role. *Source:* Rothwell, W. (2000). *ASTD Models for Human Performance Improvement: Roles, Competencies, and Outputs,* 2nd ed. Alexandria, VA: The American Society for Training and Development. Used by permission of The American Society for Training and Development.

Change Manager Competencies	Enabling Outputs
3. **Communication Channel, Informal Network, and Alliance Understanding:** Knowing how communication moves through an organization by various channels, networks, and alliances; building such channels, networks, and alliances to achieve improvements in productivity and performance.	■ Communication plans established to keep participants in change and stakeholders of change informed about the progress of the human performance improvement intervention
4. **Groups Dynamics Process Understanding:** Understanding how groups function; influencing people so that group, work, and individual needs are addressed (McLagan, 1989).	■ Groups successfully observed ■ Plans for influencing groups based on knowledge of small group development theory
5. **Process Consultation Skills:** Observing individuals and groups for their interactions and the effects of their interactions with others.	■ Group process observation forms ■ Descriptions to group members and individuals about the effects of their behavior on a group or on individuals
6. **Facilitation Skills:** Helping performers, performers' managers, process owners, and stakeholders to discover new insights.	■ Plans for facilitating group discussions ■ Plans for facilitating individual or group decision making and problem solving

Figure 4-1 *Continued*

□ Balance organization and individual needs and resolve conflicts when they arise.

□ Help the organization deal with natural resistance by surfacing issues and creating an open-door approach to change initiatives.

■ With change impetus skills, change managers may:

□ Monitor industry and organizational publications for key drivers that make a desired change more important, to communicate this information to interested stakeholders so as to reemphasize the "business case" for change.

□ Bring up the topic of the change effort as opportunity arises—with the goal being to reinforce the importance of the change effort to meeting business needs and achieving strategic objectives.

■ With communication channel, informal network, and alliance understanding, change managers may:

□ Work through existing communication channels of peers, colleagues, and others to give presentations—both formal and informal—to emphasize the importance of a change effort, the direction of it, the objectives tied to it, and the results sought from it. This may involve giving talks to groups inside and outside the organization and arranging for influential stakeholders at all levels inside and outside the organization to hear those presentations.

☐ Identify groups or individuals that have—or should have—a stake in a change effort and make them aware of it and garner their support to "make it happen."

☐ Build strategic alliances with key groups and influential individuals inside and outside the organization to serve as change champions and change supporters of the performance improvement strategy.

■ With group dynamics process understanding, change managers may:

☐ Pinpoint possible sources of resistance to a change effort and take proactive steps to address those problems so that they do not adversely affect the performance improvement strategy. (Note that a performance improvement strategy is a change effort.)

☐ Emphasize the benefits or "what's-in-it-for-me's" (WIFMs) throughout the change effort to ensure that individuals and groups appreciate the need for the change effort and support it, as much as possible, based on their own self-interests.

☐ Understand how to work with groups or teams to initiate, follow through on, and continuously assess group support (or opposition) to the direction of a change effort and take positive steps to address any issues that may serve to stall, derail, or otherwise adversely affect the performance improvement strategy.

■ With process consultation skills, change managers may:

☐ Watch group dynamics in meetings and in other group settings to identify issues in how the group(s) perform, as they may influence action in the direction of a performance improvement strategy.

☐ Take action to address group process (that is, "how group members interact") if group process issues negatively affect implementation of a performance improvement strategy.

■ With facilitation skills, change managers may help group members to:

☐ Formulate action plans and proposals to guide a performance improvement strategy.

☐ Establish measurable objectives and milestones for a performance improvement strategy.

☐ Track progress toward the objectives of the performance improvement strategy and take proactive steps for improvement when milestones are missed or when results do not match objectives or stakeholder expectations.

Of all of these, perhaps facilitation skills are the most important of all, because those competencies help participants and stakeholders in performance improvement interventions achieve agreement or consensus about how well interventions are working.

Approaches for Managing Change

There are three important approaches for managing any change effort. Those who enact the change manager role should be familiar with all three. They are: (1) *the coercive approach*, (2) *the persuasive approach*, and (3) *the normative reeducative approach* (Rothwell and Sullivan, 2005). Each deserves a brief review.

The Coercive Approach

The coercive approach to change is familiar to many people. It takes its name from the underlying driver for change that it uses—that is, coercion. People are told to "just do it." The subtle—and sometimes not-so-subtle—threat is that "if you don't do it, we will find someone who will." Most everyone with experience in organizations has heard it said that some managers adopt a philosophy that "it's my way or the highway." This phrase is indicative of the coercive approach.

The coercive approach follows this general model:

- **Step 1:** Order people to make a change.
- **Step 2:** Follow up to see if they made the change.
- **Step 3:** Take action if they did not make the change.

These steps are depicted in Figure 4-2.

The coercive approach to change is perhaps best embodied in the thinking of Scientific Management, which was founded early in the 20th century by writer-philosopher Frederick Taylor. Frederick Taylor's views were often misinterpreted, and he is often blamed for purveying such ideas as these:

- Workers are generally lazy and require a "kick butt" approach to get them to act.
- People are generally untrustworthy and will do the wrong thing—or take the easy way out—unless their actions are closely observed, monitored, and scrutinized for the slightest error.

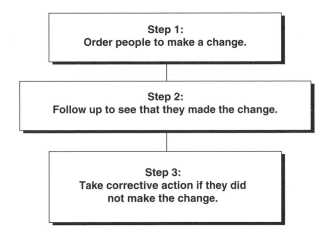

Figure 4-2   A model of the coercive approach to change.

- The manager's job requires "whipping people" to get results, and the best managers achieve results by "scaring people" more than others do.

This approach is sometimes called the "whip-and-chair" view of management, since it casts the manager in the role of lion tamer.

Of course, there are occasions when the coercive approach is quite appropriate to bring about change. Perhaps the best example is in case of an unexpected emergency or crisis. The captain of a ship does not take a vote to decide whether to abandon a sinking ship; rather, he or she orders people to do it. They are expected to act without questioning the orders or complaining about them. In any case, it is in their best interest to take action in that situation, and the dangers of not doing so are apparent to the crew.

Note that the word *unexpected* preceded *emergency or crisis* in the paragraph above. While some managers in organizations may liken their situations to those of captains on sinking ships and rationalize that a coercive approach is appropriate in today's superheated business environment, the reality is that very few crises or emergencies should exist if managers plan the work and communicate with workers. One case in which it might be appropriate is the case of an enterprisewide system implementation. It is, after all, a decision that encompasses the entire organization. Someone needs to exert leadership, make the call that it is necessary, and take action steps.

Those who do HPI work should recognize this approach, because it is too commonly used. Managers may want to "force" people to cooperate with a performance improvement strategy. Their goal is to get quick results. Unfortunately, by using this approach, effectiveness (long-term results) is sacrificed for expediency (short-term results). Effectiveness stems from obtaining worker buy-in and ownership for a change effort or a performance improvement strategy, and that requires taking the time to use another approach.

The Persuasive Approach

The persuasive approach to change should also be familiar to many people. It takes its name from the underlying driver for change that it uses—that is, persuasion. People are told to "do it because it is in your best interests to do it." The subtle message underlying this approach is that "if you don't do it, then you are acting against your own selfish interests." At its best, the persuasive approach is sincere. At its worst, the persuasive approach is a disguised form of the coercive approach in which people are told to "cooperate for your own interests—or else be prepared to accept the negative consequences stemming from your unwillingness to cooperate."

The persuasive approach follows this general model:

- **Step 1:** Give people the background of a problem or situation.
- **Step 2:** Describe for them what needs to be done to solve the problem or address the situation.
- **Step 3:** Describe, in detail, exactly what benefits the organization—and individuals—will obtain from cooperating with the change effort.
- **Step 4:** Describe the likely consequences of not taking action on the problem or situation.
- **Step 5:** Ask for their support and help to make the change happen and to solve the problem or deal with the situation.
- **Step 6:** Establish specific, measurable, and traceable performance improvement objectives and establish milestones for those objectives.
- **Step 7:** Communicate about the value of the performance improvement effort on a continuing basis and provide continuing feedback to the organization, groups, and individuals about their contributions in achieving results.

These steps are depicted in Figure 4-3.

The persuasive approach to change is perhaps best embodied in the Human Relations School of Management, which was founded early in the 20th century

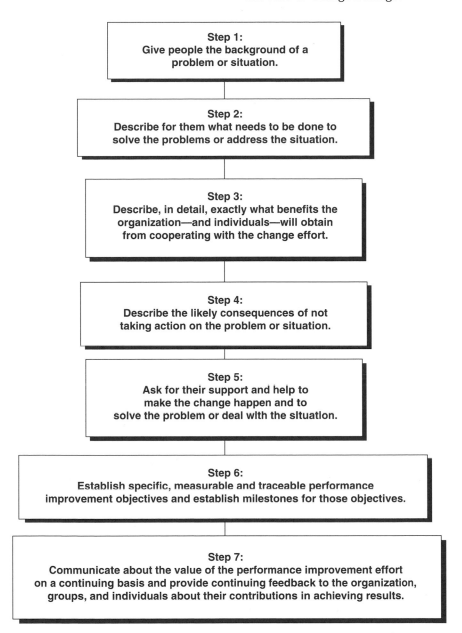

Figure 4-3 A model of the persuasive approach to change.

as a reaction to Scientific Management. It is based on such key assumptions as these:

- Workers are social beings who seek support and recognition from their peers and organizational superiors.
- People are generally trustworthy and will do the right thing—as long as they understand what to do, why to do it, and how they benefit from it.
- The manager's job requires recognizing how important social needs are in organizational settings and his or her role in "providing positive feedback" to actions by individuals or groups to achieve desired results.

The persuasive approach is frequently used in organizations today. Managers provide direction. They explain why that direction is important to the organization. They do not always, however, provide clear information about benefits—the "what's-in-it-for-me's" to workers. Nor do they always establish measurable performance targets or milestones for improvement or mount a continuing information campaign to provide feedback to workers and other stakeholders about the progress of improvement efforts.

Those who do HPI work should recognize this approach and should be prepared to help managers, workers, and stakeholders establish:

- Clear messages about the need for change and how such change relates to organizational needs and desired performance
- Clear, measurable, and well-communicated performance targets or objectives to be achieved from a performance improvement strategy or effort
- A communication plan or informational campaign to match the performance improvement strategy so that workers and other key stakeholders are given continuing feedback on how well their actions (individually and/or collectively) are helping to achieve desired results and/or what corrective actions may be necessary
- Tracking systems that permit individuals and/or groups to assess how much and how well their efforts are helping to achieve the results desired from a performance improvement strategy
- Incentive and reward systems that are tied to the desired performance results so that there is a genuine link between "performance" and "rewards"

The Normative Reeducative Approach

The normative reeducative approach to change is new to many people. It takes its name from the underlying drivers for change that it uses—that is, *norms* (unspoken rules governing action) and *education* (change resulting from new information or skills). People are not "told" anything when this approach is used; rather, they are themselves the source of the change effort. Like any other approach, however, this approach can be misused, and that is the greatest potential danger in using it.

The normative reeducative approach follows the framework of what is called the *action research model* (ARM):

- **Step 1:** Find individuals or groups who want to change or who want to improve.
- **Step 2:** Clarify the scope of the change effort. (Does this involve one or more individuals, an entire work group or team, the whole organization, the organization's approach to dealing with its external environment, or some other frame of reference? Exactly what needs to be changed?)
- **Step 3:** Conduct background research on the setting to find possible sources of performance problems or opportunities for performance improvement.
- **Step 4:** Collect information from individuals, groups, and others inside the organization and stakeholders outside the organization (such as customers, suppliers, and/or distributors) familiar with the problem or opportunity facing the individual(s) or group(s) that are attempting to improve performance.
- **Step 5:** Feed the results of the data collection effort back to individuals inside the organization.
- **Step 6:** Use the feedback effort in Step 5 (where information is gathered from individuals or groups) to energize an impetus for change by giving people a sense of different perspectives about how well the organization is doing.
- **Step 7:** Help an organization, group, or individual recognize what change is needed and why it is needed by pinpointing performance problems or opportunities for improvement.
- **Step 8:** Achieve group consensus (or individual agreement) on the performance problem or opportunity, the need for change, and the priorities desired for change.

- **Step 9:** Help an organization, group, or individual identify the best way(s) to solve the performance problem(s) or improvement opportunity(-ies) by collecting information about perceived solutions to the problems or approaches to seizing performance improvement opportunities and feeding that information back to the group.

- **Step 10:** Achieve group consensus (or individual agreement) on the most appropriate performance improvement strategies.

- **Step 11:** Establish performance or change objectives that are clear, precise, and measurable so that, when the performance objectives are met, the gap will be closed between the actual (what is happening now) and the desirable (what should be happening).

- **Step 12:** Help an organization, group, or individual identify the best way(s) to implement the performance improvement strategy to achieve the desired performance results. Do that by polling the group, benchmarking best practices in other organizations, and researching the literature on approaches used by other organizations, and other approaches.

- **Step 13:** Feed the results of Step 12 back to the group and help group members establish a proposal for a performance improvement strategy that articulates the specific, measurable performance objectives (outcomes) and solves the performance problem(s) or realizes performance improvement opportunity(-ies).

- **Step 14:** Present the proposal, including resource requirements, to key decision makers and stakeholders to secure support.

- **Step 15:** Secure approval for the proposal and launch the performance improvement intervention or performance improvement strategy.

- **Step 16:** Implement the performance improvement strategy and monitor results of the performance improvement effort over time.

- **Step 17:** Provide continuing feedback to participants and stakeholders in the performance improvement effort so that they see how well the performance improvement effort is doing and can take corrective action if results are off-target.

- **Step 18:** Complete the performance improvement strategy when results match objectives.

- **Step 19:** Evaluate results against performance objectives and report results to all key stakeholders and all participants in the performance improvement strategy.

These steps are depicted in Figure 4-4.

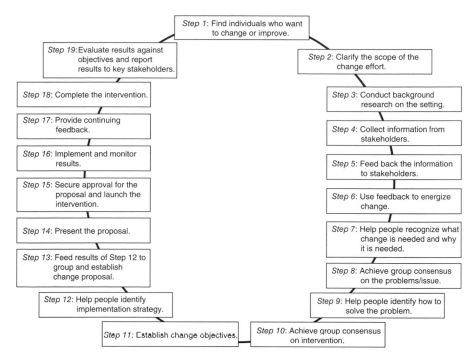

Figure 4-4 A model of the normative reeducative approach to change.

The normative reeducative approach—which is a key foundation for this book—is perhaps best embodied in the Systems School of Management. It is based on such key assumptions as these:

- Performance is best judged in the eyes of the customer or user.
- Most problems stem from management, not from individual workers. Workers, however, are well suited to advise management "what to do."
- The people who are closest to performance are usually in the best position to judge "why things go wrong" and "what would work best to fix those problems"—or else "what could be done to make things go better" and "what would work to seize opportunities that exist."
- The search for quick fixes is usually fruitless, and "the quality of the results obtained from performance improvement efforts is directly correlated to the amount of time devoted to them and the ownership in them that all key groups feel about them."

The normative reeducative approach is also known to organization development (OD) practitioners as the action research model (ARM) (Rothwell and Sullivan, 2005). It is one of several key models that should be in the toolkit of the workplace and learning and performance (WLP) practitioner (Rothwell, Sanders, and Soper, 1999). More recently, the ARM has been supplemented by *appreciative inquiry*, an approach that (appreciatively and nonjudgmentally) queries the parties concerning their beliefs about a problem situation. This is a good method for surfacing and addressing issues with regard to change initiatives in the organization as well as a way to gain support and buy-in for interventions requiring organizational change.

Those who do HPI work should recognize this approach and be prepared to use it. The normative reeducative approach model, or ARM, is suitable for use with groups of any size.

Enacting the Role of Change Manager

Change managers focus their efforts primarily around Steps 15–17 of the model described in Figure 4-4. Enacting the role of change manager thus involves the steps appearing in Figure 4-5. Each step deserves more detailed attention in this chapter.

Step 15: Securing Approval for the Proposal and Launching the Performance Improvement Intervention or Performance Improvement Strategy

Most performance improvement interventions begin when a senior manager, who may also be championing the effort, grants approval for the use of organizational resources. That is usually done upon the acceptance of a proposal that describes:

- The exact nature of the problem or improvement opportunity
- A brief description of the cause of the problem—and how that information was obtained (through the work of the analyst role)
- A brief description of the proposed solution to the problem—that is, the performance improvement intervention—and how that solution was identified as appropriate to address the problem's underlying cause and how that solution is expected to address the problem or achieve desired results

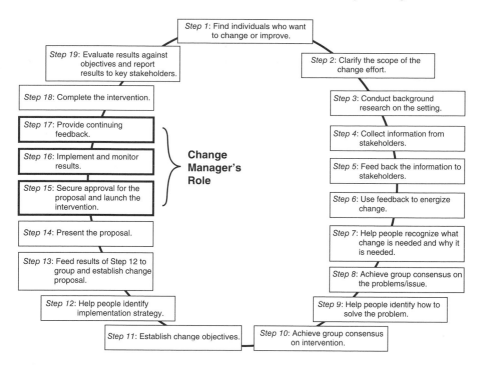

Figure 4-5 A model of the normative reeducative approach to change—the change manager's role.

- A list of the specific, measurable objectives intended to be achieved by the performance improvement intervention
- A list of time-specific, measurable milestones, which are essentially measurable signposts to show progress toward achieving the final performance improvement objectives
- A step-by-step plan to implement the performance improvement intervention, describing what will happen, what results are expected from each step, who does what, and how information about the performance improvement intervention—at each key step—will be communicated to the participants and stakeholders in the intervention
- A timeline describing when what steps will be taken
- A budget for the performance improvement intervention, showing all costs associated with the intervention
- A cost-benefit analysis to show the financial gains that are expected to be realized from the project minus the costs

- A description of all individuals—both inside and outside the organization—who are needed to implement the performance improvement intervention and how their qualifications relate to achieving intended
  objectives

Use the worksheet appearing in Figure 4-6 to prepare such a proposal.

A proposal organized like the one described above provides an excellent
foundation by which to clarify:

- What results are expected from the performance improvement
  intervention
- Who should be involved directly in the implementation of the performance
  improvement intervention
- When results should be expected
- Why the performance improvement intervention is worth undertaking
- How the performance improvement intervention will be implemented
- How much the organization's decision makers and stakeholders should
  expect to gain from the implementation effort

The proposal also supplies a means by which to communicate to others inside
and outside the organization about why the performance improvement intervention is being undertaken, what problem(s) it is intended to solve (or what opportunities are expected to result from it), and when results should be expected. It
is thus as much a persuasive tool as it is a management document intended to
guide implementation.

Step 16: Implementing the Performance Improvement Strategy and Monitoring Results of the Performance Improvement Effort Over Time

The implementation of a performance improvement strategy usually follows the
acceptance of the proposal. There are three general ways by which a performance
improvement strategy may be implemented: (1) by one person who is appointed
leader; (2) by one or more teams, committees, or task forces charged with
responsibility for planning, implementing, and evaluating the performance
improvement intervention; or (3) by giving each manager and/or worker objectives linked to the project and asking someone to track results against objectives.
Each approach is worthy of review.

Directions: Use this worksheet for drafting a proposal for a performance improvement strategy or intervention. For each question posed in the left column below, facilitate group decision making to write an answer in the right column below. When you are finished, write up the answers in narrative format and present to key decision makers.

Question	Answer
1. What is the exact nature of the problem or performance improvement opportunity?	
2. What is the cause of the problem—and how was that information obtained?	
3. What is the proposed solution to the problem—that is, the performance improvement intervention—and how was that the solution identified to be appropriate?	
4. What are the specific, measurable objectives that are intended to be achieved by the performance improvement intervention?	
5. What time-specific, measurable milestones have been (or can be) established to show progress toward achieving the final performance improvement objectives?	

Figure 4-6 A worksheet for preparing a proposal.

Question	Answer
6. What step-by-step plan can be established to implement the performance improvement intervention that will describe "what will happen," "what results are expected from each step," "who does what," and how information about the performance improvement intervention—at each key step—will be communicated to the participants and stakeholders in the intervention"?	1.
	2.
	3.
	4.
	5.
	6.
	7.
	8.
	9.
	10.
7. What time-specific, measurable milestone have been (or can be) established to show progress toward achieving the final performance improvement objectives?	

Figure 4-6 *Continued*

Question	Answer
8. What budget has been prepared for the performance improvement intervention to show all costs associated with the intervention?	
9. What financial gains are expected to be realized from the performance improvement intervention? (Benefits of project minus project costs.)	
10. What people from inside and outside the organization will be needed to implement the intervention and how do their qualifications relate to achieving intended objectives?	

Figure 4-6 *Continued*

Implementing a Performance Improvement Intervention with One Leader

An individual appointed as leader to implement a performance improvement intervention may be given specific instructions about how to implement the intervention by senior executives, or else he may "invent" the role that he is to play. In either case, this person clearly serves as change manager. Often, a change manager acting in this role has authority, without additional approvals, to expend project budgetary resources.

How the role is enacted depends, in large measure, on the nature of the performance improvement intervention that the individual has been charged to undertake. But one approach is to clarify:

- The size, scope, and nature of the problem to be solved
- The nature of the performance improvement intervention intended to achieve results
- The performance objectives and time-specific milestones intended to be achieved
- The results sought from each step in the performance improvement intervention
- The stakeholders who must be involved in and must support the effort
- The information that must be periodically communicated to stakeholders and the means by which that information is best conveyed to them

While this information should have been assembled by those who acted as analysts and as intervention selection specialists—who may not be the same individual who is charged with serving as change manager—it is important for the change manager to be very clear about what is happening, what is desired, how wide is the performance gap that exists between the two, and what must be done to close or narrow the gap.

Some change managers will find it helpful to visit the key stakeholders to secure their support for the effort and to gain their insights about what must be done to achieve those results.

Paying such visits has the added benefit of building some ownership through the personal involvement of the key stakeholders.

Implementing a Performance Improvement Intervention with a Team, Committee, or Task Force

When implementing a performance improvement strategy, some decision makers in organizations will prefer to appoint a team, committee, task force, or other group.

Members of this group should be selected for their interest in the performance improvement intervention and/or on their ability to contribute to successful implementation based on their individual knowledge, skills, and abilities.

Of course, on occasion, members are selected on the basis of their availability —which is not always the best way, since available people may (or may not) be supportive of the intervention. The individual charged with facilitating or coordinating the team, committee, or task force actions is the change manager.

The team is sometimes called a design team or an implementation team. The team members are expected to work together to achieve results on the performance improvement intervention. When a team is assembled to implement a performance improvement intervention, the change manager must help the team members progress through the predictable stages of any small group. These stages are (adapted from Tuckman, 1965):

- 1: Forming
- 2: Storming
- 3: Norming
- 4: Performing
- 5: Adjourning

During the *forming stage*, team members may not be familiar with the background leading up to the performance improvement intervention, and they may not be familiar with each other. The change manager's role during that stage should thus be to clarify the background and help members of the team become familiar with each other and the contributions they can make.

During the *storming stage*, team members are likely to question the value of the performance improvement intervention, the value of the problem leading up to it, and other such issues. The change manager should thus assemble a briefing that addresses such questions. (It may also be necessary to modify the performance improvement intervention project plan at this step to accommodate new ideas or approaches that were previously not identified.)

During the *norming stage*, team members will accept their responsibilities for the performance improvement intervention and will identify specific efforts to be achieved. The change manager's role during this stage is to ensure that team members communicate and to periodically collect information that can be compared to the project milestones.

Since team members may tend to fall into groupthink, the change manager can also play devil's advocate to encourage team members to consider new ideas or approaches that might otherwise be overlooked. During the *performing stage*, team members carry out their project responsibilities. The change manager's role during this stage is to track results against milestones and objectives and feed those back to interested stakeholders.

During the *adjourning stage* of team development, team members go through a process of disbanding. This period represents a time to reflect on performance of the improvement project and asks questions such as: What went well? What barriers did we encounter? How did we work together as a team? What would we do differently next time? What did we learn? What value did we add through our efforts?

The adjourning stage also represents a time to capture and document knowledge and learning that took place so that it can be used in the future and transmitted to other stakeholders. Knowledge management is a critical success factor in learning organizations. When HPI teams are able to capture and disseminate information about the problem and how it was solved, it's useful to others in different parts of the organization and reduces the chances of people reinventing the wheel.

During the adjournment phase, team members tie up loose ends of the project. This is a time to dot the I's and cross the T's. It is also a time to either transition back into their regular positions, if the project was a temporary assignment, or transition to a new performance improvement initiative. Adjournment is also a time for the team to celebrate success. This can help to reward and recognize individual as well as team efforts and contributions and to build momentum for future HPI work.

The change manager should help guide team members through the adjournment stage by serving as a leader. He or she facilitates the knowledge, capture, and management process. The change manager might also be involved in reassigning team members to new positions and organizing the team celebration.

Implementing a Performance Improvement Intervention with Objectives

In some organizations, decision makers may resist appointing one leader to take charge of the implementation of a performance improvement intervention or resist appointing a team, committee, or task force for that purpose. A third option is to clarify the role that each manager and worker in the organization is expected to play in the implementation effort. Such an approach may be common in organizations that use management by objectives.

This approach to implementing a performance improvement strategy is only appropriate when everyone in the organization has—or should have—a role to play in implementing the intervention and when that role can be clarified and made specific, timebound, and measurable. Lacking such information, it will be difficult to hold individuals accountable for contributing to results. In most cases, even when all or most members of the organization are given responsibility for implementing an intervention, someone will have to be appointed to track results against milestones and performance improvement intervention objectives and feed those results back to others in the organization. That individual is the change manager.

A good example for an appropriate use of this method is the implementation of a performance management process. Since all employees are expected to play some part in the successful implementation, a reasonable plan would be to communicate guidelines and expectations to all parties, and to establish measures of success. The rest of the implementation would be up to each individual in the organization.

Step 17: Providing Continuing Feedback to Participants and Stakeholders in the Performance Improvement Effort

Feedback refers to information conveyed back to performers during and following performance to permit them to correct deficiencies and highlight and celebrate successes. Feedback is properly targeted to the final results (objectives) established for a performance improvement intervention and to the milestones (measurable markers) on the way to achievement of final objectives.

One important contribution that change managers can make to the successful implementation of a performance improvement intervention is encapsulated in this step, since no system can correct problems unless some form of feedback is received that results are not matching intentions.

A simple example should dramatize this point. Suppose that an organization has been experiencing an abnormally large number of customer complaints. That is the performance problem. Suppose further that analysts have examined the problem and have determined that customers are complaining because they are not reading the directions for the use of the product made by the company. (Assume, for the sake of this fictitious case, that the company manufactures computer inkjet printers.)

Customers have been clogging technical support lines because their printers simply stop printing at some point because the customers do not regularly clean the products in conformity with instructions clearly provided to them in the manual accompanying the printer. The cause of the problem thus is that customers are not getting the message. The company takes decisive action by identifying all names of customers, obtained from product warranties, and sending them an e-mail or letter that reminds them of the need to clean their printers.

How will company decision makers know whether this performance improvement strategy—geared to conveying important information to customers—was successful and worth the sizable expense of the mailing? The answer is that they must establish some way to gather feedback. Perhaps the best way in this case is for company technical support workers to log the number and type of calls they receive to determine if the problem has been corrected. While that information is useful, it does not become feedback until it is conveyed to those who wrote and mailed out the letter and to the decision makers who made the decision to send the letter.

What might be expected from this performance improvement intervention? While it might seem that the problem would be corrected, the reality is that it is a short-term measure only. Printer customers change over time. Not everyone will have received the e-mail or letter. Consequently, additional steps must be taken to correct the problem. Such steps might include:

- Placing a sticker directly on the printer when it is manufactured to inform new users of equipment cleaning requirements
- Securing e-mail addresses from customers as they register their printers and automating an e-mail message to remind them of the product cleaning requirements and the dangers of ignoring those requirements

Each approach is essentially a performance improvement strategy intended to reduce calls about the consequences of not cleaning printers. Again, the impact of each strategy cannot be determined unless a feedback system is created.

In the future of human performance improvement, self-correcting systems are likely to become more important and more common. In a self-correcting system, measurable feedback is provided automatically to performers on a timely, specific, and concrete basis directly from participants in the change effort. Hence, if some way can be found to give the decision makers and workers in the above example information from customers as it is collected so that they can self-correct their actions, then a self-correcting system has been created.

How should change managers establish a means by which to collect information about progress toward the objectives of the performance improvement strategy? To answer that question, change managers should:

■ Clarify precisely from stakeholders what results are sought from the performance improvement intervention
■ Ensure that the results can be made specific and measurable
■ Identify who should receive feedback about performance to ensure that progress is being achieved toward the objectives
■ Work with stakeholders—and performers themselves—to identify the most effective means by which to convey feedback
■ Establish a tracking system to collect feedback and give it to performers

It is not uncommon for these interim measurements of success to get lost in the hubbub of implementation. Therefore, it's important that the change manager stay focused and ensure that these measures occur and that the data are fed back to the key stakeholders, as agreed on.

Summary

The change manager is the role that "ensures that interventions are implemented in ways consistent with desired results and that they help individuals and groups achieve results" (Rothwell, 2000). The key competencies associated with the role include: (1) change implementation skills; (2) change impetus skills; (3) communication channel, informal network, and alliance understanding; (4) group dynamics process understanding; (5) process consultation skills; and (6) facilitation skills. The terminal output associated with the role is that "performance improvement interventions [are] effectively monitored with participants and stakeholders" (Rothwell, 2000).

Change managers should be familiar with three key approaches for managing change. The coercive approach "forces" people to change under threat of coercion. The persuasive approach "encourages" people to change by appeals to self-interest. The normative reeducative approach "teaches people a new way" and taps into their desire to be productive and useful. The change manager's role is enacted by moving a project along, where "project" means performance improvement intervention or strategy. Change managers should focus attention particularly on securing approval for the proposal and launching the performance improvement intervention or performance improvement strategy, implementing the performance improvement strategy and monitoring results of the performance improvement effort over time, and providing continuing feedback to participants and stakeholders in the performance improvement effort so that they see how well the performance improvement effort is doing and can take corrective action if results are off-target.

The next chapter focuses attention on the role of evaluator. That role takes up where the change manager's role leaves off. Often, the two roles are closely related.

References

McLagan, P. (1989). *Models for HRD Practice.* 4 vols. Alexandria, VA: The American Society for Trainning and Development.

Rothwell, W. (2000). *ASTD Models for Human Performance Improvement,* 2nd ed. Alexandria, VA: The American Society for Training and Development.

Rothwell, W., and Sullivan, R. (Eds.). (2005). *Practicing Organization Development: A Guide for Consultants,* 2nd ed. San Francisco: Pfeiffer.

Tuckman, B. (1965). Development Sequence in Small Groups. *Psychological Bulletin, 63,* 284–399.

The Role of Evaluator

What is the role of the evaluator? What competencies and work outputs are associated with that role? What general approaches can be helpful in evaluating performance improvement interventions? This chapter, the last of four focusing on the roles of those performing HPI work, addresses these questions.

Managers and other stakeholders of performance improvement interventions increasingly demand accountability. They want to know what business needs were satisfied and what return on investment was received from the resources dedicated to performance improvement interventions. Determining such a return is, in part, the role of the evaluator.

According to *ASTD Models for Human Performance Improvement* (Rothwell, 2000), the evaluator "assesses the impact of interventions and follows up on changes made, actions taken, and results achieved in order to provide participants and stakeholders with information about how well interventions are being implemented." In short, the evaluator provides feedback to stakeholders about what benefits were received from a performance improvement intervention.

Competencies Associated with the Role of Evaluator

According to *ASTD Models for Human Performance Improvement* (Rothwell, 2000), the following competencies are linked to the evaluator role:

- **Performance gap evaluation skill:** Measuring, or helping others to measure, the difference between actuals and ideals
- **Ability to evaluate results against organizational goals:** Assessing how well the results of a human performance improvement intervention match intentions

- **Standard-setting skills:** Measuring desired results of organizations, processes, or individuals; helping others to establish and measure work expectations
- **Ability to assess impact on culture:** Examining the effects of human performance gaps and human performance improvement interventions on shared beliefs and assumptions about "right" and "wrong" ways of behaving and acting in one organizational setting
- **Human performance improvement intervention reviewing skills:** Finding ways to evaluate and continuously improve human performance improvement interventions before and during implementation
- **Feedback skills:** Collecting information about performance and feeding it back clearly, specifically, and on a timely basis to affected individuals or groups (McLagan, 1989)

Outputs Linked to the Role

The outputs associated with the competencies are listed in Figure 5-1.

What It All Means

Taken together, the role, competencies, and work outputs of the evaluator dramatize the importance of the role for collecting, feeding back, and emphasizing the benefits received from performance improvement interventions. In the words of one practitioner, "A good evaluator does not assume that managers and other stakeholders just intuit what benefits were received. They tell people every day *what we did for you today.*" The operative phrase here is *what we did for you.* Evaluators are under the gun to demonstrate results—in other words, measurable improvements in performance. They may also be asked to forecast, before an intervention is undertaken, what results are expected from it so that a sound investment decision can be made as to whether even to expend the time and resources to undertake the intervention.

Evaluators may apply their competencies as illustrated by the following examples:

- With performance gap evaluation skills, evaluators may:
  - ☐ Work with managers and members of a department, division, or work group to establish the performance measures before and after a performance improvement intervention.
  - ☐ Forecast the financial benefits that are expected from a performance improvement intervention before the intervention is launched.

Evaluator Role	Terminal Output
Assesses the impact of interventions and follows up on changes made, actions taken, and result achieved in order to provide participants and stakeholders with information about how well interventions are being implemented.	Written and oral reports to: ■ Participants and stakeholders about the progress of an intervention ■ The organization about performance ■ The organizations about progress of interventions ■ Work groups or teams about their performance ■ Work groups or teams about the progress of interventions ■ Management about performance ■ Management about interventions

Evaluator Competencies	Enabling Qutputs
1. **Performance Gap Evaluation Skills:** Measuring or helping others to measure the difference between actual performance and ideal performance.	■ Human performance improvement evaluation objectives ■ Human performance improvement evaluation designs and plans ■ Human performance improvement evaluation instruments ■ Pre- and post-measures of worker performance ■ Evaluation findings, conclusions and recommendations ■ Reports to management and workers on the outcomes of human performance improvement strategies
2. **Ability to Evaluate Results Against Organizational Goals:** Assessing how well the results of a human performance improvement intervention match intentions.	■ Linkage of human performance improvement interventions to other change efforts of the organization ■ Linkage of each human performance improvement intervention with other interventions ■ Linkage of human performance improvement interventions to organizational plans, goals and objectives ■ Linkage of human performance improvement interventions to organizational/business needs

Figure 5-1 Outputs associated with the evaluator role. Source: Rothwell, W. (2000). *ASTD Models for Human Performance Improvement: Roles, Competencies, and Outputs*, 2nd ed. Alexandria, VA: The American Society for Training and Development. Used by permission of the American Society for Training and Development.

Evaluator Competencies	Enabling Outputs
3. **Standard Setting Skills:** Measuring desired results of organizations, processes, or individuals; helping others to establish and measure work expectations.	■ Work standards/expectations established ■ Work standards/expectations communicated
4. **Ability to Assess Impact on Culture:** Examining the effects of human performance gaps and human performance improvement interventions and shared beliefs and assumptions about "right" and "wrong" ways of behaving and acting in one organizational setting.	■ Linkage of human performance improvement interventions to organizational culture performance improvement
5. **Human Performance Improvement Intervention Reviewing Skills:** Finding ways to evaluate and continuously improve human performance improvement interventions before and during implementation.	■ Written and oral reports to stakeholders and participants about the progress of an intervention
6. **Feedback Skills:** Collecting information about performance and feeding it back clearly, specifically, and on a timely basis to affected individuals or groups (McLagan,1989).	■ Feedback to the organization about performance ■ Feedback to the organization about progress of interventions ■ Feedback to work groups or teams about performance ■ Feedback to work groups or teams about progress of interventions ■ Feedback to management about performance ■ Feedback to management about interventions

Figure 5-1 *Continued*

- With the ability to evaluate results against organizational goals, evaluators may:
  - ☐ Clarify, with key organizational decision makers, how a performance improvement intervention can be measured against the organization's strategic business objectives before the intervention is launched.
  - ☐ Track how well a performance improvement's intervention is achieving milestones (that is, interim measures of results) during the intervention and how well those are contributing to the organization's strategic business objectives.
  - ☐ Demonstrate, and feed back information to decision makers following a performance improvement intervention, how much the intervention contributed to achievement of the organization's strategic business objectives.

- With standard-setting skills, evaluators may:
  - □ Facilitate, with key decision makers and others, the establishment of minimal and measurable performance expectations that are required of workers and others. For example, how many sales calls per day should be fairly expected of an experienced salesperson who is working at a normal pace? (The answer to that question, when posed to experienced salespersons and their immediate supervisor, may lead to the establishment of measurable performance standards that describe what should be happening.)
- With the ability to assess impact on culture, evaluators may:
  - □ Measure changes in corporate culture that result from a performance improvement intervention by soliciting stories that yield qualitative measures of change. These are positive descriptions of what happened, but without metrics associated with them. For instance, "The intervention has been helping us to get more positive comments from our customers."
- With human performance improvement intervention reviewing skills, evaluators may:
  - □ Find ways to publicize the results of performance improvement interventions during and after the intervention so that participants and stakeholders in the intervention can continuously review results achieved from the intervention(s).
- With feedback skills, evaluators may:
  - □ Find ways to feed back the costs and benefits of performance improvement interventions to participants and stakeholders in those interventions.

Of all of these, perhaps feedback skills are the most important, because feedback provides a loop back to the participants and stakeholders to demonstrate what results and benefits were realized from performance improvement interventions.

Approaches for Evaluating Performance Improvement Interventions

In the 1960s, Donald Kirkpatrick first described a model of evaluation to be used in assessing the results of training. Those who enact the evaluator role should be familiar with all four levels. They are: (1) *reaction*, (2) *learning*, (3) *behavior*, and (4) *results*. Each deserves a brief review as it applies to training and to evaluating performance improvement interventions.

Evaluating Performance Improvement Interventions at the Reaction Level

How much do participants and stakeholders involved with a performance improvement intervention like the intervention and perceive that it adds value and solves performance problems or contributes to realizing performance improvement opportunities? That is the key question posed by evaluators who examine performance improvement interventions at the reaction level. In this context, then, reaction refers to how people react to the performance improvement intervention.

How Is the Reaction Level Measured in Learning-Oriented Performance Improvement Interventions? Training, and other structured learning events, are most often measured at the reaction level. Upon completion of an off-the-job training experience, participants are asked to rate the instructor and course by means of a written survey questionnaire. Such a questionnaire, sometimes called a *smile sheet*, assesses participant feelings or attitudes about how well the training was conducted. Typical issues measured may include how well the training:

- Clarified what results were to be achieved
- Was delivered appropriately and effectively by the instructor
- Made effective use of time
- Made effective use of audiovisual aids
- Achieved the desired results

Participants may be asked to self-assess their own achievement of the program's objectives and identify any barriers to skill transfer that may exist back in the workplace. In addition, participants may be asked to describe the strengths of the training course, its weaknesses or areas needing improvement, and any other comments or suggestions they may have to make. A sample training evaluation form is shown in Figure 5-2.

How Is the Reaction Level Measured in Other Performance Improvement Interventions? Training is only one of many possible performance improvement interventions. Recall from Chapter 3 that examples of other performance improvement interventions may include (Langdon, Whiteside, and McKenna, 1999):

Directions: Please complete the following evaluation immediately upon completion of the training course. Write the course title, date, and location in the space provided below. Do not sign your name. Then, for each statement made in right column below, circle the number in the left column that best indicates your level of agreement. Use the following scale: 0 = Not Applicable; 1 = Strongly Disagree; 2 = Disagree; 3 = Neutral; 4 = Agree; and 5 = Strongly Agree. When you are finished with the evaluation, turn it in as the course instructor directs you to do. Thank you for your cooperation!

Location	Date	Course Title				
		Level of Agreement with the Statement				
Statement	Not Applicable	Strongly Disagree	Disagree	Neutral	Agree	Strongly Agree
1. The course purpose was stated clearly.	0	1	2	3	4	5
2. The objectives were described at the beginning of the course.	0	1	2	3	4	5
3. The organization of the course was clearly explained at the beginning of the course.	0	1	2	3	4	5
4. The instructor delivered the course content in a well-organized way.	0	1	2	3	4	5
5. The instructor used instructional aids, such as handouts, effectively.	0	1	2	3	4	5
6. The instructor used audiovisual aids—such as videotapes, audiotapes, and other instructional support—effectively.	0	1	2	3	4	5
7. Time in the course was used efficiently.	0	1	2	3	4	5
8. The course content was directly related to my job duties.	0	1	2	3	4	5
9. The value of the course to my work is apparent to me.	0	1	2	3	4	5
10. I would recommend this course to others who do my job because they will find it useful to help them improve their job performance.	0	1	2	3	4	5

11. What was the most valuable aspect of this course, in your opinion, for helping you do your job better?

12. What was the least valuable aspect of this course, in your opinion, for helping you do your job better?

13. What other comments do you have to make?

Figure 5-2   A sample participant training evaluation form.

- 360-degree feedback
- Assessment centers
- Communication
- Compensation systems
- Competency modeling
- Customer feedback
- Electronic performance support systems (EPSS)
- Expert systems
- Job aids
- Diversity programs
- Coaching
- Motivation systems
- Performance appraisal
- Performance management
- Policies and procedures

Many other performance improvement interventions are also possible.

A key difference between training and these other performance improvement interventions is that it is very rare for performance improvement interventions other than training to be evaluated for reactions. Organizational decision makers will take action to improve human performance using any or all performance improvement interventions listed above. Rarely, however, do they also ask participants and other stakeholders in the intervention how well they feel that it is achieving desired results.

Soliciting participant and stakeholder perceptions, though, about these performance improvement interventions other than training may also serve useful purposes. It is, after all, done to measure customer satisfaction with products or services. For instance, participants and other stakeholders may pinpoint:

- Emerging trends (or other issues) that could impact the performance improvement intervention
- Changing requirements that affect the performance objectives intended to be achieved by a performance improvement intervention
- Emerging problems with implementation efforts

Additionally, by administering periodic reaction forms, HPI practitioners and others can provide a continuing means to focus attention on the performance improvement intervention. In that way, they can garner continuing interest and support for it. Furthermore, feeding back the results of participant and stakeholder perceptions about the value of the performance improvement intervention can highlight ways to improve the intervention's implementation.

Of course, the same form that is used to collect participant reactions to training will have to be modified to keep it consistent with the nature of the performance improvement intervention. For instance, suppose that the organization is implementing an improved employee selection system. Supervisors, who are targeted to be the key participants in implementing the performance improvement intervention because they hire the most people, would be most likely to receive a reaction evaluation for the intervention (see Figure 5-3).

An evaluation form similar to that used in the organization's training could be prepared early in any performance improvement intervention. Participants and other stakeholders could be periodically assessed for their perceptions about the intervention. That information could then be summarized and fed back to participants—such as supervisors—to show what results are being achieved and uncover areas in which improvements in the intervention could be made.

What Steps Can an Evaluator Use to Establish Reaction-Level Measures for Performance Improvement Interventions? Evaluators may use the following steps to establish reaction-level measures suitable for any performance improvement intervention:

■ **Step 1:** Clarify what perceptions would be most useful to know about with the participants, key stakeholders, and decision makers of the organization. For instance, how much would they like to know, during the course of implementing a performance improvement intervention, the answers to such questions as these:

  □ How well do participants in the performance improvement intervention perceive that the goals and objectives of the intervention have been communicated to those affected by the intervention?

  □ How well do participants in the intervention perceive that the performance improvement intervention is contributing to the achievement of business strategic objectives?

  □ How well do participants in the performance improvement intervention perceive that it is solving the problem it was intended to solve?

  □ How satisfied are participants in the performance improvement intervention with the resources being devoted to implementation? Do they

Directions: Please complete the following evaluation immediately upon completion of the intervention, which is [brief description]. Write a brief description of the intervention as well as its date and location in the space provided below. Do not sign your name. Then, for each statement made in the right column below, circle the number in the left column that best indicates your level of agreement. Use the following scale: 0 = Not Applicable; 1 = Strongly Disagree; 2 = Disagree; 3 = Neutral; 4 = Agree; and 5 = Strongly Agree. When you are finished with the evaluation, mail it to [name] at [address] by [date] or fax it to [name] at [fax number] by [due date].

Location	Date	Brief Description of the Intervention				
		Level of Agreement with the Statement				
Statement	Not Applicable	Strongly Disagree	Disagree	Neutral	Agree	Strongly Agree
1. The purpose of the interventions was stated clearly at the outset.	0	1	2	3	4	5
2. The objectives of the intervention were described at the beginning.	0	1	2	3	4	5
3. Facilitators and managers were effective in communicating about the intervention to people affected by it.	0	1	2	3	4	5
4. Individuals affected by the intervention were given a say in helping to describe and troubleshoot the performance problem that the intervention was intended to solve.	0	1	2	3	4	5
5. Individuals affected by the problem and/or intervention were given a say in helping to identify the appropriate action plan to implement the intervention.	0	1	2	3	4	5
6. People were rewarded for contributing to the success of the intervention and for solving the problem.	0	1	2	3	4	5
7. The intervention was effective in solving the problem.	0	1	2	3	4	5
8. The value of the intervention to the organization's performance was apparent to me.	0	1	2	3	4	5
9. The value of the intervention to the department's performance was apparent to me.	0	1	2	3	4	5
10. The value of the intervention to my performance was apparent to me.	0	1	2	3	4	5

Figure 5-3   Reaction evaluation form for a management intervention.

11. What was the most valuable aspect of this intervention, in your opinion?

12. What was the least valuable aspect of this intervention, in your opinion?

13. What other comments do you have to make?

Figure 5-3 *Continued*

believe there is sufficient time, money, staff, and other resources necessary to implement the intervention successfully?

□ What are the major advantages being realized from the performance improvement intervention?

□ What areas for improvement are noticeable in the implementation strategy being used for the performance improvement intervention?

■ **Step 2:** Prepare a written participant questionnaire and show it to participants, key stakeholders, and decision makers to assess how well they believe it captures useful information that could be meaningfully collected during the implementation of a performance improvement intervention.

■ **Step 3:** Finalize the participant questionnaire and secure agreement from key stakeholders about:

□ Who should receive it?

□ When they should receive it?

□ What demographics should be captured for reporting purposes?

□ What translation of it may be necessary if it is to be used globally, and how will the quality of the translation be assessed?

☐ Where it should be sent (if geographical differences are important)?

☐ How often should the results of the evaluation be summarized, to whom should they be distributed, and how should improvements be made when common themes for improvement are identified?

- **Step 4:** Send out the questionnaire periodically, collect results, and feed them back.

- **Step 5:** Use the results of the questionnaire to emphasize the value gained by the performance improvement intervention, and provide written or oral reports to key decision makers and other interested people or groups periodically.

These steps are summarized in Figure 5-4.

What Are the Strengths and Weaknesses of Measuring Performance Improvement Interventions at the Reaction Level? One key strength of using participant evaluations for performance improvement interventions is that it draws attention to the results being realized based on participant opinions. Using participant evaluations for interventions also provides a means of structuring continuous feedback to stakeholders about the value being received in exchange for the resources being expended. Unfortunately, a key disadvantage of measuring perceptions is that perceptions do not always align with facts. Consequently, evaluators should supplement reaction measures—collected by written questionnaires, focus groups, or online methods—with other approaches to evaluation so that they are grounded in facts as well as attitudes and perceptions.

Evaluating Performance Improvement Interventions at the Learning Level

How much did participants in a performance improvement intervention learn from an intervention? That is the key question posed by evaluators who examine performance improvement interventions at the learning level. In this context, then, learning refers to how people changed because of new knowledge, skill, or attitude.

Of course, performance improvement interventions can be classified into two categories: (1) learning-oriented interventions and (2) management- or organizationally-oriented interventions. Examples of learning-oriented interventions include training, coaching, diversity efforts, and organization development interventions. Management- or organizationally-oriented interventions are

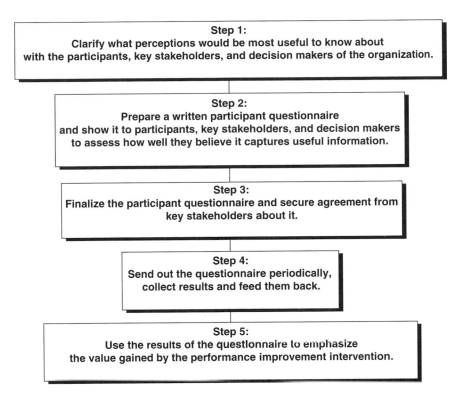

Step 1:
Clarify what perceptions would be most useful to know about
with the participants, key stakeholders, and decision makers of the organization.

Step 2:
Prepare a written participant questionnaire
and show it to participants, key stakeholders, and decision makers
to assess how well they believe it captures useful information.

Step 3:
Finalize the participant questionnaire and secure agreement from
key stakeholders about it.

Step 4:
Send out the questionnaire periodically,
collect results and feed them back.

Step 5:
Use the results of the questionnaire to emphasize
the value gained by the performance improvement intervention.

Figure 5-4 Steps in establishing reaction-level measures for performance improvement intervention.

designed to change the work environment in which individuals or other groups perform. They are thus more appropriately measured for changes in the work environment rather than for changes in individuals. Examples of management- or organizationally-oriented interventions include (to name but a few) recruitment interventions, selection interventions, reward system interventions, and feedback system interventions.

How Is the Learning Level Measured in Performance Improvement Interventions? We believe that only learning-oriented performance improvement interventions can be evaluated at the learning level. Training is evaluated at the learning level through tests or other measurements of how well participants achieved the instructional objectives established for a course or other planned learning experience.

Indeed, as training is designed, instructional designers should ensure that each instructional objective is measurable by criteria. (Criteria provide

An instructional objective describes what people should know, do, or feel at the end of a planned training experience. Instructional objectives are based on the results of a needs assessment. When an instructional objective is met, it closes a gap between what people should know, do, or feel to perform effectively and what they actually do know, do, or feel.

Effective instructional objectives have three parts:

- *Condition:* Describes what performers must have available to them to demonstrate what they know, do, or feel. As a simple example, the phrase "given a wrench" might be considered as a condition for being able to "change a tire."

- *Criterion:* Measures how well, how much, or how often a performer can demonstrate his or her knowledge, skills, or feelings. The criterion is the yardstick that is used to judge the trainee's knowledge, skill or feeling.

- *Behavior:* Describes what performers must be able to do upon completion of training. Behavior is observable—or leads to observable consequences. "Twists a lug nut" is an example of a behavior.

Figure 5-5 The basics of instructional objectives.

measurements to indicate what and how much people are expected to learn from the training.) Test items or other testing methods should be designed directly from instructional objectives and prepared before the training is designed (see Rothwell and Kazanas, 2004). Instructional objectives are described in more detail in Figure 5-5, and the basics of test development are summarized in Figure 5-6.

What Steps Can an Evaluator Use to Establish Learning-Level Measures for Performance Improvement Interventions? Evaluators may use the following steps to establish learning-level measures for training:

- **Step 1:** Use the terminal instructional objectives for a planned learning experience as a starting point to determine what individuals should know, do, or feel upon completion of training.
- **Step 2:** Select the appropriate way of measuring knowledge, skills, and attitudes based on the instructional objectives. (For instance, paper-and-pencil tests may be appropriate for testing knowledge. Performance tests

Purpose

The purpose of a test is for an individual to demonstrate his or her knowledge, skill, or attitude. Attitude surveys are usually used to measure feelings. Knowledge may be judged by an oral, paper-and-pencil or computer-based test. Skill is usually judged by a performance test that requires the individual to show what he or she knows and have it subjected to measurement.

Categorization of Tests

Tests may be categorized in many ways. They can be categorized by:

Delivery Method, such as:

• Oral test
• Paper-and-pencil test
• Performance test
• Computer-based text

Measurement Method, such as:

• *Norm referenced:* based on how well individual test takers do. If 100 people take a 100-point test and the highest score is 20, then 20 becomes the highest possible score. Individual scores are plotted in comparison to it.

• *Criterion-referenced:* based on the measurable standards established prior to the test. For instance, if all workers are supposed to demonstrate the measurable criterion of an instructional objective, then that is an absolute standard against which all learners are judged. If 100 people take a 100-point test, they may all get perfect scores—and are rated accordingly. Alternatively, they may all fail.

Figure 5-6 The basics of test development.

requiring a demonstration may be appropriate for testing skill. Attitude surveys may be appropriate for assessing changes in attitudes.)

■ **Step 3:** Create the test based on the objectives.

■ **Step 4:** Test the test by giving it to people who attend a pilot course or rehearsal. Monitor their perceptions of the clarity of directions and of test items or instructions.

■ **Step 5:** Periodically reassess the test by tracking scores on individual test items or on overall test scores.

These steps are summarized in Figure 5-7.

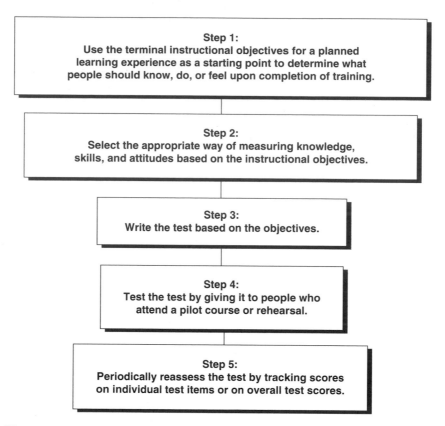

Figure 5-7 Steps in establishing learning-level measures for performance improvement interventions.

What Are the Strengths and Weaknesses of Measuring Learning-Oriented Performance Improvement Interventions at the Learning Level? One key strength of measuring learning in training (or in other learning-oriented interventions) is that it provides information about gradual improvement of individuals. The point of training is, of course, to have individuals acquire new knowledge, skills, and attitudes that they may apply on the job. Testing can thus help hold individuals accountable for meeting their responsibility to learn. Testing can also assess the relative value of training in helping individuals do just that.

One key disadvantage of measuring learning is that learning, by itself, does not ensure performance changes on the job. Factors other than individual knowledge, skill, and attitude affect how much and how well individuals apply what they learn. Those factors have to do with other issues in the work environment—such as management's ability to plan, reward, give feedback, and supply appropriate tools and equipment.

Evaluating Performance Improvement Interventions at the Behavior Level

How much did participants in a performance improvement intervention change their behavior on the job as a direct result of it? This is the key question posed by evaluators who examine performance improvement interventions at the behavior level. In this context, then, behavior refers to how people changed their work behavior as a direct result of the intervention.

As emphasized in the previous section of this chapter, performance improvement interventions can be classified into two categories: (1) learning-oriented interventions, and (2) management- or organizationally-oriented interventions. Both types of interventions will seek prescribed on-the-job behavior changes. Thus, no matter which type of intervention is administered, the behavior-level evaluation is essentially handled in the same manner.

How Is the Behavior Level Measured in Performance Improvement Interventions? No matter what performance improvement intervention is undertaken—whether it is a change in reward systems, selection methods, feedback approaches, training, or some other intervention—some behavior change should be expected to occur among those targeted for the change effort. Of course, changed behavior can occur during a performance improvement intervention by only a small number of people, and the effects can be pronounced. What is important is to determine how many people and how much behavioral change has occurred in relationship to desired results.

Two approaches are probably most effective in measuring behavioral change for performance improvement interventions. The first approach is the *questionnaire*. Participants in the performance improvement intervention are asked to specify how much behavioral change has resulted in the work setting during the intervention. Their immediate subordinates, superordinates (bosses), and peers are also given a comparable questionnaire. The results are then compared.

The second approach is *structured behavioral observation*. HPI practitioners visit the work setting and watch what happens as individuals work with the area targeted for a performance improvement intervention. If the performance improvement intervention is targeted at improved selection methods, for instance, then observers watch what happens during that process. Participants may be asked to flowchart exactly what they do. For example, how is an employee selected? The observations are then compared to the desired changes in processes from the performance improvement intervention. Differences are noted, as they are with questionnaires in the first approach, and fed back to participants and other stakeholders. In that way, continuous improvements can be made, and behaviors can be aligned with expectations.

Just as test items should be prepared before instructional materials to meet learning objectives are selected or prepared, the desired behavioral changes on the job should also be specified prior to the selection and commencement of the performance improvement intervention. In this way, evaluators know precisely what behaviors to look for when they visit work sites to observe or when they administer performance surveys on the job.

Use the worksheet appearing in Figure 5-8 to clarify what behaviors to observe on the job that will demonstrate achievement of the instructional objectives of a training program (or other planned learning experience).

What Steps Can an Evaluator Use to Establish Behavior-Level Measures for Performance Improvement Interventions? Evaluators may use the following steps to measure behavioral change that result directly from performance improvement interventions. They should:

- **Step 1:** Use the terminal performance objectives for a performance improvement intervention as a starting point to determine what behaviors should change on the work site as a direct result of the performance improvement intervention.
- **Step 2:** Ask decision makers to identify and then review a list of on-the-job behaviors that should change as a direct result of the performance improvement intervention.
- **Step 3:** Finalize the list of on-the-job behaviors that should change, as identified by decision makers and other stakeholders in the performance improvement intervention, and feed them back to decision makers.
- **Step 4:** Finalize metrics or measurement methods to assess the amount of behavior change resulting from the performance improvement interventions and feed back that information to decision makers about how behaviors will be measured on the job.
- **Step 5:** Measure behavior change in the work site that stems directly from the performance improvement intervention.

Directions: Use this Worksheet to clarify what behaviors should be observed on the performer's job to demonstrate that he or she has mastered the instructional objectives that were clarified at the outset of a training program. Begin by listing, under Column 1 below, the instructional objectives from the training course. Answer this question: *What is it that learners were supposed to know, do, or feel upon completion of the training?* Then, under Column 2, brainstorm a list of activities (or tangible products) that performers could do on the job that would demonstrate their mastery of the knowledge, skills or attitudes. Finally, under Column 3, brainstorm how those activities or products could be measured on the job to demonstrate successful on-the-job transfer of the instructional objectives. Answer this question: *How often or how well should the learner demonstrate the knowledge, skill or attitude to be using it effectively?* Use the results of this Worksheet to create an observation guide or a questionnaire to measure the transfer of training from off-the-job to on-the-job.

What were the instructional objectives of the training course?	What activities (or tangible products) could performers do on the job that would demonstrate their mastery of the knowledge, skills or attitudes? *What is it that learners were supposed to know, do, or feel upon completion of the training?*	How could those activities or products be measured on the job to demonstrate successful on-the-job transfer of the instructional objectives? *How often or how well should the learner demonstrate the knowledge, skill or attitude to be using it effectively?*
1. Example: *Upon completing the training course, the participant will be able to: Assemble a hydraulic shift in line with required specifications, given the appropriate tools*	• Assemble a hydraulic shift in line with required specification	• Using observation, the trainer could watch a performer assemble a hydraulic shift and then assess performance against a checklist created from required specifications
2.		
3.		
4.		
5.		

Figure 5-8 Worksheet to clarify what behaviors to observe on the job to demonstrate achievement of the instructional objectives of a training program.

- **Step 6:** Periodically feed back data collected about behavior change to decision makers, participants, and other stakeholders in the performance improvement intervention so that they receive feedback on the results of the intervention.
- **Step 7:** Take corrective action as necessary when behavior change does not occur as expected or desired in the work site.

These steps are summarized in Figure 5-9.

What Are the Strengths and Weaknesses of Measuring Performance Improvement Interventions at the Behavior Level? One key strength of measuring behavioral change resulting from performance improvement interventions is that it provides information about what happens in the work site. Performance improvement interventions should, of course, lead to individual behavioral changes at the work site. Measuring such change can help stakeholders determine how well the intervention has succeeded in changing behavior in the workplace.

Another key strength of measuring the results of performance improvement interventions at the behavioral level is that such measurements help to show how much corporate culture change is resulting from the performance improvement intervention. After all, corporate culture change occurs through experience over time. Behaviors give rise to, and reinforce, experience. Hence, measuring behavioral change resulting from performance improvement interventions provides clues to how much the corporate culture is changing as a result of a performance improvement intervention.

One key disadvantage of measuring behavioral change is that it may build the expectation that the performance improvement interventions will be sufficient by themselves to lead to changes in behavior. That is, of course, untrue. The work environment should also be examined for factors impeding behavioral change. Such factors may include unsupportive supervisors and coworkers, lack of rewards, or a physical work environment that does not permit the desired new behaviors.

Evaluating Performance Improvement Interventions at the Results Level

There are two key questions to consider at the results level. First, did the intervention achieve the goals it set out to accomplish? In short, was the problem

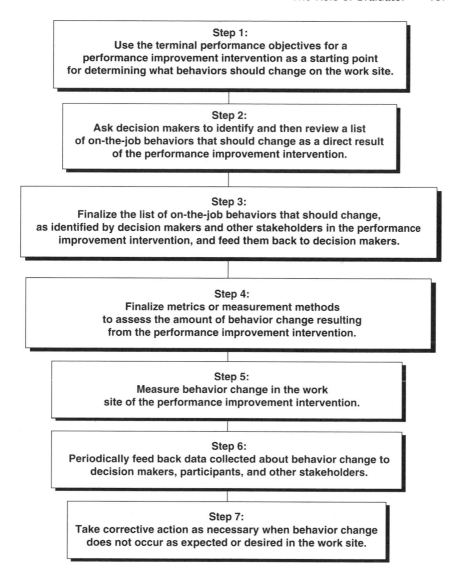

Step 1:
Use the terminal performance objectives for a
performance improvement intervention as a starting point
for determining what behaviors should change on the work site.

Step 2:
Ask decision makers to identify and then review a list
of on-the-job behaviors that should change as a direct result
of the performance improvement intervention.

Step 3:
Finalize the list of on-the-job behaviors that should change,
as identified by decision makers and other stakeholders in the performance
improvement intervention, and feed them back to decision makers.

Step 4:
Finalize metrics or measurement methods
to assess the amount of behavior change resulting
from the performance improvement intervention.

Step 5:
Measure behavior change in the work
site of the performance improvement intervention.

Step 6:
Periodically feed back data collected about behavior change to
decision makers, participants, and other stakeholders.

Step 7:
Take corrective action as necessary when behavior change
does not occur as expected or desired in the work site.

Figure 5-9 Steps in measuring performance improvement interventions at the behavior level.

solved? Second, how much did the organization gain financially—or in other ways—from a performance improvement intervention? The second question is an issue of growing concern, since trainers and others who devote time and attention to HPI are often pressured to show bottom-line financial results from their efforts.

In this context, then, *results* refer to both how well the intervention succeeded at mitigating the original identified problem (productivity, customer service, and other bottom-line measures of importance) and how much the organization gained financially as a direct result of the performance improvement intervention (cost benefit).

As was the case with the behavior-level evaluation, both learning-oriented and management- or organizationally-oriented interventions are measured at the results level in the same way. Both types of interventions attempt to bridge a performance gap. Both types of interventions have costs associated with them.

How Is the Results Level Measured in Performance Improvement Interventions? Keep the two questions at the opening of this section in mind. The first question is simply this: Was the problem solved? To answer that question, you need to identify the original performance gap and the measures that were used to determine that gap. This could be the number of customer service complaints, the number of injuries occurring, the rate of rejection due to poor quality on an assembly line, or a host of other performance measures. Then it's simply a matter of taking a pulse check using that same measure to see if the gap is trending in the right direction, or perhaps has even been eliminated altogether.

The second question—how much has the organization gained financially?—is a little more complicated to address. Much has been written about measuring financial results of performance improvement efforts. While most people who perform HPI work think of conducting cost-benefit analysis after a performance improvement intervention has been implemented, it is possible to estimate costs and benefits before an intervention is undertaken (cost-benefit forecasting) and to assess costs and benefits during an intervention (cost-benefit concurrent evaluation).

You can document financial results by measuring the costs and benefits of a performance improvement intervention. Begin by tracing all costs associated with designing, implementing, and evaluating the performance improvement intervention. Be sure to include the salary costs of trainers or other consultants who are involved in the process—as well as their travel time, materials expense, and other related expenses. Then estimate the benefits received from the intervention, which should be precisely the same as the cost of the performance problem that the performance improvement intervention is intended to solve. Subtract the costs of the intervention from the benefits received and then communicate that to decision makers.

What Steps Can an Evaluator Use to Establish Results-Level Measures for Performance Improvement Interventions? Evaluators may use the following steps to determine the costs and benefits (results) that are attributable to training or to other performance improvement interventions:

- **Step 1:** Determine all costs associated with the performance improvement interventions—including planning, implementing, and evaluating the intervention.
- **Step 2:** Estimate the benefits received from the performance improvement intervention.
- **Step 3:** Subtract the costs from the benefits.
- **Step 4:** Feed back information about the bottom-line costs and benefits of the performance improvement intervention to key stakeholders, participants, and other interested individuals and groups.

These steps are summarized in Figure 5-10.

What Are the Strengths and Weaknesses of Measuring Performance Improvement Interventions at the Results Level? Stakeholders want to know that they got the results that they were seeking and what return they received on their investment for a performance improvement intervention. Results evaluation provides that information. In addition, providing information about results tends to enhance the credibility of performance improvement interventions and those who perform HPI work. That is, therefore, a key strength of performing an evaluation of results.

Key weaknesses of evaluating results, however, tend to fall in two primary categories. First, measuring results, in some cases, can be time-consuming and expensive. Efforts devoted to measuring results tend to take away from other opportunities for improvement. There is thus an opportunity cost associated with the measurement effort itself, and that cost may—or may not—be worthwhile.

Second, measuring results rigorously is difficult. Some decision makers will not accept estimates of the benefits received from a performance improvement intervention. For that reason, HPI practitioners are well advised to get the measurement methods—that is, how the benefits will be tracked and costed and how success will be determined—*before* the performance improvement intervention is implemented. In that way, stakeholders and others involved in the process are clear about what results are desired, how they will be tracked, and how they will

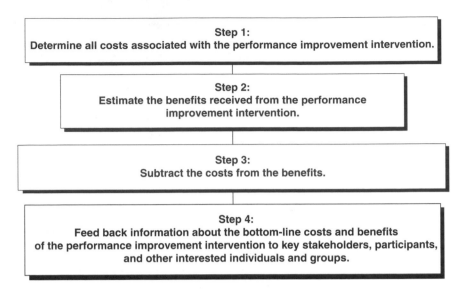

Figure 5-10 Steps in establishing results-level measures for performance improvement interventions.

be measured. Taking time during performance analysis and intervention selection to estimate the cost of problems has the additional benefit of helping to clarify the problem's parameters.

How Is the Role of Evaluator Enacted?

Recall from Chapter 4 that HPI practitioners prefer to use a normative reeducative approach to change. Evaluators tend to devote most of their efforts to Steps 18 and 19 in this model, as shown in Figure 5-11. Each step deserves more detailed attention in this chapter.

Step 18: Completing the Performance Improvement Strategy When Results Match Objectives

In this step, those who evaluate performance improvement interventions need to know when the intervention is finished because results match intentions. In short, they need to know when to call it quits. Their ability to carry out this step is directly related to the clarity of the objectives established for the intervention.

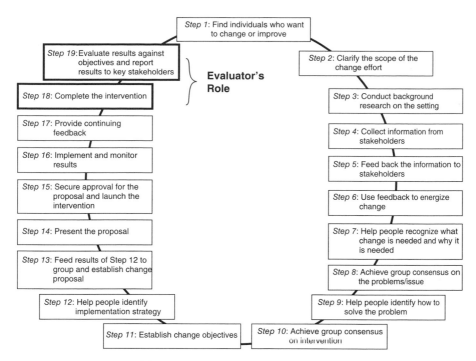

Figure 5-11   A model of the normative reeducative approach to change—the evaluator's role.

If desired results are left unclear or vague at the outset of the intervention, it will be difficult to know when to finish. If desired results are clear, specific, measurable, and well communicated, then evaluators will know when to measure.

Step 19: Evaluating Results Against Performance Objectives and Reporting Results to All Key Stakeholders and All Participants in the Performance Improvement Strategy

This step has been described in the previous part of this chapter. HPI practitioners must be able to evaluate results against objectives. It is essential to do that so as to build credibility for performance improvement interventions in the future and pinpoint when additional corrective steps are necessary to get a derailed intervention back on track.

Summary

This chapter has addressed several important questions:

- What is the role of the evaluator?
- What competencies and outputs are associated with that role?
- What approaches govern the evaluation of performance improvement interventions?

As the chapter explained, the evaluator role "assesses the impact of interventions and follows up on changes made, actions taken, and results achieved in order to provide participants and stakeholders with information about how well interventions are being implemented" (Rothwell, 2000). Key competencies associated with the role include:

- Performance gap evaluation skill
- Ability to evaluate results against organizational goals
- Standard-setting skills
- Ability to assess impact on culture
- Human performance improvement intervention reviewing skills
- Feedback skills

The work outputs associated with the role were listed in Figure 5-1.

This chapter also reviewed the evaluator's role in examining human performance improvement interventions against the backdrop of Donald Kirkpatrick's four levels of evaluation: (1) reaction, (2) learning, (3) behavior, and (4) results. Each level of evaluation was examined as it can be applied by evaluators in examining training (and other learning-oriented) interventions and management- or organizationally-oriented evaluation.

References

Langdon, D., Whiteside, K., and McKenna, M. (Eds.). (1999). *Intervention Resource Guide: 50 Performance Improvement Tools*. San Francisco: Jossey-Bass/Pfeiffer.

McLagan, P. (1989). *Models for HRD Practice*. 4 vols Alexandria, VA: The America Society for Tranning and Development.

Rothwell, W. (2000). *ASTD Models for Human Performance Improvement*, 2nd ed. Alexandria, VA: The American Society for Training and Development.

Rothwell, W., and Kazanas, H. (2004). *Mastering the Instructional Design Process: A Systematic Approach*, 3rd ed. San Francisco: Pfeiffer and Co.

6

Trends and Their Implications for HPI

This chapter offers a broad summary of current trends affecting HPI practitioners. The trends are classified into three categories. The first category consists of business and public sector trends, and that section of the chapter describes how corporations and government agencies are changing or are being forced to change to remain competitive. The second category consists of workforce trends, and that section reviews how the U.S. workforce is changing. The third category consists of human resource trends, and that section describes how the human resource function is changing. Taken together, the three parts of this chapter summarize key drivers of change that affect performance in organizational settings and how HPI practitioners can respond in a proactive way.

Business and Public Sector Trends

While each industry has its unique characteristics and unique responses to the global economy and other corporate challenges, there are several trends that appear to be true for most corporations and public sector agencies. This section will discuss these corporate and public sector trends and their implications for HPI practitioners.

> **Key Trend 1:** Organizations Are Placing Innovation at the Top of Their Priority Lists

In the early 1990s, companies responded to increased competition by taking decisive action to reduce costs, leading to greater profits. Today, organizations realize that one of the keys to business success is innovation. *Innovation* is the term used to describe how organizations create value by developing new knowledge and/or using existing knowledge in new ways. Innovation can lead to growth in new markets, customer loyalty in existing markets, and a workforce culture that can respond effectively to the changes that organizations face over time. Innovation has become a vital management mandate for both private and public enterprises. A 2006 American Management Association/Human Resource Institute survey found that 67 percent of the 1,356 global business leader respondents identified innovation as either "extremely important" or "highly important" to their organizations today. More significant is that 85 percent think that innovation will be "extremely important" or "highly important" to their organizations in 10 years (AMA/HRI, 2006).

Organizations can be innovative in many different ways. One way is to provide new products and/or services to new or existing customers. While this type of activity has been typically housed in the research and development division of organizations, more and more companies are looking for these types of innovations to come from throughout the organization. Another way organizations can innovate is to implement new business models that allow for reductions in time-to-market, reductions in cost-to-produce, increased customer service levels, etc. Doing things faster and smarter with less than the competition can lead to market growth and an expansion of profit margins. Meeting customer needs is the key to any company's success. Innovations in identifying and responding to changing customer needs can have a great effect on a company's ability to stay on top or gain additional market share.

While it should be obvious that in order to become an innovative company, organizations must craft and foster a more creative corporate culture, this is something that typically gets overlooked. A creative corporate culture encourages appropriate risk taking, values teamwork and collaboration over individual heroics, and encourages open communication up and down throughout the organization. Amabile and Sensabaugh (1992) cited freedom and control, good project management, sufficient resources, and creative cultural attributes (collaborative atmosphere, a high expectation of creativity, an acceptance of failure, and a nonbureaucratic structure) as keys to providing a workplace that is supportive of innovative behaviors. Conversely, lack of freedom or choice in deciding what to do or how to do it, lack of interest or psychological support within the organization, and poor project management can lead to the minimization or elimination of innovative behaviors.

The need for innovation is important for the public sector as well. As pressures to reduce taxes increase, funding for government agencies is always in jeopardy. Agencies need to find innovative new ways to meet constituent needs.

Improving customer service while reducing costs will require a great deal of innovation. In a bureaucracy as large as our government, creating a culture that cultivates innovation could prove most challenging.

There are many ways HPI practitioners can help organizations become more innovative. We can review the recruitment process to be sure that our organization is hiring people via personality assessments who exhibit attributes for creativity that can lead to innovation. We can ensure that our organizations are more diverse in terms of race, ethnicity, and even collegiate degree programs. We can be sure that the ability to foster creativity and innovation becomes a valued competency of all leaders in our organization. We can create succession plans in the organization to be sure that we promote leaders who exhibit management styles that encourage innovation. Performance management tools as well as simulation assessment labs can be used to identify the most effective leaders. We need to review the employee reward systems to be sure that they align with the company's innovation strategies. That assumes that the organization has an innovation strategy. If it doesn't, we can help them formulate one and communicate it effectively throughout the organization. We can help our organizations analyze their internal business processes, looking for ways to modify, enhance, or completely rewrite the way they do business. Reorganization and the reengineering of work processes can help companies implement innovation strategies. Communication channels up, down, and across the organization are vital for a company to be innovative. It is essential to create a culture where open communication, even sharing of mistakes and failures, is not only possible but is expected and rewarded. An innovative company will generate countless ideas for change, and our organizations will need a process for evaluating those ideas for their potential impact on the organization. HPI practitioners can help their organizations identify the key success criteria that can be used to create a stage-gate process by which "go"/"no-go" decisions can be made in an objective manner at various stages of new idea exploration.

> **Key Trend 2:** Organizations Are Faced with Increased Security Concerns

We live in a post–September 11th era. That day changed not just the way businesses and governments handle security in the United States, but worldwide.

Statistics confirm anecdotal evidence that corporate security has leaped to the top of many businesses to-do lists. Before the attacks and the anthrax scare, only 35 percent of the companies polled had a plan to deal with biological, chemical or nuclear contamination, according to the International Security Management Association, which surveyed its membership of corporate security executives. Since then, an additional 39 percent of those businesses have put plans in place. Most of those polled also were confident their companies would earmark more funds for security at home and overseas—with about half of the funds directed at physical security, a quarter toward IT, and the remainder for security staff (Poletz, 2002).

While the airlines and other transportation modes have obvious security concerns, in general, the biggest areas of concern for most organizations are building access, business continuity, and data security.

Security system enhancements are being made all over the world. HPI practitioners can be catalysts for the changes that new procedures will require. This might include training programs for all employees, measurement systems, and cultural shifts where security becomes part of everyone's job.

Does your organization have a disaster recovery plan? Chances are it does not. When asked the status of their organization's disaster recovery plan in an online poll, 64 percent of 642 respondents answered, "Does not exist yet." Only 7 percent said that their plan was current and complete (disaster-recovery-guide.com, 2006). (See Figure 6-1.) Business continuity in the event of a disaster is in jeopardy without a disaster recovery plan. HPI practitioners can help their

What is the status of your disaster recovery plan?

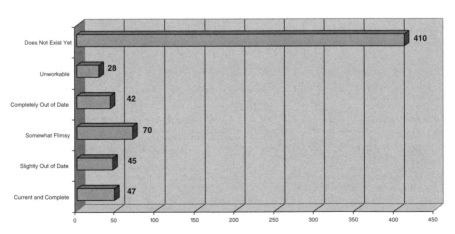

Figure 6-1 What is the status of your disaster recovery plan? Source: http://poll.pollhost.com/ZHJndWlkZQkxMDc1MDI4MTU2CUVFRUVFRQkw MDAwMDAJQXJpYWwwJQXNzb3J0ZWQkMA/.

organizations identify the business processes that are vital to the company or agency. We can also produce job aids that will help the company respond appropriately in the event of a natural or man-made disaster. We can be sure that our leadership development programs prepare our leaders to function in the event of a disruption to normal operations.

HPI practitioners can help their businesses or agencies maintain data security by working with their information technology organizations to make sure employees understand the implications of a breach of data security and the various ways that those breaches can occur unintentionally. This practice is called social engineering. Social engineering is when confidential information is obtained by manipulation of legitimate users. A social engineer will commonly use the telephone or Internet to trick people into revealing sensitive information or getting them to do something that is against typical policies. By this method, social engineers exploit the natural tendency of a person to trust his or her word, rather than exploiting computer security holes. It is generally agreed upon that "users are the weak link" in security and this principle is what makes social engineering possible. All employees who have access to data are responsible for the security of that data. HPI practitioners can help strengthen the former "weak links" in their organizations to ensure data security.

Key Trend 3:   Organizations Are Growing via Mergers and Acquisitions

---

There was a near record volume of mergers and acquisitions in 2005. The value of mergers and acquisitions worldwide totaled over $2.7 trillion. According to Thompson Financial, a leading provider of financial data, this recent resurgence in M&A activity is due to increased demand for energy assets, easy access to capital, and a record amount of private equity funding. While the largest sectors affected by mergers and acquisitions during the first boom in M&A in the late 1990s were technologies and banking, today, worldwide, the industries most commonly affected include energy and power companies, financial companies, and telecommunications companies. In the United States, there has been a high rate of mergers and acquisitions in the energy and power sector, the financial sector, the media and entertainment sector, and in the health care sector (Thompson Financial, 2006).

Unfortunately, many mergers and acquisitions occurring in recent years have not included HPI practitioners or other human resource personnel in the planning stages. Company leaders focus more on the financial end of the deal and neglect the key people-related and knowledge management-related issues that are so important to eventual success of the venture. According to a longitudinal study of 125 mergers that occurred between 1996 and 2000, ". . . there was a large and significant difference between the stock performance of companies where executives proactively tackled cultural issues during the integration process and those who did not. A proactive approach netted 5.1 percent higher stock price performance versus a minus 4.4 percent share price underperformance in deals where companies failed to identify and negotiate cultural hurdles" (Vestring, King, Rouse, and Critchlow, 2006). HPI practitioners can facilitate the identification of the desired culture for the newly formed corporation and assist in efforts to communicate about that desired culture. HPI practitioners can also play key roles in improving retention and redeployment in the wake of mergers and acquisitions as well as provide help in retraining skilled employees and leaders. HPI practitioners have the skills needed to foster teambuilding, and assist with the new organization's design. The key is to become part of the M&A team early in the process; even assisting with the due diligence prior to the merger to anticipate the human resource challenges that lie ahead.

Key Trend 4: Businesses and Agencies Are Paying Closer Attention to Business Ethics

---

What do company names like Enron, Worldcom, and Tyco make you think of? How about the name Jayson Blair, former writer for the New York Times? Did you hear about the Pennsylvania legislature's 2 a.m. vote for a 16 percent pay hike? Nothing can grab headlines quicker than a corporate or government scandal. In some cases, a business is unable to survive such negative publicity. In the case of the Pennsylvania legislature, it didn't take long for the backlash to hit, and the reversal of the raise to take place, but not before the ethics of the leaders was scrutinized severely by their constituents. Organizations and individuals cannot afford these types of scandals. While most companies have a code of ethics in place, few have paid much attention to its compliance in the past.

Most of the leading MBA schools have cited an increase in interest and enrollment in the Business Ethics classes. Sometimes it takes a major collapse, like Enron, to wake people up to the importance of ethics in business. But what about those leaders who are already in the workforce? HPI practitioners can be instrumental in identifying knowledge gaps when it comes to business ethics. Does the workforce know how the organization's code of ethics applies to them? Do they know what to do if they become aware of a violation of the code of ethics? Does your organization's code of ethics meet accepted standards? Does a code of ethics even exist? If not, as HPI practitioners we can facilitate the creation of one.

As HPI practitioners, this code of ethics applies to us, too. In our work, we become privy to lots of confidential and personal information. We must uphold our confidences strongly to ensure our credibility and trustworthiness with our clients, whether we are internal or external to the organization with which we are working.

> **Key Trend 5:** Public Sector Organizations Are Recognizing the Need to Become High-Performing Organizations

A 2005 General Accounting Office report entitled "21st Century Challenges: Transforming Government to Meet Current and Emerging Challenges," declares that "reexamining the base of all major existing federal spending and tax programs, policies, functions, and activities offers compelling opportunities to redress our current and projected fiscal imbalances while better positioning government to meet the new challenges and opportunities of this new century" (GAO, 2005). The report calls for all agencies to become high-performing organizations. It challenges government agencies to become more results-oriented. Agencies are strongly encouraged to reexamine their business processes, organizational structures, management approaches, and even missions (see Figure 6-2).

A previous GAO report identified the following key characteristics of a high-performing organization:

A clear, well-articulated, and compelling mission. High-performing organizations have a clear, well-articulated, and compelling mission, the strategic goals to achieve it, and a performance management system that aligns with these goals to show employees how their performance can contribute to overall organizational results.
Strategic use of partnerships. Since the federal government is increasingly reliant on partners to achieve its outcomes, becoming a high-performing organization requires that federal agencies effectively manage relationships with other organizations outside of their direct control.
Focus on needs of clients and customers. Serving the needs of clients and customers involves identifying their needs, striving to meet them, measuring

Current State		High Performing Organizations
• Hierarchical • Stovepipes • Process and output-oriented • Reactive behavior • Inwardly focused • Avoiding technology • Hoarding knowledge • Avoiding risk • Protecting turf • Employee direction	**Summary of Key Practices** • Committed, persistent, and consistent leadership • Strategic planning • Organizational alignment • Integrated performance management systems • Modern human capital approaches • Effective communications • Employee involvement	• Flatter and more horizontal • Matrixes • Results-oriented • Proactive approaches • Externally focused • Leveraging technology • Sharing knowledge • Managing risk • Forming partnerships • Employee empowerment

Figure 6-2 Cultural changes and key practices necessary for successful transformation. Source: GAO-05-830t.

performance, and publicly reporting on progress to help assure appropriate transparency and accountability.

Strategic management of people. Most high-performing organizations have strong, charismatic, visionary, and sustained leadership, the capability to identify what skills and competencies the employees and the organization need, and other key characteristics including effective recruiting, comprehensive training and development, retention of high-performing employees, and a streamlined hiring process (GAO, 2004).

This sounds like a job for an HPI practitioner! This major transformation of government could be the largest human performance improvement project ever. We have the skills to guide the shift in leadership approaches. We can translate strategic plans into implications for the workforce. We can be sure that organizations are designed effectively. We can help design and implement effective performance management systems. We can help identify the gaps that currently exist and propose ways to fill them. This approach to government will be a huge cultural shift and will not take place overnight, but the time has come to begin to make this transformation, and HPI practitioners can play key roles in making it happen.

Key Trend 6: Businesses and the Public Sector Are Experiencing the Effects of Global Interdependence

From environmental factors such as the ozone layer, global warming, and acid rain to the social concerns of poverty, genocide, and human pandemics, most everyone can recognize the increase in global interdependence. Businesses and public sector organizations are not immune to these factors. Organizations have been influenced by global economies for decades, but the degree of that influence has never been greater than it is now, and there is no sign that it will lessen anytime in the near future. As such, organizational leaders need to learn how to "play" in the "global sandbox."

Hewlett-Packard is a company that has learned to leverage globalization to its advantage. They now produce printers that print in Chinese, Japanese, and Korean. They've also designed battery-operated digital cameras and printing systems that operate completely without electricity, to meet the needs of developing countries where an electrical grid may or may not exist. It's no longer good enough to be number one in the United States. The race is on to be number one in the world.

The Pacific Rim countries of China, Indonesia, Singapore, Thailand, Japan, Malaysia, South Korea, Taiwan, and Vietnam represent a tremendous opportunity for most businesses. Economic growth in this region is expected to at least double in the coming years. International investment in this region is great. The success or struggle of these economies will have a ripple effect around the world. Being successful in these countries could be the most obvious way to increase revenues for a business, and most CEOs would agree that revenue growth is the most important way to increase overall financial performance.

The increase in the number of companies that have sent whole business functions offshore is another example of growing global interdependence. A natural disaster in India could send shock waves through the world economy. A pandemic in Thailand could interfere with supply chains around the globe. A government coup in China could send the world economies spiraling downward. No longer is a stable global economy controlled by the fiscal policy of a single country.

What does this mean for HPI practitioners? First of all, interactions with different cultures will pose a challenge for business leaders. Knowing the customs and traditions of foreign nations could prove to be the difference in a deal succeeding or failing. Something as simple as how to greet a foreign leader, i.e., a handshake or a bow, can help to establish a positive atmosphere for doing business. HPI practitioners can be instrumental in developing "cultural boot camps" for executives who will be interfacing with leaders from other countries.

Being able to identify the global interdependencies within an organization will help that organization be able to respond to crises when they occur or proactively, before they occur. HPI practitioners can help diagram the linkages and their implications worldwide for any organization. We can help identify those functions that are "mission critical" and make sure that these functions have redundancy in another part of the world.

HPI practitioners can design performance management and reward systems that are adaptable to the various world cultures. While individual evaluations and performance-based pay is typically acceptable in a Western society, they may not be acceptable practices in an Eastern society, where "team" is more highly regarded than "individual."

Key Trend 7: Corporations Are Outsourcing Tasks and Large-Scale Functions

---

Outsourcing is the strategic use of outside resources to perform activities traditionally handled by internal staff and resources. Outsourcing is a management strategy by which an organization farms out major, noncore functions to specialized, efficient service providers. A 1996 *Fortune* article cited outsourcing as one of the eight learnable skills leaders need to advance in their careers (Faircloth, 1996).

Any function not directly associated with a business's core competencies— that is, what it does better than any other organization and is key to its competitiveness—is a candidate for outsourcing. According to the Outsourcing Institute, a professional association and executive network with a mission to provide timely information exchange and services on outsourcing and related sourcing strategies, the fastest growing area for outsourcing is information technology (IT). More specifically, areas of IT that companies have outsourced in large numbers to date include application management and maintenance, helpdesks, data entry, capture, and records management (Outsourcing Institute, 2005). Non-IT functions that have been outsourced involve many of the human resource functions, including benefits, payroll, relocation, and worker's compensation (see Figure 6-3).

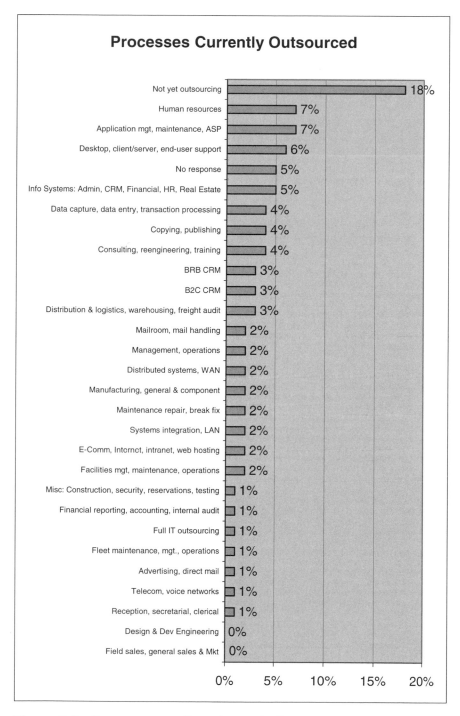

Figure 6-3 Processes currently outsourced. Source: www.outsourcing.com, 2005.

Many more companies are considering outsourcing various noncore functions of their business. Ten percent of companies responding to a Outsourcing Institute survey indicate that they are considering outsourcing the entire human resource function. Nine percent indicate an interest in considering outsourcing their security, testing, purchasing, records, and travel functions (see Figure 6-4).

In the late 1990s, companies were mostly outsourcing certain subtasks of a function, like the help desk in the IT department. Today, they are more willing to let go of entire functions. We're seeing more and more companies outsource their entire human resource function or their entire information technology function.

There are many reasons why companies choose to outsource. Dennis Rogers of Resource Outcomes says that there are strategic and tactical reasons to outsource: "Outsourcing becomes *Strategic Outsourcing* when the external firm provides a management function and manages the work to deliver the outcome your business requires rather than perform a task" (Roger, 2006). Resource Outcomes identified the top 5 strategic and tactical reasons for outsourcing (see Figure 6-5). The Outsourcing Institute surveys new buyers of outsourcing each year. In 2005, 1,410 new members cited the reduction and control of operating costs and the improvement of company focus as the top two reasons that they were either currently outsourcing or planning to outsource in the near future (see Figure 6-6).

Gartner Inc. projects that business process outsourcing will grow from $112.9 billion in 2003 to $176.1 billion in 2008 (Gamble, 2005). With the rate of outsourcing expected to increase, HPI practitioners can help their organizations successfully identify outsourcing opportunities, select the right vendor, and manage issues associated with transitioning to a new supplier—including redeploying displaced personnel. We can also help to establish measures and procedures that will track and monitor the performance of outsourcing vendors. One of the pitfalls with outsourcing can be poor communication to the workforce. This can lead to poor morale and the loss of valuable employees. HPI practitioners can put communication vehicles in place to avoid this pitfall.

In many cases, we may find ourselves being in the function that is being outsourced. We have several choices: (1) We can seek employment elsewhere; (2) We can approach the organization that is taking over our role about employment (either full time or contract); (3) We can try to reposition our role in another part of the organization, such as the operations division; or (4) We can use it as an opportunity to "hang out our shingle" and start our own consulting business or freelance.

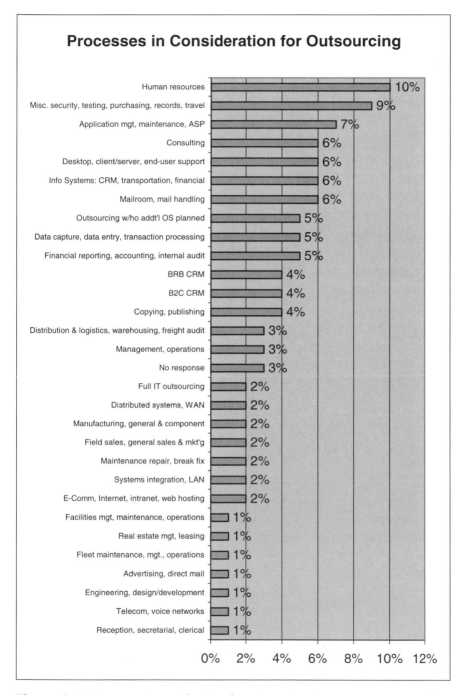

Figure 6-4   Processes in consideration for outsourcing. Source: www.outsourcing.com, 2005.

Reasons to Outsource	
Strategic	Tactical
1. Improve business focus. Outsourcing allows organizations to focus on their business issues. 2. Free up resources for core activities. 3. Gain access to world-class capabilities. Specialists have expertise. 4. Gain benefits from re-engineering. Experts take over the process and quickly deliver benefits 5. Share risks. Let the experts manage the risk of investing in changing technology.	1. Secure resources not available within the organization. 2. Gain control of difficult to manage functions. Give your problems to someone who has the expertise to solve them. 3. Reduce and control operating costs. Experts know how to lower the costs. 4. Make capital funds available. No need to invest in noncore functions, so funds can be allocated where they will have the greatest effect on profit. 5. Provide cash injection. Where outsourcing involves the transfer and sale of equipment, facilities, and other assets from the organization to the outsourcing provider.

Figure 6-5   Reasons to outsource. Source: http://www.resourceoutcomes.co.nz/outsourcing.htm.

Workforce Trends

Several important trends are affecting the global workforce at precisely the same time as organizations are coping with—and trying to anticipate—the trends described in the previous section of this chapter. This section will review the workforce trends and their implications for HPI practitioners.

Key Trend 1:   The Emergence of a Knowledge-Based Economy Is Driving Skill Requirements Up

---

A knowledge-based economy is one that is based on the production, distribution, and use of knowledge and information. Technology plays a key role in the capture, use, and dissemination of knowledge. It's not surprising, then, that a knowledge-based economy would require workers to have higher skills and

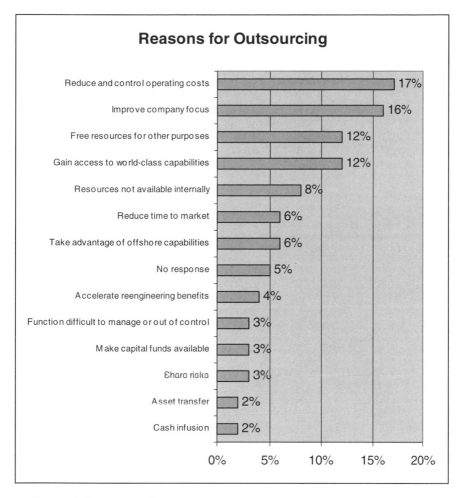

Figure 6-6 Reasons for outsourcing. Source: www.outsourcing.com, 2005.

higher levels of education than in the past. For example, manufacturing supervisors used to be selected from veteran manufacturing employees. Today, they are recruited from two-year degree programs. In addition to strong math and other technical skills, supervisors also need to be good team builders, communicators, motivators, and problem solvers.

Recruitment and retention of skilled talent will become more of a challenge. Once skilled talent is in place, it is important to create and maintain a positive culture and to keep employees engaged in the goals and objectives of the organization. This presumes that goals and objectives exist and are adequately communicated. If not, there's an obvious role for the HPI practitioner.

Today, schools are not necessarily preparing our future workforce with the skills needed to be successful. As it becomes more and more difficult to find and hire skilled workers, there will be an increased need for training to "build" a skilled workforce. This will be a shift, as fewer companies in the recent past have been willing to expand training initiatives with the exception of leadership training. Cost-effective training solutions will need to be employed and made available for all employees, not just the leaders of the company.

We can also help facilitate the creation and use of formal and informal networks for the sharing of knowledge. These can be both internal to the organization and external. Caution needs to be used with external networks. Not all countries respect intellectual property rights. The sharing of any knowledge or information with those outside your organization should always be scrutinized. Just because you hold a patent doesn't necessarily protect you in all countries. Employees need to be cautioned on the sharing of information with people from these areas of the world.

Key Trend 2:   We Have an Aging Workforce That Is Soon to Be on Its Way Out of the Labor Pool

---

The high birth rate that followed the end of World War II resulted in a swell of the population. This era produced the "baby boom" generation. Most define baby boomers as those who were born 1946–1964. The majority of these people will be approaching retirement age in the next 2 to 20 years. The 55-and-older age group made up 13 percent of the workforce in 2000. By 2020, they are estimated to be 20 percent of the workforce. Their exit from the labor pool has many implications.

The first implication, which has grabbed headlines for many years, is the increased financial pressure on currently underfunded pension plans, Social Security, and Medicare in the United States. The worker-to-retiree ratio will shrink to its lowest point ever. This deficit between deposits and withdrawals from the social systems of our country will put increased pressure on already tight public funds.

Second, certain industries could experience talent shortages. The nuclear industry, for example, will be losing many top engineers. This is not a popular field of study for those in the next generation. Most manufacturing workforces already are seeing average ages in the 50s. Health care will suffer continued nursing shortages. The airline industry is likely to have a shortage of pilots and navigators. Education could feel the effects the earliest, as most teachers are eligible to retire at age 55. Social workers and police officers both have an aging workforce with relatively fewer people entering those fields. A creative approach to the projected skilled labor shortage is to have government change the pension regulations to allow for partial retirement. This would allow workers to work part-time and collect a portion of their pension to subsidize their incomes, keeping skilled workers in the workforce longer. HPI practitioners can be supportive of these and other creative approaches to keeping the veteran talent and skills and knowledge in the workplace until we can capture and pass along this information to the next generations.

While an overall growing population will help to fill these vacancies, the challenge will be to fill them with skilled workers. A lot of expertise will be departing the workforce through a revolving door. HPI practitioners can help to capture the expertise before it leaves by making sure that standard operating procedures (SOPs) are up-to-date and accurate. They can also capture the subject matter expertise and create curriculum that can be used to build skills in the next generation of workers. Establishing mentoring programs that pair younger workers with older workers can be effective at passing along necessary skills and knowledge.

Having the overall workforce age poses its own set of challenges. Due to older workers remaining in the workforce longer, for the first time in history, there are four generations in the workforce: (1) The traditionalists (born 1922–1945); (2) The baby boomers (born 1946–1964); (3) Generation X (born 1965–1979); and (4) Generation Y, sometimes referred to as the Millennium Generation (born 1980–2000). Generational differences pose significant challenges to organizations:

> As workers reach mid-life, their concerns about child care often diminish and are replaced by concerns about elder care (for their aging parents and loved ones), savings and investment for their own retirement, health issues, and job security. Their "world views" shift as well, and they place more value on personal freedom, greater control over how they spend their time and energy, and reconnecting with interests that they've put off to raise a family (Weil, 2003).

This realization has prompted several companies to begin to offer training for leaders to better respond to the challenges of the generational gaps. Constellation Energy currently offers a course entitled "Engaging the Generations" (see Figure 6-7). Being proactive about the challenges of the wide range of values can help an organization be more successful.

Engaging the Generations

For the first time in modern history, there are four generations in the workplace. And just like a multigenerational family, each group has different motivators, communication styles, and work values. Generational differences are one of the greatest challenges facing organizations today. They are also one of the greatest potential sources of opportunity and creative strength. Creating an inclusive, generations-friendly climate that will engage talented members of each generation is a business and a leadership imperative.

Who should attend this course:

Leaders at all levels, including Project Team Leaders and Project Managers. Also appropriate for professionals who must work closely with others to accomplish work.

What you will learn:

During this highly interactive workshop, you will examine the generational forces that shape individuals, teams, departments, and work groups. You will gain practical tips and tools you can apply immediately to bridge the generation gaps, build an inclusive work environment, and tap into the creative potential of our multigenerational workforce.

At the end of this course you will be able to:

- Explain the forces that shape values and behaviors at work
- Identify the critical differences among the four generations in today's workforce
- Apply specific strategies and tactics to address generational differences
- Communicate more effectively to bridge the generation gap (do's and don'ts)
- Create a workplace climate that motivates each generation
- Retain talent across the generations

Figure 6-7   "Engaging the generations" course description. Source: Constellation Energy, 2006.

Key Trend 3:   Offshoring Is Changing the Ethnicity and Culture of the Workforce

---

Offshoring is the relocation of business processes to another country, especially a country overseas. Initially, companies were offshoring mostly low-waged, low-skilled jobs, and the primary reason for offshoring was lower wages and benefits. However as education and skill levels increased in other countries, more and more organizations are deciding to offshore higher-skilled tasks or full processes. The reasons for offshoring have started to shift as well. Today companies are still offshoring work to save money, but they are also offshoring to reduce time-to-market, and to free up highly skilled labor for more important and strategic activities. The work is going to workforces in India, China, Malaysia, Czech Republic, Singapore, the Philippines, and many other countries.

"The most important aspect of any effective offshore relationship is to treat the vendor as a true partner, rather than an independent contractor" (Klingshirn and Wisniewski, 2006). This means that a strong relationship between the process owner and the offshore provider of goods and services needs to be established and maintained. For this relationship to prosper, both parties need to understand the cultural norms and traditions of the other. They also need to have common goals and integrated work processes.

HPI practitioners can help identify the cultural norms and traditions and can provide training in the work processes that will be shared. We can study any breakdowns that occur between the organization and the offshorer, to determine their root causes and propose solutions to those issues. We can establish measures that can be used to evaluate the performance of the offshorer. We can help our organizations modify their organizational structures and assist with manpower planning. We can be sure that the leaders in our organizations have the additional skills required to manage a remote workforce, especially one from a different part of the world where time zones and languages could add to the challenge. We can help establish an internal communication strategy. We can help to redesign the new jobs that will be created as a result of the offshoring. We also have the skills to manage the overall change process.

> **Key Trend 4:** Workers Are Increasingly Considering Job Changes

A 2004 Society for Human Resource Management survey found that 35 percent of current employees are actively seeking a new job; an additional 40 percent are keeping their eyes open in case something better comes along (Burke and Collison, 2004). Intentions are one thing; actuality quite another. According to a Watson Wyatt Data Services study, the percent of voluntary separations overall was 11.4 percent—a far cry from the 35 percent that are actively hoping to change jobs. Some industries fare better than others. The retail and wholesale industry leads the rest with a 35 percent voluntary turnover rate. The most stable workforce is in the utilities and energy industry, where the voluntary turnover rate is only 6.5 percent (see Figure 6-8) (Watson, 2000/2001).

These numbers are cause for concern, as the difficulty to recruit skilled labor increases. Rebecca Clark, an advisor for Chartered Institute of Personnel &

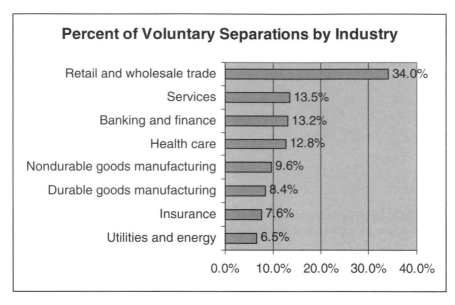

Figure 6-8 Percent of voluntary separations by industry. Source: Watson Wyatt Data Services.

Development in London, states that 93 percent of organizations in the UK are citing difficulties with recruiting. Companies are responding by implementing special retention strategies. Salary, promotions, and career development opportunities top the list of the strategies most used to keep talented employees in organizations (see Figure 6-9) (Clark, 2003).

HPI practitioners can help their organizations hire the right people in the first place. We can study the top performers in any given role and determine what it is that makes them succeed. Then we can make sure that these qualities and skills are sought during the recruiting process. Once we've hired the best people, the focus shifts to retaining them. Google recruits and retains its employees using its company culture. Employees have access to free beverages and free lunches, and bean bags and large balls are available as alternate chairs. A desk at Google isn't complete without a lava lamp; and that's just the beginning. The conference rooms are named after famous rock stars, including John Lennon and David Bowie. And what would a Friday afternoon be without a company happy hour, complete with subsidized beer? And don't forget the free massages. Google has found an effective way to retain its workforce.

HPI practitioners can help their organizations respond to the needs of their workforces. It might not be lava lamps and beer that keeps your employees happy.

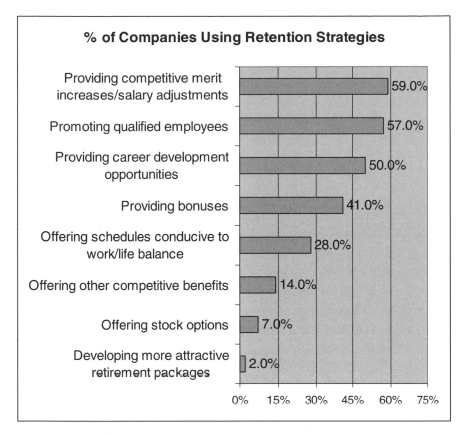

% of Companies Using Retention Strategies

Providing competitive merit increases/salary adjustments — 59.0%

Promoting qualified employees — 57.0%

Providing career development opportunities — 50.0%

Providing bonuses — 41.0%

Offering schedules conducive to work/life balance — 28.0%

Offering other competitive benefits — 14.0%

Offering stock options — 7.0%

Developing more attractive retirement packages — 2.0%

0%   15%   30%   45%   60%   75%

Figure 6-9   Percent of companies using retention strategies. Source: Society for Strategic Human Resource Management.

Perhaps it's flex-time, opportunities for advancement, and telecommuting. Some companies are offering compensation incentives. For example, an energy company offers quarterly bonuses to its workers. There's always incentive to hang on for three more months, then three more months, and so on.

Human Resource Trends

Several important trends are also affecting human resource functions at precisely the same time as the other trends, described previously in this chapter, are also occurring. These trends and their implications for HPI practitioners will be discussed in this section.

Key Trend 1: The Training and Development Industry Is Spending a Greater Percent of Their Budget on External Services (Including Tuition)

The *2005 State of the Industry Report* from the American Society for Training and Development (ASTD) (Sugrue and Rivera, 2005) compared three groups of U.S. corporations, which they refer to as Benchmarking Survey, Benchmarking Forum, and BEST Award Winners. Their Benchmarking Survey group consists of 281 companies that participated in the benchmarking survey process. The Benchmarking Forum is a select group of 24 companies that represent very large global organizations, most of which are based in the United States. The 29 BEST Award Winners are a group of organizations that have demonstrated a clear link between learning and performance.

Many organizations are utilizing resources external to the training function to meet the growing demand for training—including nontraining staff employees, outside training firms, independent training consultants, product suppliers, community colleges, other educational institutions, unions, trade or professional associations, and government organizations. Typical companies are spending slightly more on external resources, while the Forum and BEST Award companies are spending about the same or less (see Figure 6-10) (Sugrue and Rivera, 2005). In the past, the top learning and performance organizations were utilizing external resources in greater numbers than then general population. Today, the best of the best seem to be doing a higher percentage of their work by utilizing internal practitioners. This could be explained by the fact that larger organizations tend to have more internal practitioners to call upon when projects are identified. However, a 2005 ASTD and IBM survey of 174 learning executives indicates that learning organizations anticipate increasing the amount of external resources utilized in the future (see Figure 6-11). Executives cited operating cost reductions, lack of internal capability, and access to best practices and talent as the primary reasons for utilizing external resources (see Figure 6-12) (Deviney and Sugrue, 2005).

This trend has many implications for HPI practitioners. Internal HPI practitioners must be skilled to effectively select and manage external providers of training and other performance improvement services. Utilizing external practitioners for most of the learning development and delivery will free up the HPI practitioners to focus on strategic performance improvement.

External HPI practitioners should see an increase in demand for their services, especially for learning design and development and learning technology infrastructure. Skilled internal HPI practitioners might consider entrepreneurship.

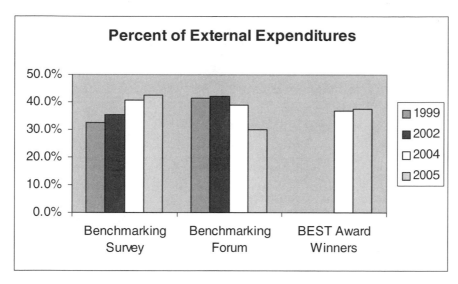

Figure 6-10   Percent of external expenditures. Source: ASTD *2005 State of the Industry Report.*

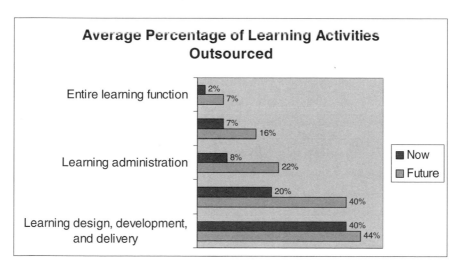

Figure 6-11   Average percentage of learning activities outsourced. Source: ASTD/IBM Learning Outsourcing Research Report, 2005.

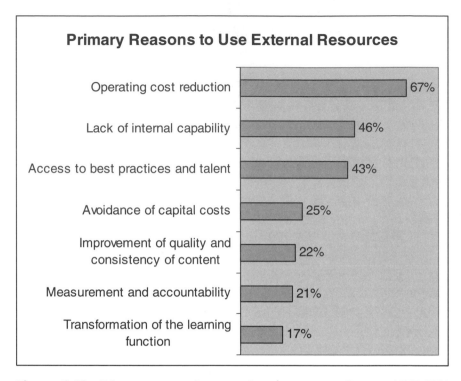

Figure 6-12 Primary reasons to use external resources. Source: ASTD/IBM *Learning Outsourcing Research Report*, 2005.

Key Trend 2: Human Resources Is Being Innovative with the Methods for Delivering Services Throughout Their Organizations

Classroom training has always been the primary method of training delivery utilized in the American workplace. The ASTD *2005 State of the Industry Report* confirms that it is still the primary method, but technology-based learning is rapidly gaining widespread utilization (see Figure 6-13). Examples of technology-based delivery methods gaining broader acceptance and use include CD-ROM–based training, video teleconferencing, satellite broadcasts, and Internet-based training (both synchronous and asynchronous). HPI practitioners must be ready to manage, design, develop or select, and use learning technologies that support learning and development for their organizations.

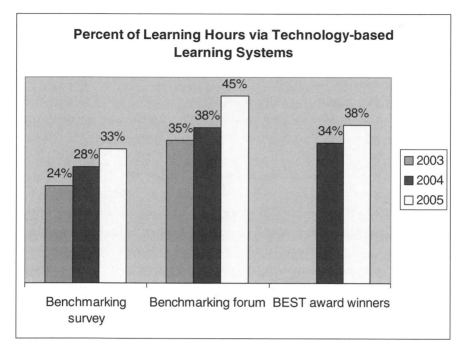

Figure 6-13   Percent of learning hours via technology-based learning systems. Source: ASTD 2005 State of the Industry Report.

In addition to technology-based training delivery vehicles, nontraditional structured learning approaches are finding favor with U.S. businesses. Group-ware and knowledge management systems are innovative technological approaches to putting information and knowledge into the hands of the work-force. Action learning and large group interventions, such as open space technology, are new approaches that can accomplish business objectives while at the same time provide a structured vehicle for learning (Rothwell and Sensenig, 1999). Self-directed learning, group-based instruction, job rotation, mentoring, and coaching programs all can be effective in the right circumstances (Rothwell and Sensenig, 1999). As a result of this trend, HPI practitioners will need to be able to study the circumstances of a particular learning, and challenge, make appropriate recommendations for the approach to learning, and design, manage, and in some cases, facilitate the learning event. The HPI practitioners must be comfortable selecting and implementing a full range of high-quality training and nontraining solutions.

Key Trend 3:   Organizations Are Making More Demands to Demonstrate Measurable Results and ROI for Human Resource Initiatives

Our customers are increasingly asking us to prove that the services that we provide produce the results that they seek. Using the terminology of Donald Kirkpatrick and Jack Phillips, no longer are our customers satisfied with success at Level 1 (Did they like it?) and Level 2 (Did they learn it?) evaluations. Now we're asked to demonstrate success at Level 3 (Did they use it?), Level 4 (Did it make a difference?), and Level 5 (Did the outcome justify the cost?). According to the ASTD *2005 State of the Industry Report*, HPI practitioners are still not routinely completing Level 2 and above evaluations (see Figure 6-14).

This is not cause for alarm. There can be many explanations as to why only 2.1 percent of us calculate actual Level 5, return on investment, figures. First of all, making this sort of calculation can be time-consuming and, with current workloads, finding the extra time to calculate this figure may not be the best use of your time if you're not being asked for it from management. Secondly, it is often difficult to isolate the effect of the intervention to determine the true

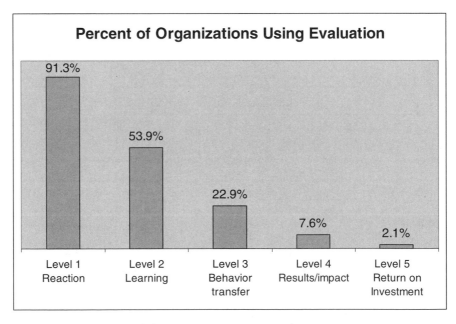

Figure 6-14   Percent of organizations using evaluation. Source: ASTD *2005 State of the Industry Report.*

impact to the organization. Knowing this, many executives categorize ROI calculations that are shared with them as "fuzzy math." Still, there are many times when this measurement is not only easy to obtain, but it's in our best interest to calculate and publicize it.

Key Trend 4:   An Increasing Percent of Learning Function Resources Are Being Used for Human Performance Improvement

---

Trainers have long recognized that simply providing workers with new skills and knowledge in a classroom will not necessarily result in those new skills being applied in the workplace. Many other factors in the workplace—such as appropriate tools, practice, feedback, reward, work processes, and other factors—should be in place for new skills and knowledge to transfer from instructional to work settings. Beyond that, trainers have also realized that training cannot solve all performance problems identified in the workplace. In fact, very few performance challenges can be met by training alone. That's why it's great to see that more and more formerly training resources are being used to do performance improvement analysis and interventions (see Figure 6-15).

In many organizations, HPI practitioners are helping to create workforce strategies (Rothwell and Kazanas, 2004). Their input is being sought on how to establish and achieve organizational goals and their metrics, how to cascade those goals down through the organization, and, ultimately, how to enable the

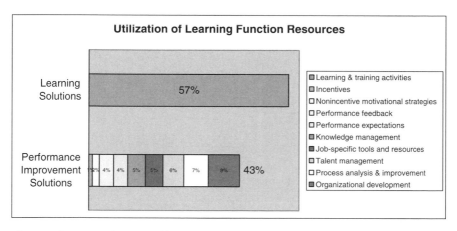

Figure 6-15   Utilization of learning function resources. Source: ASTD *2005 State of the Industry Report.*

workforce to achieve those goals. This level of consulting requires a rigorous understanding of how the business operates, what the long- and short-term strategies are for achieving organizational goals, recognizing the current challenges to success, and identifying the intervention(s) necessary to enable workers to perform in line with organizational performance goals.

The other related trend is that HPI practitioners aren't necessarily part of the human resources function. Many are strategic partners and serve on the management teams in the business operations units. This is happening for various reasons, but one major reason is that sometimes training executives are reluctant to allow their traditional training personnel to step outside of the box to try their hands at performance improvement. Another reason is that many human resource executives are more compensation- and benefits-oriented, rather than performance improvement–oriented. When we put our HPI practitioner hats on, we begin to speak in the language of our customers. We can build our own credibility with our customers, even if we can't manage to build it with our own function's leadership.

On the other hand, there are many examples where learning organizations are spinning off a team of internal practitioners to tackle the large-scale performance improvement projects in the organization. In many cases, human resources is 100 percent supportive in this shift in roles.

Key Trend 5: There Is an Increasing Demand for Employee Development

---

Several trends cited earlier in this chapter result in an increase in the demand for employee development. Skilled labor is increasingly in short supply. Workers are demanding that career development opportunities be a condition of employment. New technology creates a constant demand for skill-upgrading efforts. Increasing skill requirements for most jobs provides an endless source for employee development opportunities.

Our educational institutions are not expected to be able to meet the demands for skilled labor in the future, in part because those demands are so quickly changing. Organizations will need to bridge this skill gap with programs of their own or to work with educational institutions to supply the future talent. Employees will also need to take charge of their own development and will exert greater pressure on their organizations than they have traditionally done in the past to provide planned and unplanned learning opportunities.

HPI practitioners need to be prepared to meet this increase in demand for employee development by providing access to employee development tools and resources. These can take many forms, including onsite and offsite training seminars, structured on-the-job training programs, job-specific training curricula, job rotation initiatives, career counseling, and the creation and application of knowledge management systems.

Key Trend 6: Leadership Development Is Seen as Critical to Organizational Success

---

Decisions on how to respond to all the trends identified in this chapter have to be facilitated by today's leaders. HR practitioners—including HPI practitioners—have an important role to play in this process (Rothwell, Prescott, and Taylor, 2005). It should come as no surprise that U.S. corporations, as well as their global counterparts, are recognizing the key role that leadership development plays in competitive success.

With the help of HPI practitioners, organizations can identify the individual competencies and the organizational factors contributing to leadership success within unique corporate and national cultures and lines of business. They can then propose leadership development initiatives that support this vision of leadership (Rothwell and Kazanas, 1999). These can take the form of training programs, coaching, action learning, and developmental assignments. One critical factor remains constant for the success of a leadership development program—dedication and commitment from the top of the organization.

Jack Welch, former CEO of General Electric, attended workshops and planning sessions and conducted biweekly sessions with managers for the last 16 years of his career. PepsiCo's former CEO, Roger Enrico, believes that proven leaders are the best developers of other leaders and devoted a great deal of his time to PepsiCo's leadership development programs. This is what support from the top of the organization looks like.

Albert Vicere and Robert Fulmer (1995), from Pennsylvania State University, believe that leadership development programs are becoming more customized and strategic, shorter and more focused, and are being done on a larger scale and then cascaded down to all levels of the organization. They are seeing more action learning projects being assigned with measurable results. The idea is to provide people with opportunities to learn from their work rather than taking them away from their work to learn.

Leaders who are hesitant to take the necessary business risks, are arrogant and insensitive, demonstrate a controlling leadership style, and are reluctant to tackle difficult people issues will not survive in organizations in the future. The successful leaders of the future will be master strategists, change managers, relationship/network builders, and talent developers (Barrett and Beeson, 2002).

Key Trend 7:   HPI Projects Will Be More Focused on Business Results

---

Traditional performance improvement case studies typically involve a performance gap for a workgroup or small part of the overall organization. Today, we can no longer settle for just picking the low-hanging fruit. We need to take on larger-scale projects and really go after improving overall business results that are directly aligned with the organizations goals and objectives. Increasingly, our customers should be senior level management and our results should be clearly measured at all 5 levels of evaluation—reaction, learning (if applicable), transfer, results, and ROI.

Key Trend 8:   HPI Certification Is Available

Both the American Society for Training and Development (ASTD) and the International Society for Performance Improvement (ISPI) have established certificate and certification programs that HPI practitioners can use to add skills and knowledge and build credibility with their peers and customers. ASTD offers both a Human Performance Improvement Certificate Program and a certification program for Certified Professional in Learning and Performance (CPLP). The HPI Certificate program consists of five core courses. These can be taken at local college campuses or at a host of other locations. The CPLP designation can be obtained by passing a rigorous test that demonstrates your level of expertise and qualifications to work in the workplace learning and performance field. Self-study test preparation materials are available for purchase.

ISPI offers a certification program to become a Certified Performance Technologist. The application process is rigorous and follows a set of ten standards of performance technology. Applicants must complete at least seven performance improvement projects while adhering to the standards. Both project documentation and customer contact information for verification must be submitted to a review board.

Whether you should pursue an advanced degree, a certificate, or certification will depend on your career goals and what qualifications your future employers and customers seek.

In conclusion, the future is bright for those in the HPI field. We have our work cut out for us. The challenges are ample and large, but we have the skills and knowledge necessary to lead our organizations to greatness.

Use the worksheet appearing in Figure 6-16 to structure your own thinking about what these trends will mean for HPI practitioners.

Summary

This chapter summarized key trends in three areas that affect HPI practitioners. The trends were classified into three categories: (1) business and public sector trends, (2) workforce trends, and (3) human resource trends.

The key business and public sector trends identified in the chapter were:

- **Key Trend 1:** Organizations are placing innovation at the top of their priority lists.
- **Key Trend 2:** Organizations are faced with increased security concerns.
- **Key Trend 3:** Organizations are growing via mergers and acquisitions.
- **Key Trend 4:** Businesses and agencies are paying closer attention to business ethics.
- **Key Trend 5:** Public sector organizations are recognizing the need to become high-performing organizations.
- **Key Trend 6:** Businesses and the public sector are experiencing the effects of global interdependence.
- **Key Trend 7:** Corporations are outsourcing tasks and large-scale functions.

The key workforce trends identified in the chapter were:

- **Key Trend 1:** The emergence of a knowledge-based economy is driving skill requirements up.
- **Key Trend 2:** We have an aging workforce that is soon to be on its way out of the labor pool.
- **Key Trend 3:** Offshoring is changing the ethnicity and culture of the workforce.
- **Key Trend 4:** Workers are increasingly considering job changes.

Directions:

Use this worksheet to structure your thinking about the trends described in this chapter and how they may influence the competencies needed by HPI practitioners to help their organizations cope with these trends. For each trend listed below, brainstorm what you think the most important competencies will be in order for you to help your organization react to the trend or even to take competitive advantage of the trend. There are no "right" or "wrong" answers in any absolute sense.

Type	Trend	Competencies
Business and Public Sector	1. Organizations are placing innovation at the top of their priority lists.	
	2. Organizations are faced with increased security concerns.	
	3. Organizations are growing via mergers and acquisitions.	
	4. Businesses and agencies are paying closer attention to business ethics.	
	5. Public sector organizations are recognizing the need to become high-performing organizations.	
	6. Businesses and the public sector are experiencing the effects of global interdependence.	
	7. Corporations are outsourcing tasks and large-scale functions.	

Figure 6-16 Worksheet for trends and competencies needed to cope with these trends.

Type	Trend	Competencies
Workforce	1. The emergence of a knowledge-based economy is driving skill requirements up.	
	2. We have an aging workforce that is soon to be on its way out of the labor pool.	
	3. Offshoring is changing the ethnicity and culture of the workforce.	
	4. Workers are increasingly considering job changes.	

Type	Trend	Competencies
Human Resource	1. The training and development industry is spending a greater percent of their budget on external services (including tuition).	
	2. Human Resources is being innovative with the methods for delivering services throughout their organizations.	
	3. Organizations are making more demands to demonstrate measurable results and ROI for Human Resource initiatives.	
	4. An increasing percent of learning function resources are being used for human performance improvement.	
	5. There is an increasing demand for employee development.	
	6. Leadership development is seen as critical to organizational success.	
	7. HPI projects will be more focused on business results.	
	8. HPI certification is available.	

Figure 6-16 *Continued*

The key human resource trends identified in this chapter were:

- **Key Trend 1:** The training and development industry is spending a greater percent of their budget on external services (including tuition).
- **Key Trend 2:** Human resources is being innovative with the methods for delivering services throughout their organizations.
- **Key Trend 3:** Organizations are making more demands to demonstrate measurable results and ROI for human resource initiatives.
- **Key Trend 4:** An increasing percent of learning function resources are being used for human performance improvement.
- **Key Trend 5:** There is an increasing demand for employee development.
- **Key Trend 6:** Leadership development is seen as critical to organizational success.
- **Key Trend 7:** HPI projects will be more focused on business results.
- **Key Trend 8:** HPI certification is available.

References

Amabile, T.M., and Sensabaugh, S.J. (1992). High Creativity versus Low Creativity: What Makes the Difference? In S.S. Gryskiewics and D.A. Hills (Eds.), *Readings in Innovation*. Greensboro, NC: Center for Creative Leadership.

American Management Association. (2005). Leading into the Future, American Management Association/Human Resource Institute, p. 26.

American Management Association. (2006). The Question for Innovation: A Global Study of Innovation Management 2006–2016. Retrieved from http://www.amanet.org/research/pdfs/hri_innovation.pdf.

Barrett, A., and Beeson, J. (2002). Developing Business Leaders for the Future, *The Conference Board*, New York.

Burke, M., and Collison, J. (2004). 2004 U.S. Job Recovery and Retention Poll Findings, Society for Human Resource Management and Career Journal.com, retrieved from www.SHRM.org/surveys/results.

Clark, R. (2003). Turning Round Turnover Trends. *People Management*, December 18, 2003, pp. 22–24.

Deviney, N., and Sugrue, B. (2005). Learning Outsourcing: A Reality Cheat, *T & D Magazine*, *58*(12), 40–45.

Disaster Recovery Guide (2006). What Is the Status of Your Disaster Recovery Plan? www.disaster-recovery-guide.com.

Dolliver, M. (2004). Job Hopping. *Adweek*, *45*(12), 34.

Faircloth, A. (1996). Really Important Things You Need to Know. *Fortune.*

Families and Work Institute. (1998). Press release. www.familiesandwork. org/press/p2.html.

Fulmer, R., and Vicere, A. (1995). *Executive Education and Leadership Development: State of the Practice.* University Park, IN: The Penn State Institute for the Study of Organizational Effectiveness.

Gamble, Richard. (2005). The Rise of BPO, Outsourcing Essentials, *3*(1), retrieved from www.outsourcing.com.

General Accounting Office. (2004). *High-Performing Organizations: Metrics, Means, and Mechanisms for Achieving High Performance in the 21st Century Public Management Environment.* GAO-04-343SP, retrieved from www.gao. gov.

General Accounting Office. (2005). *21st Century Challenges: Transforming Government to Meet Current and Emerging Challenges,* GAO-05-830T, retrieved from www.GAO.gov.

Hernze-Broome, G., and Hughes, Richard L. (2004). Leadership Development: Past, Present, and Future. *Human Resource Planning, 27*(1), 24–26.

Institute of Management & Administrations, Inc. (2005). Why the Turnover Threat Is Real—and What to Do About It. *HR Focus,* 2005(3).

Kirkpatrick, D. (1994). Evaluating Training Programs: The Four Levels. San Francisco: Berrett-Koehter Publishers.

Klingshirn, R.G., and Wisniewski, B. (2006). Solving the Offshoring Dilemma. *Training and Development Magazine, 60*(6), 49–52.

Outsourcing Institute. (2005). Processes Currently Outsourced, retrieved from www.outsourcing.com.

Poletz, L. (2002). Corporate Insecurity: Big Companies Seek Greater Protection Against Terrorism Post-9/11. *Reuters Journal.* Retrieved from http://www.jrn. columbia.edu/studentwork/reutersjournal/2002/poletz.asp.

Rogers, Dennis. (2006). Outsourcing, retrieved from www.resourceoutcomes. co.nz/outsourcing.htm.

Rothwell, W., and Kazanas, H. (1999). *Building Successful In-house Leadership and Management Development Programs.* Westport, CT: Greenwood Press.

Rothwell, W., and Kazanas, H. (2004). *Planning and Managing Human Resources: Strategic Planning for Personnel Management,* 2nd ed. Amherst, MA: Human Resource Development Press.

Rothwell, W., Prescott, R., and Taylor, M. (2005). *Strategic Human Resource Leader: How to Prepare Your Organization for the Six Key Trends Shaping the Future.* Mumbai: Jaico Publishing House.

Rothwell, W., and Sensenig, K. (Eds.). (1999). *The Sourcebook for Self-Directed Learning.* Amherst, MA: Human Resource Development Press.

Sugrue, B., and Deviney, N. (2005). Learning Outsourcing Research Report, Alexandria, VA: The American Society for Training and Development and IBM.

Sugrue, B., and Rivera, R.J. (2005). *The 2005 State of the Industry Report: ASTD's Annual Review of Trends in Workplace Learning and Support.* Retrieved from www.astd.org.

Thompson Financial. (2006). Retrieved from www.thompson.com.

Vestring, T., King, B., Rouse, T., and Critchlow, J. (2003). Merger Integration: Why the "Soft Issues" Matter Most. *European Business Forum, 13,* 28–32.

Watson Wyalt. (2000/2001). ECS Survey Report on Employee Efficiency. Rochelle Park, NJ: Watson Wyalt Data Services.

Weil, J.B. (2003). Navigating the Perfect Storm. *Work and Family Connection.* http://www.workfamily.com/GuestColumns/Weil.asp.

7

Transforming the Training Department into an HPI Function

Chapter 6 illustrated the changes that are occurring throughout corporate America and their implications to HPI practitioners. These trends are driving the need for corporate training departments to transition into full-service performance improvement organizations. Training professionals are moving away from training as the sole solution for all human performance problems or improvement opportunities when, in fact, many performance improvement strategies are possible. Countless books, articles, college courses, conference presentations, and workshops bear witness to this trend.

Such a transition does not occur rapidly and without challenges. In fact, it can easily take two years or more to convert a traditional training department into an HPI function—and perhaps longer, depending on the current status of the training department in the organization. Not only must the training department change and be prepared to offer additional HPI services, but the clients—internal or external—must recognize and value the additional services. This could prove to be quite a challenge in some organizations where the human resource function has enjoyed a less than stellar reputation.

"How is it that, after 20 years of steadily developing professionalism and lofty vision, in many companies, HR is still regarded—rightly or wrongly—as the department where all good things come to an end?" (Finney, 1997). One need only read Scott Adams' *Dilbert* comic strip featuring Catbert, the "evil" HR director, to get a sense of what many people in corporate America think of the human resource function and such related functions as human performance improvement, human resource development, and workplace learning and performance.

One Approach to Transforming a Traditional Training Department into an HPI Department

This chapter provides a rudimentary list of action steps that are needed to transform a traditional training function into a full-service human performance improvement organization. The order may vary somewhat for different organizations. The steps are shown in Figure 7-1.

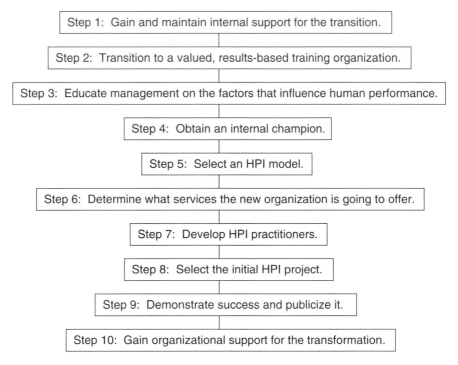

Step 1: Gain and maintain internal support for the transition.

Step 2: Transition to a valued, results-based training organization.

Step 3: Educate management on the factors that influence human performance.

Step 4: Obtain an internal champion.

Step 5: Select an HPI model.

Step 6: Determine what services the new organization is going to offer.

Step 7: Develop HPI practitioners.

Step 8: Select the initial HPI project.

Step 9: Demonstrate success and publicize it.

Step 10: Gain organizational support for the transformation.

Figure 7-1   Possible action steps for transforming a traditional training department into an HPI department.

Step 1: Gain and Maintain Internal Support for the Transformation

Speak to those who have tried to lead a transformation from training to HPI and they will tell you that one of the biggest challenges is securing and sustaining the advocacy of the practitioners in their own training organization. The transition will require many in the training function to upgrade, or in some cases completely change, their skill sets. This can prove to be very exciting to some, threatening to others, and downright heresy to a few. It is critical to get the organization aligned and supportive of the change initiative.

At this early stage, one way to build support is to create the vision of the transformed training organization collectively. It is important to identify the many benefits of moving to a full-service HPI organization. These benefits should include expanded opportunities for professional growth, increased credibility within the organization, greater variety in project tasks, increased skills, and many others. It is also important to capture those aspects of the transformation that are likely to prompt the most concern. Examples of such issues might include loss of specialization, lack of clarity in individuals' future roles, and lack of experience with nontraining interventions. Addressing these concerns in an open manner will encourage the support of internal practitioners. Maintaining an open dialogue can dissuade "negative speak" that can escalate to internal sabotage. Negative "hallway talk" with potential internal clients could stall—or even defeat—transformation efforts.

Too much enthusiasm for the transformation can hurt your efforts. Why? A shift in the functionality of the organizational unit takes time—time for your organizational unit to make the shift and time for your clients to understand and accept the change. Being overzealous by trying to do too much too fast damages your overall transformation effort. Building too much enthusiasm in your client base before you are staffed to respond, or trying to initiate HPI projects in organizations where you have not earned credibility with management, could also prove destructive to your mission.

Therefore, it is important to establish a timeline for the transformation and establish consensus among those in the department for sticking to it. The remaining nine steps are suggested milestones for the timeline.

— Step 2: Transition to a Valued, Results-Based Training Organization

Establishing the training organization as one that is focused on performance will help management recognize the function's role in helping the organization achieve its goals. This will help to establish credibility for transforming the training function into an HPI function.

Many training organizations today offer many internally and externally designed training programs. Managers and employees are accustomed to picking up the training catalogue and searching for the program that will provide the skills and knowledge they need to succeed in the workplace. That is one of the more optimistic scenarios. In many cases, the company course catalogue is an easy solution to the mandatory employee development effort of the company. Employees flip through the listing of courses, looking for interesting topics that may or may not have much relevance to their current knowledge or skill gaps or, more importantly, anything to do with their current job tasks.

The role of traditional training departments has been to identify the training needs within the organization and to provide training opportunities that will help meet those needs. They often schedule the programs, manage registration and logistics, and, in some cases, even deliver the content. There are many outstanding training departments in corporations today that not only provide standard off-the-shelf training programs but also design and develop customized training for their organizations.

In order to increase our value to the organizations that we serve, we must first offer training that is strategic, i.e., that aligns with the organization's key business strategies. This means that we need to be very clear on what those strategies are. We need to be able to step into the role of analyst and determine those skills and knowledge that the workforce needs in order to achieve their goals. Then we need to design effective training that will bridge those gaps. Finally, we need to be able to quantify our impact on business results.

To win the support of management to transform a training function into a performance improvement function, the training organization must first measure and publicize the effectiveness of their most recognizable human performance intervention—training. It is not good enough to just report the number of classroom hours delivered. The training department must measure and report the ability of the learning events to produce behavior change back on the job and the impact of behavior change in meeting the organization's goals. This information is vital to communicating the training organization's commitment to producing measurable business results rather than just filling classrooms.

In general, the training profession has made significant improvements to demonstrate their training's effectiveness in terms that business leaders can understand (see Figure 7-2). The Kirkpatrick model for evaluation, discussed in Chapter 5, has been historically used for demonstrating training effectiveness. Jack Phillips, of the ROI Institute, has written extensively on a fifth level—return on investment. The ASTD *2005 State of the Industry Report* (Sugrue and Rivera, 2005) indicates that 91 percent of courses offered by leading-edge firms are evaluated at Level 1. Fifty-four percent of courses at these firms are evaluated at Level 2. Twenty-three percent of courses offered by leading-edge firms are evaluated at Level 3, and only 8 percent at Level 4 (see Figure 7-3). In general, orga-

Kirkpatrick Model for Training Evaluation

Level of Evaluation	Measures	Answers the Question
Level 1	Reaction	Did they like it?
Level 2	Learning	Did they learn it?
Level 3	Behavior	Did they use it?
Level 4	Results	Did it make a difference?

Figure 7-2 The Kirkpatrick model for training evaluation.

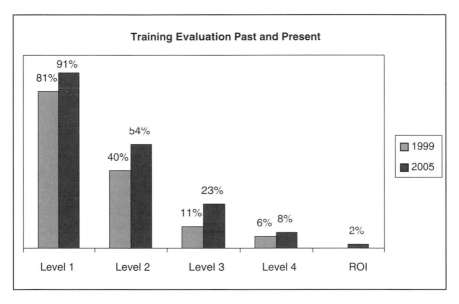

Figure 7-3 Increase in levels of evaluation. Source: ASTD *2005 State of the Industry Report.*

nizations should conduct Level 3 evaluations for 20–30 percent of course offerings and Level 4 evaluations for 10 percent of course offerings. However, those are just guidelines. If your training department is having a credibility problem within your organization, you may choose to conduct Level 3 and Level 4 evaluations for most of your training initiatives until you firmly resolve the image problem. Why not 100 percent all of the time? The answer is that it is a practical matter of resources. We are operating within budget constraints; not just of dollars, but with limited training personnel to meet our organization's needs. Level 3 and 4 evaluations can be time consuming to complete.

However, being able to transform the traditional training function into a valued performance-oriented training function requires that professionals in the training department design and implement effective Level 3 and Level 4 evaluations. Chapter 8 provides several options for building this competency in the training organization. Successful execution of Level 3 and Level 4 evaluations also requires that management support the implementation of these evaluations by their own participation and by providing access to the employees whose behavior is being measured.

If it's quantifiable, you should also calculate the return on investment. This calculation clearly defines your financial value to the organization and is in the language of your customers.

When the training department has a success story, publicize it. Describe it in newsletters, websites, e-mail, and presentations to employees and management. You can even submit the success story to a local or national trade journal. The communication should identify the knowledge or skill gap that existed, the structured learning event that was selected, the behavior change that was achieved, and the benefits received by the organization. The more success stories your department can share, the greater the confidence your customers will have that you're committed not to just training, but to their overall business success. Once you've established that you're both on the same team trying to achieve the same goal, you'll have an easier time selling your services—not just training services, but other performance improvement services.

Step 3: Educate Management on the Factors That Influence Human Performance

A well-designed Level 3 evaluation not only can measure the behavior change that has occurred as a result of a learning event but also can determine what barriers to performance, if any, still exist in the workplace. Both data are important to communicate to management. The first part helps management recognize the training function's commitment to follow-up and ensure that the new skills and knowledge transfer to the workplace. Identifying the remaining barriers to performance is the first step in educating management that training is not necessarily the sole solution to all performance problems. It gives you the opportunity to communicate the other factors in the workplace that can lead to less-than-acceptable performance.

The ability to educate management requires the HPI practitioner to identify the myriad factors influencing workplace performance. These may include:

- Clarity of expectations
- Level of empowerment
- Completeness of data, information, or feedback available to performers when they need it and in the form they need it
- Quality of documentation
- Quality of job aids for simple, infrequently performed tasks
- Workplace design
- Organizational structure
- Conflicting, or nonexistent, consequences of performance
- Efficiency of work processes
- Employee ability

By identifying organizational performance gaps, decision makers can take proactive steps to build a high-performance workplace (HPW), where individuals are supported in all ways to perform to their peak. You can establish yourself and your colleagues as the ones in the organization who have the expertise to bridge these gaps. Try to avoid HPI jargon like, "interventions" and "terminal objectives." Rather, you should talk to the managers about "solutions" and "what's most important" (Willmore, 2003). One caution: Many times, management sees most of these types of performance gaps as "their issues" to address. Be prepared for this attitude. Seeing the former training person as someone who can help them with these types of organizational issues may take some getting used to. Be patient, but diligent. Susan Fehl, an HPI practitioner who has over 25 years of experience in the field, says, "There are very few enlightened managers out there that realize that (human) performance improvement is a foundational piece to their business." Part of our job is to help them not only to accept this role, but to embrace it and value it. Eventually, you'll find a manager who will welcome your help. And that brings us to Step 4.

Step 4: Obtain an Internal Champion

To make a successful transition from a traditional training function to an HPI function, you first need to have a success story. Seek an internal champion—

that is, a manager who has shown interest in the results of training offered in his or her organization or a manager who has shown an interest in factors influencing human performance. Choosing a manager who is one to two levels above you on the organization chart has proven to be successful (Fuller and Farrington, 1999). If you go too high in the organization, the project that gets defined may prove to be too challenging and complex for novice HPI practitioners. Too broad a project may require the involvement of a large population of nonbelievers—those who do not understand why trainers should poke around in the business process. For these reasons, "think small" on your first effort.

You want a champion who will support the initial organizational analysis that will result in baseline measurements of performance and will also commit to post-intervention evaluation so you can measure the overall improvement in performance. Your champion should be ready to remove barriers that you encounter during the course of the project. The champion will also be a key partner in communicating the success of the HPI intervention.

The key to maintaining the support of a champion is to form a partnership with him or her. You form that partnership by asking a lot of questions about their organization. What are the challenges that they face? What kinds of solutions have been tried in the past? What were the results of those solutions? What are the measures of success? How will we know if we've achieved our project goals? The HPI practitioner needs to demonstrate his or her true commitment to achieving the organization's goals, and the champion needs to demonstrate his or her true commitment to the project.

Step 5: Select an HPI Model

Chapter 2 featured several models for HPI. It is essential that your training organization select a model that will be utilized by the new HPI function. While it could be argued that using only one model is too restrictive, it is critical at this stage of transformation that the organization gains a thorough understanding of only one HPI model and the procedural tasks accompanying it. Your organization must interface with the client base in a consistent manner. Settling on one model will encourage this. And remember, the model is to guide all HPI practitioners to follow the same process with the organization's client. It's not necessary to explain the model to the client. Your interactions with the client should be kept in terms that the client can relate to. "Effective performance consultants make sure that the performance model, language, and process don't distract from the focus on the performance issues and business priorities that initially mattered to the client" (Willmore, 2003). The model you choose to operate within does not need to be taken right out of some textbook. In fact, most organizations find it a useful exercise to develop their own customized model for HPI. Keep in mind, however, that the model should include the following elements (Fuller and Farrington, 1999):

- Identification of a business need
- Determination of the performance required to meet the business need
- Identification of the performance gap(s)
- Determination of the root cause(s) of the performance gap(s)
- Selection and implementation of interventions to remove or reduce the root cause(s)
- Evaluation of performance to determine the success of the intervention

This model will not only serve as the blueprint by which you approach all HPI projects, but it will also be the primary tool you use to communicate your function's transformation to the rest of the organization. Over time—and with experience—the original model will most likely be modified to better fit the idiosyncrasies of the key personalities and corporate culture of your organization.

Step 6: Determine What Services the New Organization Is Going to Offer

Before a traditional training department can begin to transform to a human performance improvement function, it must define what that means. There are a host of interventions that a full-service HPI function can offer to an organization. It must be determined which interventions will be included in the service offerings. Of those, determine which will be resourced internally and which will be resourced utilizing external service providers.

Mager (1992) cites several services that might be included in the newly defined organization (see Figure 7-4). Langdon, Whiteside, and McKenna (1999) cite 50 performance improvement tools that you might include as services in your new organization. The checklist appearing in Figure 7-5 will help you define the new organizational unit services.

Here is a list of some of the services that might be offered by a performance-oriented full-service department.

Needs analyses	A review of organizational plans to identify needs for training and nontraining services.
Performance analyses	Onsite review to identify causes of discrepancies between actual and desired performance, with recommendations for solutions.
Feedback review	An onsite review to ensure that all tasks include sources of feedback to the performers.
Consequence review	An onsite review to ensure that all tasks include sources of feedback to the performers.
Task analyses	Onsite analyses intended to generate descriptions of actual and/or exemplary performance.
Goal analyses	A technique intended to assist managers in developing usable definitions of abstract intents.
Organizational analyses	A review of the organizational structure within and around a job, intended to determine whether the organizational structure facilitates or impedes peak performance.
Documentation	Manuals, and so on, designed to be used to facilitate job performance.
Job/performance aids	Design and development of items that will prompt desired performance.
Performance management systems	Development of mechanisms and procedures intended to ensure a supportive environment.
Workplace review	Onsite review intended to identify obstacles caused by awkward workplace design.
Orientation sessions	Sessions that allow people to become familiar with target concepts and information.
Training sessions	Sessions intended to teach people what they do not currently know but need to know.
Coaching instruction	Training sessions for nontrainers who will be expected to conduct on-the-job training.

Figure 7-4 The full-service training and performance services department. © 1999, "What Every Manager Should Know About Training". The Center for Effective Performance, Inc., 1100 Johnson Ferry Road, Suite 150, Atlanta, GA 30342. www. cepworldwide.com. 800-558-4237. Reprinted with permission. All rights reserved. No portion of these materials may be reproduced in any manner without the express written consent from The Center for Effective Performance, Inc.

Step 7: Develop HPI Practitioners

Just as additional competencies are required to transition from a traditional training function to a results-based training function, so too are new

Services We Offer	Intervention	Internally Sourced	Externally Sourced	External Source Options
√	**Sample**	√		
	360-Degree Feedback			
	Accelerated Learning			
	Action Learning			
	Assessment Center			
	Automated Resume Tracking System			
	Challenge Education			
	Change Style Preference Models			
	Cognitive Ergonomics			
	Communication			
	Compensation Systems			
	Competency Modeling			
	Conflict Management			
	Critical Thinking Systems			
	Cultural Change			
	Customer Feedback			
	Electronic Performance Support Systems			
	Employee Orientation			
	Expert Systems			
	Flowcharts			
	Fluency Development			
	Human Resource Information Systems			
	Job Aids			
	Leadership Development Programs			
	Learner-controlled instruction			
	Leveraging Diversity			
	Mentoring/Coaching			
	Motivation Systems			
	Needs Assessment			
	On-the-Job Training			
	Organizational Development			
	Organizational Scan			
	Outplacement			
	Partnering Agreements			
	Performance Analysis			
	Performance Appraisal			
	Performance Management			
	Policies and Procedures			
	Process Mapping			
	Recognition Programs			
	Reengineering			
	Results-based Management			
	Safety Management			
	Simulation			

Figure 7-5 A checklist for defining the interventions offered by an HPI function/department.

Services We Offer	Intervention	Internally Sourced	Externally Sourced	External Source Options
√	**Sample**	√		
	Strategic Planning and Visioning			
	Structured Writing			
	Team Performance			
	Teaming			
	Training			
	Usability Assessments			
	Work Group Alignment			

Figure 7-5 *Continued*

competencies required to transform into a full-service HPI organization. The initial HPI project will define priorities for development for your organization. Initially, you will want to develop one or two HPI practitioners. Your selection of these candidates should be based upon their enthusiasm to grow in their profession and their proven success at organizational analysis.

As Jim Fuller (Fuller and Farrington, 1999) writes, "Potential candidates within the organization typically have backgrounds that are strong in either systems thinking or people development. If you must choose between the two, select the candidates with the systems thinking backgrounds." Each HPI project that is launched will provide additional opportunities for the staff to develop new skills. See Chapter 8 for additional information on how to develop HPI practitioners.

Step 8: Select the Initial HPI Project

Once you have your champion and your newly trained HPI practitioners, you are ready to identify an HPI project that will allow the transformed department to demonstrate its value to others in the organization. Ideally, the initial project should meet the criteria described below.

First, the project should provide an opportunity to improve performance that is easy to define and measure. For example, it should reduce injuries, reduce merchandise return rate, increase production, improve quality, or address some other pressing organizational problem—preferably one of high visibility and one tied to the organization's strategic objectives. While efforts to increase empowerment or improve the leadership of an organization are outstanding HPI goals, these would not be wise choices for the initial HPI project, since they are more challenging to measure and more difficult to demonstrate short-term results.

Second, the project timeline should be six months or less. Remember that the goal of the initial project should be to create a success story—and testimony from a credible manager that you can use to promote the desired transformation of the training function. The longer the project timeline, the longer it will take to achieve this transformation.

Third, the project should be relatively straightforward and not complex. Keep in mind that, in most cases, HPI practitioners assigned to the project will be novices and will still be on a learning curve. Avoid projects that are too ambitious in scope and that have too many uncontrollable or politically sensitive issues associated with them.

Fourth, the root cause of the problem or opportunity should be something other than—or in addition to—lack of skill or knowledge. Since a goal is to feature your organization's capability to select and implement interventions beyond training, it is critical that your initial project be highly likely to result in nontraining interventions.

These are guidelines and not absolute requirements for the initial project. Adhering to these guidelines will help your organization rapidly gain credibility for its new direction.

Step 9: Demonstrate Success and Publicize It

Many public case studies demonstrate successful HPI projects at major corporations (see, for instance, Rothwell and Dubois, 1998). Why not just use these to convince management to support your organization's new direction? After all, if it was successful at Motorola, it will be successful in your organization, right? Managers are quick to point out how these corporations differ from their own. It is unlikely that you would ever gain support for your desired transformation by sharing these case studies with management. What is required to gain the support of management is an *internal* success story.

Follow the HPI model that your organization selected in Step 3. It is critical to obtain baseline performance measures as your project commences. Success is achieved when the desired performance is achieved or improved in the workplace. Therefore, it is also imperative to conduct a postintervention performance evaluation to demonstrate the success of the intervention(s).

In addition to measuring overall performance improvement, you should complete a cost-benefit analysis or ROI. To do this, track all costs—both direct and indirect. *Direct costs* are out-of-pocket expenses, such as the cost of materials or external resources. *Indirect* or *opportunity costs* are less easily measurable costs, such as the value of internal consultants and other resources used in the project that would be productive in other ways in the organization.

Communicate to such key stakeholders as managers and affected employees both the improvement in performance that occurred as well as the results of the cost-benefit analysis. Organizational leaders must recognize that HPI practitioners can produce measurable results in the workplace with interventions other than training, and that they can do it in a fiscally responsible way. Use company newsletters, websites, e-mail, and presentations to employees and management. Share the success stories with anyone who will listen. When the success case is communicated, it should:

- Identify the problem or challenge
- Describe the intervention(s) that were selected
- Clarify the behavior change that was achieved
- Estimate the net impact on the organization's goals and the return on investment projections

Charles Harpham, a Six Sigma Blackbelt with Constellation Energy, says, "I feel like I'm valued more and more with every successful project." The only way this happens is if the business leaders of his organization know about his successes. This is not the time to be humble. Be proud of your accomplishments, and be sure to share the role that others played in your success.

Step 10: Gain Organizational Support for the Transformation

When you are equipped with a successful case, you are ready to spread the word about your HPI function's new capabilities. There are many ways to get the word out and thereby build support throughout your company. First, everyone on the staff must be capable of describing the vision for the new organization in 30 seconds or less. One effective way to solicit support for your transformation is informally via "elevator" or "water cooler chats." These conversations tend to be very brief. Therefore, you must be able to succinctly communicate what it is that you are trying to do.

Here is an example of an early-stage conversation:

Chris: Barbara, what's been going on over in your area?
Barbara: We're beginning to measure training's impact on the achievement of organizational goals.

A later-stage conversation:

Chris: How are things in training these days, Barbara?

Barbara: We're trying to change our focus from one that just provides skills and knowledge to the organization to one that offers multiple solutions, in addition to, or in lieu of, training that helps our businesses achieve their goals.

Chris: What's wrong with training?

Barbara: Nothing really, if the reason you're not making your numbers is because people don't know how to do certain aspects of their job, but we've found that many times, that's not the case. In fact, training is a pretty expensive solution, so we only want to use it if we need to. We try to improve performance with less costly solutions, if we can. We use a systematic approach to analyze what's really going on in the workplace and offer the most cost-effective solutions that will bring the desired results.

As you can see, individuals can communicate the overall gist of the transformation from a training-oriented to a performance-oriented approach in just a few short sentences. Occasionally, people like Chris in your organization will show more interest. That opens the door to schedule some time to share the model and approach that you use to improve human performance, as well as your success story. Remember to lose the jargon and talk in terms of how you can help "Chris" with his or her business challenges.

In addition to these informal opportunities to share what you are doing, seek out formal avenues of communication. You should "create a comprehensive marketing plan with the goal of creating mindshare and transforming the way [the training function] is viewed by the organization" (Spirgi, 2005). Newsletters, websites, e-mail, and presentations to managers and employees are all good ways to share your success story. Be careful not to promote the new approach beyond your means. In other words, do not solicit project work that you are not staffed to complete. Make sure that your communication includes your current and future capabilities to implement the model in other parts of the organization.

Consider, at this point, changing the name of your department. Harless (1995), in survey research he conducted, notes that the word *performance* appeared in the names of many in-house departments. He cited the following list of department names provided by respondents:

Human Performance Enhancement, Performance Systems, Performance Support, Performance Support & Training, Performance Design, Performance & Organizational Support, and Performance Technology.

An argument against changing the title of a department is made by Sorohan (1996). She notes that some people—and especially managers—may become confused with such terms as *performance technology* and *performance consulting*. Sorohan states that "some performance consultants report that they've had more trouble winning support for the term than the practice." You need to make the decision about changing—or not changing—the name of your organization to reflect your new service offerings based on your knowledge of your client base.

Recognize that some in your organization might perceive the new model as infringing on the job responsibilities of others. When an executive at a Wall Street financial firm received a recommendation to expand the capabilities of the training function to include analysis of human performance, her response was that she expected her managers to be performing that function. She was not supportive of the concept to have traditional training people performing the analysis she expected from the leaders in her organization. In fact, it's been suggested that it won't be long before human performance improvement becomes part of the leading MBA programs.

There may be other functions inside or outside of the human resource organization that perform similar roles. Organization development and quality departments, in particular, are just two of many departments that might regard themselves as already providing this service to the organization. It would be advantageous to engage these departments early in your process, share approaches, and determine if there are overlaps in your strategies to improve performance. Reorganization or merging of similar functions, either on the organization chart or virtually, may prove beneficial as time goes by.

Alternative Paths for Transforming a Traditional Training Department into an HPI Department

Other HPI authors have recommended similar, yet different, paths. Smalley and DeJong (1995) reflected on the transformation of their traditional HRD department at Amway and cited five phases in the evolution to HPI formulated by Harless (1992). These progressive stages included "conventional training, performance-based instruction, job-aided training, front-end analysis and measuring results, and performance planning." Fuller (1998) described a five-step approach for preparing to transition to a focus on performance improvement. These were to:

1. Determine who needs to be involved as advisers
2. Form a definition of HPI
3. Select a single HPI model to use
4. Identify specific people who will perform the HPI work
5. Position HPI into the organization, illustrating its benefits

As with any road map, there are always alternative routes that can be taken. The 10 elements featured in this chapter are simply guidelines that can be modified to fit your organization. They are intended to help you identify a path that will successfully guide your organization from a training function to a human performance improvement organization.

Common Mistakes to Avoid

While there is no one right way to navigate the transition from a traditional training organization to a human performance improvement organization, there are some pitfalls that you can avoid when leading this transformation in your company. To list just a few:

- Don't wait for the client to come to you; be proactive in identifying performance improvement projects.
- Don't assume that you can make the case for transformation by citing external case studies.
- Don't widely publicize the intended transformation before you can respond with resources.
- Do not treat the transformation as a project; treat it as an ongoing process. Don't form a task force. Don't form a project team. It's an ongoing evolution that will be impacted by an ever-changing environment. The players will need to change depending on current needs.
- Don't get discouraged. There will be setbacks. A champion may be promoted or leave the company. An emergency, such as a merger, could occur that will alter your focus. Or a host of other changes could occur that might have a negative impact on your course of action.

- Don't speak of your transformation using human resource jargon. Use business language—language that your potential clients will understand (Graham, 1998).

- Don't seek perfection. Make a judgment about how much change an organization can handle.

- Don't try to sell HPI . . . just start asking the right questions.

- Don't take on too large or too small of an initial project. You want a project that will have significant organizational impact and attain some visibility, without exceeding the capabilities of your young organization.

- Don't ignore the naysayers—especially those within your own department. There is almost always value in listening to the objections of others. Some degree of truth is typically expressed and ought to be addressed.

- Don't spend time selling the process of HPI. Focus on selling the potential for results.

- Don't assume that having the support of the vice president of human resources will assure the support of line management.

- Don't try to make the transition overnight. A change like this will take years to occur.

Success Stories

Many companies can serve as examples where a traditional training organization has been transformed into a full-service HPI organization. There are many more in the process, and still more that have yet to begin this adventurous journey. This section will share the transformation experiences of four companies that have successfully migrated the path to HPI.

Mallinckrodt, Inc.

Mallinckrodt, Inc. manufactures health-care products that diagnose disease, sustain breathing, and relieve pain. The training function at Mallinckrodt completed their transformation to a performance improvement organization over approximately a one-year period. Recognizing that their greatest challenge was to gain management's support and confidence, they began their transition by building relationships with managers in the field.

They asked managers many questions and listened carefully to their answers. They asked such questions as, "What are your issues?" "What have you done about it?" and "If you could change things, what would you change?" They did not try to sell a program or a process. Their intention was to convey that they were credible and wanted to be partners in business success. It was not long before they had managers valuing the new services and making new requests. Instead of getting phone calls asking for training, the department members were getting calls asking for help to achieve business goals.

The new Organizational Development Department (formerly the Individual and Organizational Development Department) attributes some of their early success to their consistent use of an eight-step process, which they developed early in their transition. Additionally, they partnered with their clients to measure their success at both Level 3 and Level 4 (see Figure 7-3).

As the demand for the department's services grew, so did the department. The new, growing organization was staffed strategically. Practitioners with varied backgrounds and experiences were sought so that the overall organization could provide an array of services to the organization. This breadth of talent, together with the HPI department's client-centered focus, has sustained its reputation within the company as a valued partner for success.

Prudential Health Care Systems

Prudential Health Care Systems made the transition from training to performance over an approximate two-year period. The key to the success was the dedication and support of the internal staff and upper-level management. The fledgling HPI function, however, suffered several setbacks in its progress due to management changes. Each time a change occurred, new managers needed to be educated and convinced of the merits of the new direction. Despite these challenges, the HPI function has successfully completed many projects.

Steelcase

Steelcase is the world's leading manufacturer of office productivity furniture and services dedicated to providing high-performance work environments that help people work more effectively. A few members of the Corporate Learning and Development Department had the passion and determination to transform themselves into an HPI service organization known as Performance Planning Services.

Their transition took approximately two and a half years. There were many challenges. One was ongoing clarification about how HPI could benefit and work in conjunction with existing human resource department functions. A second was getting the clientele of the function to think of it as something more than a learning resource. A third was acquiring the necessary resources that were in short supply throughout the entire human resource organization.

Performance Planning Services credits its successful transformation to the existing HPI expertise and work ethic and to its selection of initial projects targeted to the middle of the organization—which proved to be neither too high nor too low in the organization. The members of the HPI function also believe that their success was due to the selection and use of one specified HPI model to provide structure to their work and the adaption of that model to meet the needs of their internal clients.

Additionally, they found that Tom Gilbert's performance matrix (see Chapter 2) proved to be an excellent tool to explain the concept of HPI to leaders. While members of the Steelcase Performance Planning Services group were mostly receiving requests for training and instructional design before their transition, today they find themselves responding to true performance analyses and recommending business-focused solutions for multiple clients within the organization. A true indication of their successful transformation is a recent move of the entire group from within the human resource organization into the corporate quality function, where fast action and results have traditionally been recognized by company leadership.

Compaq

The Compaq Services' Information and Performance Solutions Group has been making its transition from a full-service training, development, and documentation entity into a performance improvement organization over the past three years. The original organization had an outstanding reputation for delivering high-quality training and documentation so, not surprisingly, these HPI practitioners encountered some early hurdles in convincing both internal management and internal practitioners that the shift in focus from training and documentation to performance improvement was advantageous.

The successful transformation of the function is due to several factors, including the sheer tenacity of those who initiated and pioneered the change. Though the group experienced repetitive challenges—including a merger—the group recovered and continued on its path toward performance improvement. Another key to success was the development of the group's own model for HPI, which group members use consistently within their organization.

While the group notes a change in the actual deliverables offered now, the more notable shift is in the way that the services are offered. Group members address client needs and requests from a performance improvement viewpoint. Rather than being mere "order takers" for training, group members have become performance solutions partners who understand the client's business, environment, and resources and provide the most appropriate combination of training and nontraining products and services to address individual and organizational performance.

Assessing Your Progress

As your department begins this transformation process, you may wish to take occasional pulse checks to see how you're progressing. Appendix I contains an assessment instrument that you can use to assess your department's success. It will help you and your clients determine how frequently and how well the department is producing outputs associated with human performance improvement work. Annually completing this assessment, or one similar, will help you monitor your progress and decide where to focus your efforts for improvement.

Summary

There are 10 possible steps that can be taken to guide your organization in the transformation from traditional training to human performance improvement:

1. Gain and maintain internal support for the transformation
2. Transition to a valued, results-based training organization
3. Educate management on the factors that influence human performance
4. Obtain an internal champion
5. Select an HPI model
6. Determine what services the new organization is going to offer
7. Develop HPI practitioners
8. Select the initial HPI project
9. Demonstrate success and publicize it
10. Gain organizational support for the transformation

Ensuring that each occurs will increase your overall chances of success.

References

Bassi, L.J., and Van Buren, M.E. (1999). The 1999 ASTD State of the Industry Report. Supplement to *Training and Development Magazine, 53*(1), 1–27.

Coe, R., and Lake, P. (2003). Effectively Managing Nuclear Risk Through Human Performance Improvement. *Nuclear Plant Journal, 21*(5), 40.

Finney, M. (1997). The Catbert Dilemma. *HR Magazine, 42*(2), 70–76.

Fuller, J., and Farrington, J. (1999). *From Training to Performance Improvement: Navigating the Transition.* San Francisco: Jossey-Bass Pfeiffer.

Fuller, J.L. (1998). Making the Transition to a Focus on Performance. In J. Robinson and D.G. Robinson (Eds.), *Moving from Training to Performance: A Practical Guide.* San Francisco: Berrett-Koehler.

Graham, C. (1998). From Reengineering to Performance Consulting. In J. Robinson and D.G. Rocinson (Eds.), *Moving from Training to Performance: A Practical Guide.* San Francisco: Berrett-Koehler.

Harless, J. (1992). Whither Performance Technology? *Performance and Instruction, 31*(2), 4–8.

Harless, J. (1995). Performance Technology Skills in Business: Implications for Preparation. *Performance Improvement Quarterly, 8*(4), 75–88.

Langdon, D.G., Whiteside, K.S., and McKenna, M.M. (1999). *Intervention Resource Guide: 50 Performance Improvement Tools.* San Francisco: Jossey-Bass Publishers.

Mager, R.F. (1992). *What Every Manager Should Know About Training or "I've Got a Training Problem" . . . and Other Odd Ideas.* Belmont, CA: Lake Publishing Company.

Robinson, D.G., and Robinson, J.C. (Eds.). (1998). *Moving from Training to Performance: A Practical Guidebook.* San Francisco: Berrett-Koehler Publishers.

Rothwell, W., and Dubois, D. (Eds.). (1998). *In Action: Improving Performance in Organizations.* Alexandria, VA: The American Society for Training and Development.

Smalley, K.A., and DeJong, M.J. (1995). Strategic Planning: From Training to Performance Technology Within Three Years. *Performance Improvement Quarterly, 8*(2), 114–124.

Sorohan, E.G. (1996). The Performance Consultant at Work. *Training and Development, 50*, 34–38.

Spirgi, H. (2005). Workforce Performance Improvement: Impacting Business Goals. *Chief Learning Officer, 4*(9), 38–43.

Stolovich, H. (2001). Survival Guide for the Future: Make Sure Your Training Delivers Improved Performance. *Managing Training & Development, 1*(12), 5.

Sugrue, B., and Rivera, R.J. (2005). *The 2005 State of the Industry Report: ASTD's Annual Review of Trends in Workplace Learning and Support.* Retrieved from www.astd.org.

Trout, T. (2005). How to Make Performance Consulting an Integral Part of Your Training Landscape. *Managing Training and Development, 5*(2), 1–14.

Willmore, J. (2003). The Seven (Actually Nine) Deadly Sins of New Performance Consultants. *T + D, 57*(8), 28.

Willmore, J. (2004). The Future of Performance. *T + D, 58*(8), 27–31.

8

Building Your Competence as an HPI Practitioner

While Chapter 7 focused on transforming an organization from one that offers traditional training solutions to one that offers performance improvement solutions to address organizational problems and opportunities, this chapter focuses on transforming an individual from a traditional trainer (or other related role) into a HPI practitioner. This chapter discusses the reasons why you might consider this expansion of the traditional trainer role. It also shares true stories of the transitions that others have made from previous careers to HPI. The chapter then outlines a three-step process for making the transformation.

Making the Shift in Role

Chapter 6 made the case that the demand for HPI services in the workplace will steadily increase. Thus, the demand for those who are skilled to deliver those services will also increase. Settle (1995) highlights some consequences for those who continue to focus on training for the sake of training alone. He cites criticism from other organizational members as to their value, budget vulnerability, potential to be outsourced, and detachment from the business as potential consequences of not heeding the move to a performance orientation.

Gill (1995) stresses that a shift in paradigms is needed among trainers to help them rethink their role and purpose. To accomplish this shift in perspective, Rummler (1996) offers a simple starting point when he states that "the essence of the relationship between training and performance lies in how a trainer responds to a training request." He then follows with three questions with which a trainer who is operating from a performance paradigm should respond: (1) Is training the solution? (2) Is training in this area the best return on the training dollar? (3) Will training alone make a difference?

This notion of responding to a request is echoed by Gordon (1992), who believes that trainers' responses are determined largely by how they view their role: as a "provider of instructional programs" or as a "person in charge of helping this organization succeed by improving the performance of its people." McLagan (1996) identifies the role of performance consultant as one of nine key roles that must be played by HRD professionals now and in the future.

Mager (1996) goes beyond that by contending that trainers must be performance-oriented to survive into the 21st century. He contends: "First and foremost, survivors will think of themselves as being in the performance business, not the training or education business. Successful trainers will understand that, regardless of their job titles, regardless of their specialties, they have one role: to help improve performance aimed at accomplishing important organizational goals."

Research has been conducted to study this transformation from training to human performance improvement. As mentioned in Chapter 1, Bassi, Cheney, and Van Buren (1997) report that "89 percent of training professionals 'strongly agreed' or 'agreed' that a shift from training to performance improvement is a top trend." In addition, a survey conducted in July 1997 among national HRD executives revealed that the shift from training to performance was currently the number three trend, but that it would emerge as the number one trend within three years. In another survey, however, Galagan and Wulf (1996) noted that "73 percent of HRD executives agree that current training managers and staff are ill prepared for performance support." So, the demand is there, but the skills are not there—yet!

You can't just assume that employees in a traditional training role will want to make the shift. There will always be a role for a traditional trainer and/or instructional designer in any organization. You can help persuade those in your organization to make the transformation by giving them the business case for change:

1. There will be opportunities for greater rewards and recognition, not just in the training organization, but companywide.
2. Practitioners will become valued and credible partners with the line instead of being seen as merely an overhead expense.
3. The benefits to the client and the organization are quantifiable and observable in the client's improved operational and performance results (LaBonte and Robinson, 2000).

The Transformation to HPI Practitioner—True Stories

HPI practitioners find their way into the profession from many different backgrounds. Susan Fehl, VP of Enterprise to Value at Pillar Technology, was a traditional technical trainer. She led a team that conducted classroom-based software training for almost 10 years. She became frustrated and began to question the effectiveness of training. She asked herself, "How can you give people the best tools and the best training and support, but not get the business results that you desire?" She interviewed for and accepted a relational database instructor position at a new company and, when given the offer, she negotiated the terms. She requested that the manager allow her to transition her role to HPI within the first year. While the manager wasn't too familiar with this new field, she had faith in Susan and agreed to the terms. It was during this year that a manager who was familiar with and highly valued performance consulting was hired into a senior technology role. Susan quickly paired up with this manager and began to serve as an HPI practitioner. Just a few years later, the manager became the CIO and made the IT executive team Susan's primary customer. Then her company merged with another. As most of the executives she served were leaving the company, she decided it was a good time to go out on her own. She spent almost six years as an external consultant before joining Pillar Technology. Today she leads the Enterprise to Value practice, Pillar's cultural transformation and performance improvement practice. There, Susan designs solutions for their clients with software construction and other sorts of performance challenges.

Susan is a long-term member of the International Society for Performance Improvement (ISPI) and serves on her local chapter board. She continues to develop in the field by networking with her peers and reading articles and books. She often contacts the authors of those articles and books to further discuss ideas that she finds more interesting and helpful. When asked what she finds most rewarding about a career in HPI, Susan quoted Bob Myers, Pillar's president, who said, "Here's what I see in you: You get a super charge out of bringing managers and employees together on the same plane." Susan continued, "Hierarchy imposes restrictions that don't need to be there and impede success. Everyone provides value—you simply need to tap into it." She really enjoys teaching others how to intentionally refine the culture of their organization.

Lou Roberts, a partner with Christensen Roberts Solutions, has been an HPI practitioner for over 11 years. In the early 1980s, Lou completed his master's in instructional design from Columbia University, Teachers College. He became a technical director at EPIE Institute, a unit of *Consumer Reports* magazine, primarily responsible for testing the first generation of microcomputers to be used in schools. For two years, he appeared in the monthly PBS television program *Educational Computing* to discuss the application of microcomputers in educational applications. After a former professor asked Lou to work with him on client projects, Lou became a full-time instructional design consultant working on long-term projects at Minolta, AT&T, Lucent Technologies, and Avaya. He's now in a partnership designing electronic performance support systems with Christensen Roberts Solutions and is currently working on a large-scale EPSS project at Memorial Sloan Kettering Cancer Center. Lou finds reading books and interviewing experts in the field to be the best way for him to continue to grow in the field of HPI. He likes to participate in webinars. He rarely goes to formal training, but spends a lot of time exploring websites that feature good articles and information on the latest trends and research in HPI. When Lou was asked what he found most rewarding about his career as an HPI practitioner, Lou said, "The promise that I'm going to make a difference."

When asked, Joe Monaco will tell you that he has been doing performance improvement his entire life. He couldn't remember a time when he wasn't constantly trying to improve upon some outcome by improving or fixing its process. For Joe, it seemed natural to always looking for ways to do things better. He believes his vantage point is one he learned growing up in the family bakery business, where opportunities for improvement were abundant. He always naturally worked from a systems view of things. In an early job as a production supervisor for a large paint company, he began to experiment. From that job, he moved on to become an operations trainer for a large cosmetics company. He was responsible for all operations training—from designing industrial skills to delivering supervisory and management practices training. Discovering instructional design models for the first time, Joe started developing formal ways to do things that he had been thinking about and experimenting with for years. Soon thereafter, Joe read Robert Mager's work and was turned on to performance improvement. He eventually adopted the performance improvement vantage points of notable contributors such as Tom Gilbert, Geary Rummler, Joe Harless, Ogden Lindsley, and William R. Daniels.

In his career, he never felt limited to instructional design. Joe could always see the big picture and the systems view of things. Back then, there wasn't a lot of formal performance management processes in place. It basically worked like this: "I'll pay you and you will do what I say." Joe introduced a different approach: "If you just train people in the expected methods, provide them with adequate resources, and get them talking to each other about the work, they'll go out and do the stuff." And he found a way to convince the supervisors that it was all their idea. His method was to perform detailed performance/process analysis by interviewing the very people who needed to change their own way of doing things. His early lessons were that you had to use data that people already had about themselves; and that people were more likely to follow new process "rules" if they derived the rules from that data.

Joe spent 10 years heading up a corporate OD and training department where he was able to work throughout the organization. He reported to French executives, which posed some interesting challenges and unique opportunities. The French business executives were cautious, if they didn't just flat-out reject "flavor-of-the-month" interventions. They were too serious for that. But they would easily embrace and support new initiatives that were clearly intended to improve upon the core process or the effectiveness of their organization. Joe says, "For me, that focused business perspective was like being in performance improvement heaven." Joe would share with them what other companies like IBM, Johnson & Johnson, and others were doing, but the French managers were unimpressed. He took a lot of risks to continue to implement performance improvement strategies, mostly because the strategies required persuading the non-French managers who were used to seeing flavor-of-the-month offerings and had come to expect it. Fortunately, Joe's boss was a power broker in the company with lots of influence. Joe began to work primarily as a personal consultant for his boss. When his boss returned to France, Joe admitted, "I enjoyed more autonomy than anyone should." There was continued pressure for him to move into the HR function, but he felt strongly that he needed to reside in operations.

He next reported to the chief financial officer (CFO). This became challenging, as this boss was mostly focused on the financial costs for *all* training initiatives, with little apparent interest in organizational process. Because the CFO was very demanding from the financial point of view, Joe says that he was forced to learn things about corporate finance that he eventually embraced as a unique and welcomed contribution to his own perspective. His new boss stopped in one day and announced that during the last board meeting, Joe's location on the organizational chart was called into question. Joe was told that from now on, his department would be reporting to HR. This was a mismatch from the beginning. Joe knew he was in trouble during his first meeting, when he asked the top HR manager to discuss objectives—only to find that he didn't have any he was willing to share. Joe was convinced that the HR manager didn't believe it was the proper role of his new subordinate to focus their reporting relationship in this way. Joe was used to being an "intrepreneur," someone who acts like an external consultant, but is actually working for the company full-time. The HR manager did not like Joe's free-ranging style. Seeing the writing on the wall, Joe began to update his resume and plan for the possibility that he might one day be "downsized." By the mid-1990s, the final bomb dropped: The board had decided to get rid of Joe's department, and he had one year to find another job.

Then Joe had an idea. He went to the French chief executive officer (CEO), offered to resign at the end of the month instead of a year later, and instead of them buying him out, he offered to buy them out. He asked the CEO to take the dollars they would have spent on his department's cost center and write him a retainer check. The retainer check would fund current projects to their conclusion, with Joe now acting as the CEO of his own consulting firm. The CEO thought that this was a very clever proposal, and ten minutes later, Joe was an external HPI consultant.

Joe is still on retainer with that company, and it accounts for a large percentage of his current company revenues. He continues to develop in the field of HPI by utilizing his great network of peers. He also is active in the International Society for Performance Improvement (ISPI), having recently chaired the Society's awards committee for honoring exemplary work in the field of human performance technology. When asked what he enjoyed most about his career in HPI, Joe said, "When I know and can verify that I've made a difference and that I've been part of some worthy accomplishment."

Dennis Mankin, who's been in the HPI field for about 20 years, started off with an undergraduate degree in behavioral psychology. He studied Gilbert and Skinner and touched base with the works of Joe Harless as part of his studies. Upon graduating, Dennis took a job in sales and marketing with ABC Television and then with Ameritech. He rose to a position of leadership, which required him to coach and develop his own skills and those of others in the organization. In 1986, Dennis decided that he no longer wanted to be in sales and marketing, so he started his own business, delivering time management and project management training. About the same time, Paul Elliott was starting RWD Technologies. Dennis found the work that Paul was doing very interesting and watched Paul grow RWD Technologies into a pretty large organization. Dennis began to realize that training was only taking his clients part of the way. He wanted to apply what he knew from his degree program, so he started to get connected with those in the HPI field. Dennis joined Paul Elliott at a firm called Human Performance Technologies. HPT purchased the rights to Joe Harless's tools and materials and began to offer workshops to teach other practitioners how to apply HPT in the workplace. Today, Paul and Dennis are managing partners in a company called Outcome Systems, along with two other partners, Mason Holloway and Dr. Karen McGraw. Dennis and Mason are also the managing partners of Platinum Performance Group.

In 2003 Dennis and Mason cowrote, and then copublished with ASTD, a set of paper-based tools and job aids for performance analysis called *Performance DNA*. These HPI tools and processes have been taught to thousands of people from at least 16 countries in just over three years since their launch. An electronic version of these tools was created through Outcome Systems, and they are described as

> a software toolset to help the human performance improvement professional conduct complex analyses to improve performance more efficiently and effectively. *Performance DNA Desktop* provides support from project set up and management and reporting through the analysis phases:
>
> - Business Analysis
> - Performance Analysis
> - Key Performer Analysis
> - Influence Analysis
> - Analysis Consolidation and Reporting

Performance DNA Desktop was developed to align with ASTD's HPI certification program and provides the tools and templates the HPI professional needs to vastly improve the efficiency of data collection, analysis, integration, and reporting (www.outcomesys.com/products_desktop.htm).

Dennis likes to pick the brains of his colleagues in order to stay current in the field of HPI. He reads the most recent books and surfs the Internet for the latest articles and research on occasion. Dennis says that the best way to develop your skills is to use them and practice, practice, practice. He says that the most rewarding thing about a career in HPI is when "I see positive change and I see people getting past those barriers."

Charles "Chuck" Harpham's career began in public education. He taught at both secondary schools and community colleges. He eventually left the teaching profession to accept a training manager position in the manufacturing industry. His next step was to become a business HR manager. Chuck's Manager of Human Resources at Baltimore Gas and Electric Company eventually asked Chuck and another colleague to become internal performance improvement consultants. Then, about three years ago, Chuck was asked if he'd like to get involved with the company's Six Sigma initiatives. Today, Chuck is a Six Sigma Blackbelt working in the HR department at Baltimore Gas and Electric Company, a Constellation Energy Company. He is active with the Society for Human Resource Management (SHRM), ISPI, and the local chapter of the ASQ. He likes to network with other operations-based Blackbelts in the company to see the details of their projects.

"There's a lot to be learned from seeing what others in the field do," says Chuck. Chuck finds the variety of work the most rewarding part of his job as a Blackbelt. "As an HR generalist, you tend to get spread pretty thin but in *this* job, I can focus on select projects and I get the opportunity to really sink my teeth into specific problems and work on them until they're solved," says Chuck.

Carol Panza today calls herself a management consultant, but that's not how her career started. Carol received her undergraduate degree in marketing. She went on to earn her MBA in industrial relations. Soon after completing her MBA, Carol went to work for a tiny management firm that focused on training. She was asked to join a job study and quickly took on a leadership role based on her business focus. Immediately following the job study, Carol was assigned to an important training design project that was already underway for a very large client. She was the only one on the project team who had a genuine business focus, and ended up designing the entire course. After this, Carol joined another small company, which had just been awarded a project to design a performance appraisal system for use onboard oil tankers operated by a large petrochemical company. She had to learn all of the business processes and understand four different nationality groups so that her finished product could be used cross-culturally.

Carol started her own consulting company in 1985. She describes herself as a very analytical person who likes working with people. She comes at projects with questions rather than answers. She says that she often takes what has been politically and emotionally charged, and converts it into objective information that actually brings diverse people and processes together and, importantly, that the client can use to make improvements. Carol continues to grow and develop in the field by talking with her network of colleagues. She learns every day on her projects by asking lots of questions. Carol cites the ability to form life-long relationships with people as one of the best parts of being in the field of HPI. Carol says, "Being a management consultant allows me to feel like I'm making a difference, that I can help people to be more successful."

Steps for Transforming to an HPI Practitioner

The remainder of this chapter is designed to help you successfully make the transformation from whatever it is that you do now, to a HPI practitioner by using the following three-step process:

1. Assess your competencies
2. Plan for your development
3. Take action

Step 1: Assess Your Competencies

The new role of an HPI practitioner is quite different from that of a traditional trainer who designs and/or delivers classroom-based instruction. This transformation will not occur any more rapidly for individuals than for organizations. The timeline to get there will depend on your current level of competence and experience. You may have a gut feeling for your readiness for this new role from reading earlier chapters in this book. While there is much need for "trusting your gut" in this field, true success is realized when decisions are derived from good, solid data.

With that in mind, an HPI competency assessment tool and instructions for completing the assessment tool can be found in Appendix II. The instrument contains the 40 competencies of the HPI field, as they were identified in *ASTD Models for Human Performance Improvement* (1996). There is a six-point scale for identifying your current level of expertise for each one.

It is recommended that you not only complete the assessment for yourself but also that you make several copies of the assessment tool and seek input from managers, peers, and direct reports (if applicable). If you are currently an external consultant, you may choose to have past or current clients complete an assessment for you. The feedback you derive from having others give you input on your current competency levels will help you identify your strengths and areas requiring improvement.

Step 2: Plan for Your Development

Armed with the results of the competency assessment, you can then identify ways to build your competencies. Appendix III contains a resource guide for the competencies associated with HPI. There you will also find a partial listing of graduate degree programs that will help you develop many of the competencies listed in *ASTD Models for Human Performance Improvement*. You will also find comprehensive HPI development options. In addition, each of the 40 competencies from *ASTD Models for Human Performance Improvement* is listed. For each competency area, you will find:

- **Recommended readings:** Current publications that will provide knowledge and the foundation for skill development for the competency
- **Workshops:** Publicly offered workshops that will help to development the competency
- **Self-study options:** Nonclassroom training solutions, including self-study text, video, audio, computer-based training (CBT), and CD-ROM
- **Other development opportunities:** A list of nontraditional ways to develop the competency

Armed with these resources, you will be able to begin identifying the optimal development path for yourself. It could be attending conferences and workshops, getting involved with cross-functional teams, receiving coaching from an experienced HPI practitioner, and/or sharing best practices with others in the field.

Many factors—including time, cost, and learning preference—will go into deciding your overall development plan. You will need to determine the following:

- What are your individual development priorities? Consider such issues as the size of your skill gap, organizational needs, and personal interests.
- What is your time frame for development?
- How much do you need to achieve? By when?
- What are the most likely barriers to the successful completion of your development plan? (Think about cost, time, or lack of support.) How can you overcome them?
- What are your learning preferences?
- Who can support your development effort (manager, coach, spouse, etc.)?
- What does success look like? What opportunities exist in the workplace to demonstrate new or existing competencies?

Whatever format you decide upon, the development plan should be formalized in writing (paper or electronic), and should include the following elements:

Competency	Method(s) for Development	Target Date	Practice On-the-Job
Performance Analysis Skills	■ Read *First Things Fast: A Handbook for Performance Analysis* by Allison Rossett ■ Attend Analyzing Human Performance, ASTD, (703) 683-8100	■ Purchase by: 9/1; Read by: 10/1 ■ Register by: 9/15 for 10/25–28 workshop	■ Determine performance gaps for printing services department
Questioning Skills	■ Attend Data Collection Techniques workshop, Management Concepts, (703) 790-9595	■ Register 8/1 for 8/15 workshop	■ Develop survey for printing services department.

Figure 8-1   Portion of a sample individual development plan.

- Competencies to be developed
- Method for development
- Target date
- On-the-job practice opportunity

A portion of a development plan appears in Figure 8-1.

One final step is to review the entire plan and determine if it is achievable. Over-committing is easy to do in your eagerness to achieve success. The repercussions of an unachievable development plan can be self-defeating. Trying to acquire too much knowledge too fast could lead you to feel overwhelmed and thus discourage future development efforts. Trying to commit to more development opportunities than you have time or funding for could also prove to be disappointing. On the other hand, not committing to short-term development goals can lead to apathy about the transformation. Review your plan and make adjustments, as necessary. Keep in mind that an individual development plan is not a static document. It should be updated as your priorities shift and as your resources for development change.

Step 3: Take Action

Once you have your development plan formulated, it is then time to put those plans into action. Buy the books and enroll in the workshops. Schedule time for reading or other self-study options. Look for creative ways to practice new skills in the workplace. Keep managers, peers, and direct reports informed of the new competencies that you are acquiring and hoping to demonstrate in the workplace. Solicit feedback from those who can observe you in action.

Continually revisit (at least monthly) your development plan, and make adjustments as necessary. You may want to consider seeking a development coach who can keep you focused on your long-range development goals and who will continually encourage and support your development efforts. This could be your manager, a colleague, a mentor, or an external coach who can help you stick to your development plan and ultimately guide you to a successful transformation into your broadened performance improvement role.

Following this prescribed process will have you placing on your business card, before you know it, a title like Performance Consultant, Performance Technologist, Performance Improvement Consultant, HPI Consultant, or whatever seems to work for you and your organization.

Summary

This chapter shared the true stories of how some experienced HPI practitioners transitioned into the field of HPI from previous careers. This chapter went on to describe a three-step process for individual development. The steps are: (1) assess your competencies, (2) plan for your development, and (3) take action. The chapter described some strategies for carrying out each step in that process. Use Appendix II to assess your competencies. Use the resources in Appendix III to help you—and your training department—to build your HPI competencies and thereby provide the foundation for improving performance in your organization.

References

Bassi, L.J., Cheney, S., and Van Buren, M. (1997). Training Industry Trends 1997. *Training & Development*, *51*(11), 46–59.

Galagan, P., and Wulf, K. (1996). Sign of the Times, *Training and Development*, *50*(2), 32–34.

Gill, S.J. (1995). Shifting Gears for High Performance. *Training & Development*, *49*(5), 25–31.

Gordon, J. (1992). Performance Technology: Blueprint for the Learning Organization? *Training*, *29*(5), 27–36.

Labonte, T., and Robinson, J. (1999). Performance Consulting: One Organization. One Process. *Training & Development*, *53*(8), 32–37.

Mager, R.F. (1996). Morphing Into a 21st Century Trainer. *Training*, *33*(6), 47–54.

McLagan, P. (1996). Great Ideas Revisited. *Training & Development*, *50*(1), 60–65.

Moser, M.E. (2001). Calibrating Texas Instruments: Business Effectiveness Regulates Training Solutions. *The New Corporate University Review*, *9*(2), 17–21.

Rummler, G. (1996). In Search of the Holy Performance Grail. *Training & Development*, *50*(4), 26–32.

Settle, T.J. (1995). Evolution of a Trainer. *Training & Development*, *49*(9), 15–16.

9

From Theory to Practice: Real-World HPI Projects

This book has shared with you the roles and competencies for human performance improvement. It's shared the models and best practices in the field of HPI. While the book provided many examples to illustrate how these models and best practices are put to use in the workplace, nothing illustrates better how it all comes together than actual projects that have been completed by experienced HPI practitioners. This chapter will share the details of five HPI projects. It concludes with "words of wisdom" from experienced HPI practitioners for those of you who are new to the field.

Safe Forklift Operation

Sometimes it takes an accident to draw attention to a problem. That's exactly what happened at a large cosmetics company. A forklift operator drove her forklift into a steel support column en route to the cafeteria. The accident resulted in a crushed leg. It should come as no surprise that the manager in charge had great concerns about the growing number of safety incidents with forklifts and came to the HPI practitioner requesting training for all forklift operators.

The operations manager gave the HPI practitioner some freedom to look into the root causes of the incidents. His position: "Solve my problem so that it stays solved. Fix it so that it stays fixed."

The major stakeholders for the project initially were the operations manager and the forklift operators. The project team consisted of three forklift operators, the senior manager, and the HPI consultant. The project team was not constrained by time or budget.

The first step was to conduct the performance analysis. The team also reviewed accident reports, training literature, and the National Institute for Occupational

Safety and Health (NIOSH) research on forklifts. The team identified root causes, which included a lack of operating skill and knowledge by forklift operators, some minor warehouse engineering items that needed to be changed, and some safety policy gaps.

The following interventions were proposed and carried out:

- Instruction and testing of operator skill and knowledge
- Specific management policies
- Supervisory practices
- Engineering standards, which covered things like painting safety lines on the ground for pedestrians who traveled in and around forklift operations
- Maintenance practices for brake repair, etc.

As you can see, the supervisors, engineers, and maintenance workers became stakeholders of the projects, too.

To determine the project's success, a list of about 50 safe behaviors were identified and measured. Seven to eight years later, studies showed that serious injuries were greater for those who were not trained in the system. The long-term outcome of this project was the development of a forklift safety system (www. LIFTOR.com) that has been marketed and sold to other companies for the past 20 years.

When asked what led to the project's success, the HPI practitioner cited the initial lack of budget constraints and the personal interest that extended all the way to the top of the company. But most of all, it was the detailed and systematic analysis of the forklift operators' performance that continues to focus improvements to this day.

Call Center Makeover

Most everyone recognizes the challenges of managing a call center. Spending all day talking with people who are mostly unhappy and frustrated could make anyone, well, unhappy and frustrated. It's not surprising that most call center operations have a high level of employee turnover.

An HPI practitioner was approached and asked to conduct two one-day meetings to create a new Service Excellence Strategy for the call center. When the HPI consultant asked why they needed a Service Excellence Strategy, she quickly discovered some underlying problems. The environment was hostile. Employees were slamming down phones and screaming in the aisles. There were frequent shouting matches between employees and managers. The only feedback provided to call-center employees was negative and untimely. They didn't have modern call center tools and technology. The managers didn't receive much training on how to manage. The major decision makers for the project were the call center director and the next-level managers.

The key stakeholders were the call center employees, the customer service rep auditors, the technical support staff, and all other employees within the company who had technical questions.

The project team consisted of the entire call center management team, a project manager, an interpersonal communications coach, an organizational communications person, a metrics and survey method consultant, a life skills coach, and an HPI practitioner.

While the call center management wanted the quick fix of training, the HPI consultant was able to convince all levels of management that a complete make-over was needed. A complete analysis was authorized. The team studied the call center auditors, whose role was to listen in on the calls, and report what they observed. The team observed that the auditors would basically focus narrowly on call standards, criticize the calls, and write people up. The call center employees would receive the negative feedback from their managers weeks later. The process was ineffective at driving excellent customer service or a productive work environment.

The team also looked at the metrics that were used to measure performance. The measure of "average speed of answer" was found to be more of a measure of staffing than of individual performance. The measure was encouraging customer service reps to get off the phone quickly, sometimes without resolving the customer issue. There were no guidelines for what made a good customer service rep. Managers were not well equipped with call center management skills or people coaching skills. The call center tools that were being utilized were antiquated.

The team proposed the following solutions: (1) install new tools for call monitoring and incident reporting; (2) develop a competency model for call center reps; (3) create a department communication strategy with goals and metrics for the department and for individuals; (4) change the role of auditor from policing to coaching for improvement (and change the name of the role from auditor to coach!); (5) build relationships between management and call center reps and their customers.

All of the proposed solutions were implemented. In many cases, new people needed to be hired into the role of coach, since the job requirements had significantly changed. The new coaches were observing call center reps as they were answering calls, and would ask the call center reps to assess the call based on the competency model before providing additional feedback and suggestions for how to handle situations better and more efficiently. There was an intentional teaming process put into place. This consisted of managers and coaches participating in workshops, large-group facilitations, one-on-one coaching, and even small-group coaching.

The six-month result was that customer satisfaction levels rose from 83 percent to 90 percent. There was a 33 percent improvement indicated by the employee engagement survey, issued multiple times throughout the year.

The HPI practitioner cited many factors that led to the overall success of this project. First, the call center director played an active leadership role in the effort. Second, the skill set of the project team was diverse and was selected specifically to address each of the multiple root causes of the problems identified. And finally, the solution addressed the three different levels of the organization—the organization, the workgroup, and the individual—as this HPT practitioner believes all sustainable solutions should.

Department of Transportation Construction Safety Improvements

One of the state Departments of Transportation (DOT) was experiencing more than its share of lawsuits (in their eyes) due to people being injured on road construction sites, safety and injuries on the job, or just long delays in getting a job accomplished. There are many safety precautions that road crews are to employ to ensure the safety of the workers and motorists who have to travel through a construction zone. The DOT employs approximately 750 construction inspectors whose job it is to make sure that each job site is complying with all safety measures, using a high quality of construction, and meeting all environmental concerns at a building site. The request to the HPI practitioner was to make sure that all large DOT projects were completed on time, within budget, and met all state and federal guidelines.

The primary decision makers for the project were the state DOT commissioner and the chief of learning and development. The key stakeholders were the 750 construction site inspectors, their managers, and some district managers.

The project team consisted of three external HPI practitioners who also had project management skills and three members of the DOT learning and development department, who were skilled in the specific HPI processes and tools used by the external HPI practitioners. This team had to be innovative, as they only had three weeks within which to do their analysis. They employed a set of HPI tools called *Performance DNA* to guide them in their front-end analysis.

The team quickly conducted 25 interviews using the *Performance DNA* tools. What they learned was that construction inspectors need to be working onsite to do their jobs effectively, yet they were spending much of their time in the office doing paperwork and entering data into the computer, along with other process and training needs. The technology that was in place was not working effectively for all construction inspectors. The agency did not have high-speed Internet access in some locations, and the construction inspectors (in some cases) had limited computer skills, coupled with cumbersome and somewhat technical software to contend with. There were computer crashes and excessive time invested reading manuals to use the technology. The failing technology was costing the organization a lot of money in wasted employee time. The team also learned that many of the construction inspectors were not trained in blueprint reading and other skills needed to do their job effectively. Those that were able to read blueprints got their training at local community colleges, even though there was a course offered by the organization. Inspector supervisors were reluctant to inform the inspectors about the availability of the training because they wanted to inspectors to be in the field, not attending training, and because the additional cost to send inspectors to the training site was prohibitive to their district budget.

The project team proposed the following solutions: (1) add administrative staff to do the paperwork and free up inspectors to get back into the field where most of their productive work takes place; (2) encourage the construction inspectors to attend the blueprint reading training already available, and work with management to ensure that people could attend these classes; (3) improve technologies by getting the inspectors cell phones (where they were needed), high-speed Internet access, etc. The team also proposed another 15 or so changes.

While this project is relatively recent, already the organization is experiencing less anxiety among its construction inspectors, and they suspect it will also result in a reduced rate of turnover. The overall goal for reducing lawsuits and getting construction projects completed on time and within budget has not been measured at this time.

Meter Reader Retention

Meter readers are the people who go house to house, and business to business, to read the meters that monitor gas and electricity usage for billing purposes. While technologies are beginning to change the job, today, it still requires a human being to make the rounds. Some meter readers walk in excess of eight miles per day. And that's year round. It doesn't matter if it's 98 degrees, or −10 degrees; the job needs to get done. It should come as no surprise then, that retention proves challenging in this entry-level job.

This particular company had quite a bit of experience and confidence in its HPI practitioners. Meter reader leadership went beyond requesting a particular solution. The request was more business oriented—reduce turnover.

The decision makers for the project included the manager of the department, the director in charge of the meter readers, the supervisors in charge of meter readers, and the human resource manager. The key stakeholders were the leaders in the meter reader department, the HR recruiters who had to continually recruit meter readers, and the candidates who were interviewing for the position of meter reader.

The project team included one of the supervisors in charge of the meter readers, the director of the department, the HR consultant for the meter reading department, the recruiter for meter readers, the HPI consultant, and an HR graduate assistant.

The team used an internal process (or model) called SIRIUS. *SIRIUS* stands for scope, investigate, reason, innovate, undertake, and sustain.

The results of the process were as follows. The *Scope* of the project was to reduce turnover. During the *Investigate* stage, the team collected all of the information that they could relating to the turnover problem. They determined the current turnover rate, the times of the year that were better and worse for turnover, the reasons that employees gave for leaving the job, and the thoughts of supervisors about why people leave the job. The team took a look at the current recruiting process. They also looked at the wages and other incentives.

What the team found was that approximately 50 percent of the people being hired into the entry-level position were employee referrals, while the others had no connection with the company. The job is entry-level and extremely physical, but one that can lead to positions requiring basic utility knowledge that are critical jobs in a great company to work for. But the team found that the employees who were referring candidates didn't always have the information necessary to inform the candidates about the requirements of the position well. The team also found some bottlenecks in the recruiting process. When examining the data, the team was able to determine that those candidates who had had previous physical jobs in the past or were athletes seemed to do better in the role. When interviewing the supervisors, the team quickly learned that interview questions being used by the supervisors didn't consistently yield all the information needed to make sound hiring decisions. In addition, very little if any time was being given to explaining the Power Rating System (PPRS). The Power Rating System is the quarterly incentive awards program that provides additional income for meter readers based on their performance. New meter reader trainees indicated that they weren't clear about how much incentive money they could actually earn via the incentive program when they were candidates. The team also discovered that more meter readers leave the company during July/August and January/February for obvious weather-related reasons. The team was also able to document a starting wage issue among the new employees. Finally, the team discovered that there appeared to be some communication issues between the meter readers, who were mostly young Generation X and Y employees, and their supervisors, who were mostly baby boomers.

As the team entered the *Innovate* stage, they began to brainstorm ways to overcome the issues uncovered in the *Investigate* stage. They looked into what other companies did and tried to think "out of the box" for creative solutions for the problems encountered. The team then proposed several solutions or interventions, and those that were approved by the decision makers were implemented during the *Undertake* stage.

The team developed a candidate referral specification sheet that included a list of all of the attributes of good meter readers. The sheet was provided to employees who might want to make a referral. The team also produced a job aid for supervisors during the interview process. This job aid included guidelines for discussion about the employee incentive plan and specifically how meter readers could add as much as 12 percent to their annual salary via bonuses. They gained support from management to examine the need for extra people just prior to the two "high turnover" times of the year and to hire them, if warranted. The team hired a consultant to improve interview questions and the overall interview process. Starting salary is being reviewed to ensure it is competitive with market, to both attract and retain employees. As well, the amount of time meter readers have to work before getting a salary increase is proposed to be shortened. Pending approval, department leaders will be provided access to a course offered by the learning and OD department on the characteristics of Generations X and Y plus mitigating strategies. In order to clarify job expectations, a slide presentation featuring all of the conditions of the job, including dogs, bad weather, etc., as well as positive aspects of the position, is now shown to all prospective candidates. An online assessment tool will likely be added to the recruitment and interview process. It only takes 10 minutes to complete, and will quickly eliminate those candidates who don't possess the right attributes to succeed on the job. The team proposed that, if the candidates pass this assessment, they should take a behavioral psychological battery to determine if their personal traits include reliability, follow-up, ability to follow directions, etc. These assessments are meant to help managers make better decisions about who they put into the job in the first place. The project provided for tracking turnover data on a rolling 12-month cycle, rather than quarterly or annually. This change is really part of the *Sustain* stage of the project. It will help management monitor the turnover situation to make sure that the changes made will lead to overall improvement in the turnover rate.

Although not all of the solutions have been fully implemented at the time of this writing, progress has been made. The goal of the project was to reduce turnover to a rolling 12-month rate of 15 percent or less. The current rate is 31 percent, but the rate has been as high as 74 percent during the last 12 months. The HPI practitioner cautions that this noteworthy improvement could be partly explained by the Hawthorn effect and other factors not related to the project. But clearly, these recommendations and recent improvements in the turnover rate have things headed in the right direction.

Medicare Reimbursement Coding Errors

Hospitals have to file paperwork in order to obtain reimbursement from Medicare. It's up to the physicians to place the appropriate codes onto the forms so that the proper reimbursement is requested. Improper coding has both legal and financial implications. If you are audited by the government and they find errors, then you are subjected to a major audit. This is a huge investment of time and should be avoided.

The initial request from the compliance office was for online training for physicians on how to properly code office visits for Medicare reimbursement. This project would affect over 400 physicians at the hospital.

The project team consisted of a physician, a project manager, and the HPI practitioner. The team had an advisory council made up of the head administrator of the hospital, the head of medicine, the head of surgery, the head of neurology, the compliance officer, and the technology officer. There was yet another team who was charged with handling the change management process that included the head of training and the head of nursing.

The project began with a meeting with the senior executives of the hospital. They didn't like the idea of pulling 400+ doctors off of the floor to participate in the training. The HPI practitioner began a root cause analysis by asking the physician on the team to look at all of the coding errors that had occurred. The team was able to determine that 11 root causes caused 90 percent of the errors. They also concluded that most of the causes required a small intervention to correct the problem. They resolved that a short 15-minute intervention could solve 80 percent of the coding errors.

One of the solutions proposed was to hire professional coders. A second alternative solution was to devise an electronic performance support system (EPSS) that a group of auditors could use when randomly selecting charts to determine if there were coding problems. The tool would track error rates. It would then pull from over 100 different feedback statements that would deal with a particular physician error. This, ultimately, was the solution that the client entertained.

The team added a technology designer who could create the very sophisticated database. It needed to be web-based and have high security. But when the design of the system was begun, it became apparent that not all auditors interpreted the coding rules the same way. So the first step was to have a large meeting to determine the hospital's stance on each rule. Once those rule interpretations were agreed upon, the system could be developed.

The final electronic tool would produce an audit report for each physician. In the past, it would take two to three hours to audit a physician, and all 400+ physicians required an audit. With the new tool in place, the hospital will be able to audit all 400+ physicians in six months. The goal is for each physician to have the results of two audits per year. With the new tool, practically anyone can conduct the audits. In fact, the audit process has been offshored to a company in India.

The role of the internal auditor is now that of coach. After the physicians attend an initial 90-minute service meeting to explain the new system and the importance of accurate coding, the auditors need only spend about 15 minutes to review the audits with each physician in the future to coach the physician on any errors that were made. The tool also provides all sorts of trend reports so that larger issues can be addressed proactively.

The HPI practitioner took a risk by abandoning the initial request for training, but it paid off. When the project concluded, the client admitted that she had been trying to solve the coding problem for over 10 years. Using HPI methodologies, they found a cost-effective solution in less than two years.

All of the case studies shared in this chapter have some common themes:

- It takes multiple interventions to resolve most business challenges.
- Success comes when you involve the key stakeholders and decision makers on the project team.
- HPI practitioners have to have the courage to look beyond the initial request to determine the root cause of the business problem.

Words of Wisdom

The authors of this book interviewed many experienced HPI practitioners. We asked them to provide novice HPI practitioners with the benefit of their experience. What follows is a list of "words of wisdom" from some of the leaders in the HPI field.

- "Stay close to the classroom, even if you just teach one workshop per year."
- "Don't assume that you've got a good process, unless you've taken a good hard look at it and have examined it from every angle."
- "You must understand business. You need to have a basic understanding of the financials and some idea about operations."
- "Study the principles of change management. There is no project that I'm involved with that doesn't involve change."
- "Find a mentor, someone who has been doing HPI for a while."
- "Practice, practice, practice; in your church, with your schools, with your family."
- "If you don't feel passionate about what you're doing, consider changing careers. This field takes a lot of passion and commitment."
- "Always partner with your stakeholders."
- "Avoid partnering too low in the organization. We are a limited resource and we should work on large-scale issues that will make a significant improvement."
- "Don't shortchange your analysis due to time pressures."
- "Try to convert HPI terminology into business terms, i.e., talk about solutions not interventions."
- "Be flexible; follow the model in general terms."

- "Pull in talent who is credible with your organization."
- "Limit data collection to that which you're likely to take action upon."
- "Focus on troubleshooting the performance problem."
- "HPI needs to move beyond troubleshooting to include creative thinking about ways to foster breakthrough leaps—even quantum leaps—in productivity improvement."
- "Start small; build some success stories."
- "Identify a mentor (formal or informal) from the business to be your champion and to help you learn the business."
- "Immerse yourself in the business to build your acumen and credibility."
- "Wear a marketing hat. Think about ways to promote your services and successes. Think multiple channels and multiple mediums."
- "Remember that your relationships are your most important assets. The HPI practitioner who no one wants to work with will not be successful. Likewise, the HPI practitioner with clients who like them will succeed because their clients will have a vested interested in seeing them succeed."
- "Client involvement – client commitment = change = improvement. Keep your client thoroughly informed minimally and ideally fully engaged."
- "Build thoughtful reflection time or even journaling into your process to ensure full learning from your experiences."
- "Practice what you preach. Focus on results, not activity. Make sure that you're making progress and getting results quickly."
- "Build your network so that you can tap into the talents and expertise of others."
- "Be generous. Open doors for others. Provide resources. Help where you can. You will reap what you sow."

We hope that you can put this good advice to use and avoid some of the common mistakes that novice HPI practitioners tend to make.

Summary

This chapter shared five examples of HPI in action in the workplace. It also shared "words of wisdom" from experienced HPI practitioners.

Appendix I

Reengineering the Training Department Assessment Instrument

Instructions: Training departments must do more than just training in the future. One possible role is for them to function as human performance improvement departments.

When that idea is first raised, however, it is not always clear to human resource development (HRD) practitioners, line managers, or others what a training department should be doing if it is to function frequently and effectively in doing human performance improvement work. That is the purpose of this instrument.

The instrument can be used to poll HRD practitioners in the organization regarding their perceptions of how often and how well the training department does human performance improvement work. The instrument can also be used to poll line managers about how often and how well they perceive the training department to be doing human performance work. Once the instrument has been administered to one or both groups, it can be a starting point for establishing action plans to "reinvent" or "reengineer" the training department as a human performance improvement department.

In the items that follow, ask the respondents to rate *how frequently* and *how well* they believe the training department produces the outputs associated with human performance improvement work. In the center column, ask the respondents to rate, by circling a number, how frequently they believe the output is produced by the training department. Advise them to use the following scale for the center column:

1 = Never
2 = Seldom

3 = Occasionally
4 = Often
5 = Very Often

Then, in the right column, ask the respondents to rate how well they believe the output is produced by the training department by circling a number. Advise them to use the following scale for the right column:

1 = Very Poorly
2 = Poorly
3 = Adequately
4 = Well
5 = Very Well

As the respondents complete each page of the instrument, they should add up the numbers in each column and place the subtotal in the appropriate position in the box at the bottom of each page. When they finish the entire instrument, they should compile a total score for the center and right columns from all pages and place the total score in the box at the end of the instrument. They should then continue reading for instructions about how to interpret their scores and set priorities for reengineering the training department to function as a human performance improvement department.

(*text continues on p. 273*)

Table Appendix I-1

Output	How Often Does the Training Department Produce This Output?					How Well Does the Training Department Produce This Output?				
	Never	Seldom	Occasionally	Often	Very Often	Very Poorly	Poorly	Adequately	Well	Very Well
	1	2	3	4	5	1	2	3	4	5
1. Descriptions of industry/organizational status	1	2	3	4	5	1	2	3	4	5
2. Positive influence on others exhibited	1	2	3	4	5	1	2	3	4	5
3. Positive relationships established and maintained with clients, stakeholders and decision-makers	1	2	3	4	5	1	2	3	4	5
4. Facility in using technology	1	2	3	4	5	1	2	3	4	5
5. Written and oral briefings to performers, performers' managers, process owners and other stakeholders about performance gaps	1	2	3	4	5	1	2	3	4	5
6. Problem-solving activities to lead performers, performers' managers, process owners and other stakeholders to discover/forecast the likely impact of multiple interventions on processes, individuals or the organization	1	2	3	4	5	1	2	3	4	5
7. Strategies for groups, teams or individuals to discover present or anticipated performance gaps	1	2	3	4	5	1	2	3	4	5
8. Application of quality tools to identify special and general causes (histograms, trend charts, etc.)	1	2	3	4	5	1	2	3	4	5
9. Systems flowcharts showing the impact of interventions on processes, individuals or the organization	1	2	3	4	5	1	2	3	4	5
10. Written and oral descriptions of performance	1	2	3	4	5	1	2	3	4	5
Subtotal										

Table Appendix I-1 *Continued*

Output	How Often Does the Training Department Produce This Output?					How Well Does the Training Department Produce This Output?				
	Never	Seldom	Occasionally	Often	Very Often	Very Poorly	Poorly	Adequately	Well	Very Well
	1	2	3	4	5	1	2	3	4	5
11. Visual charts or other aids to show performance	1	2	3	4	5	1	2	3	4	5
12. Plans for employee recruitment programs	1	2	3	4	5	1	2	3	4	5
13. Plans for employee orientation programs	1	2	3	4	5	1	2	3	4	5
14. Plans for employee training programs using systematic approaches	1	2	3	4	5	1	2	3	4	5
15. Plans for establishing learning organizations	1	2	3	4	5	1	2	3	4	5
17. Plans for employee performance appraisal practices and programs	1	2	3	4	5	1	2	3	4	5
18. Plans for career development programs	1	2	3	4	5	1	2	3	4	5
19. Plans for organization development interventions	1	2	3	4	5	1	2	3	4	5
20. Plans for compensation, reward and incentive programs	1	2	3	4	5	1	2	3	4	5
21. Plans for employee feedback programs	1	2	3	4	5	1	2	3	4	5
22. Plans for employee discipline programs	1	2	3	4	5	1	2	3	4	5
23. Plans for employee counseling and wellness programs	1	2	3	4	5	1	2	3	4	5
24. Plans for safety programs	1	2	3	4	5	1	2	3	4	5
25. Plans for improved tools and equipment	1	2	3	4	5	1	2	3	4	5
26. Plans for improved on-the-job training	1	2	3	4	5	1	2	3	4	5
27. Plans for improved on-the-job learning	1	2	3	4	5	1	2	3	4	5
28. Plans for job aids	1	2	3	4	5	1	2	3	4	5
Subtotal										

	1	2	3	4	5	1	2	3	4	5
29. Plans for organizational design	1	2	3	4	5	1	2	3	4	5
30. Plans for job design	1	2	3	4	5	1	2	3	4	5
31. Plans for task design	1	2	3	4	5	1	2	3	4	5
32. Plans for ergonomic improvements	1	2	3	4	5	1	2	3	4	5
33. Plans for improved employee staff planning and forecasting programs	1	2	3	4	5	1	2	3	4	5
34. Flowcharts of work processes	1	2	3	4	5	1	2	3	4	5
35. Flowcharts of organizational operations/networks	1	2	3	4	5	1	2	3	4	5
36. Flowcharts of interactions with customers and other stakeholders	1	2	3	4	5	1	2	3	4	5
37. Cash flow statements	1	2	3	4	5	1	2	3	4	5
38. Budget documents	1	2	3	4	5	1	2	3	4	5
39. Income sheets and balance statements	1	2	3	4	5	1	2	3	4	5
40. Stories about organizational culture/history and experiences	1	2	3	4	5	1	2	3	4	5
41. Descriptions of the likely impact of changes ons different parts of an organization, work processes or individual	1	2	3	4	5	1	2	3	4	5
42. Requests for proposals	1	2	3	4	5	1	2	3	4	5
43. Written or oral proposals to management or to clients	1	2	3	4	5	1	2	3	4	5
44. Written and oral agreements	1	2	3	4	5	1	2	3	4	5
Subtotal										

Table Appendix I-1 *Continued*

Output	How Often Does the Training Department Produce This Output?					How Well Does the Training Department Produce This Output?				
	Never	Seldom	Occasionally	Often	Very Often	Very Poorly	Poorly	Adequately	Well	Very Well
	1	2	3	4	5	1	2	3	4	5
45. Management plans for oversight of vendors, contingent workers or outsourcing agents	1	2	3	4	5	1	2	3	4	5
47. Action plans	1	2	3	4	5	1	2	3	4	5
48. Agreements for action	1	2	3	4	5	1	2	3	4	5
49. Support for change voiced by performers, performers' managers, process owners and/or stakeholders	1	2	3	4	5	1	2	3	4	5
50. Strategies for managing stress and ambiguity	1	2	3	4	5	1	2	3	4	5
51. Strategies for helping others manage stress and ambiguity	1	2	3	4	5	1	2	3	4	5
52. Strategies for addressing resistance to change	1	2	3	4	5	1	2	3	4	5
53. Descriptions of the impact of human performance improvement strategy on organizational plans, work processes and individuals	1	2	3	4	5	1	2	3	4	5
64. Statistical summaries of needs analysis results	1	2	3	4	5	1	2	3	4	5
65. Content analysis summaries of needs analysis results	1	2	3	4	5	1	2	3	4	5
66. Work portfolios	1	2	3	4	5	1	2	3	4	5
67. Job descriptions	1	2	3	4	5	1	2	3	4	5
68. Behavioral events interview guides	1	2	3	4	5	1	2	3	4	5
69. Written critical incident survey questionnaires	1	2	3	4	5	1	2	3	4	5
70. Competency models by function, process, organization or work category	1	2	3	4	5	1	2	3	4	5
71. 360-degree assessments	1	2	3	4	5	1	2	3	4	5

	1	2	3	4	5		1	2	3	4	5
72. Interview guides	1	2	3	4	5		1	2	3	4	5
73. Interview administration plans	1	2	3	4	5		1	2	3	4	5
74. Content analyses of interview results	1	2	3	4	5		1	2	3	4	5
75. Statistical summaries of interview results	1	2	3	4	5		1	2	3	4	5
76. Team meeting agendas and plans	1	2	3	4	5		1	2	3	4	5
77. Strategies for analyzing the root cause(s) of performance gaps	1	2	3	4	5		1	2	3	4	5
78. Fishbone diagrams	1	2	3	4	5		1	2	3	4	5
79. Storyboards of problem events	1	2	3	4	5		1	2	3	4	5
80. Flowcharts	1	2	3	4	5		1	2	3	4	5
81. Policy and procedure preparation	1	2	3	4	5		1	2	3	4	5
82. Written policies	1	2	3	4	5		1	2	3	4	5
83. Written procedures	1	2	3	4	5		1	2	3	4	5
84. Preparation of work standards/expectations	1	2	3	4	5		1	2	3	4	5
85. Environmental scans	1	2	3	4	5		1	2	3	4	5
86. Business/organization plans	1	2	3	4	5		1	2	3	4	5
87. Team/group plans	1	2	3	4	5		1	2	3	4	5
88. Process improvement strategies/plans	1	2	3	4	5		1	2	3	4	5
89. Persuasive reports to stakeholders about past, present and future performance gaps and their cause(s)	1	2	3	4	5		1	2	3	4	5
Subtotal											

Table Appendix I-1 *Continued*

Output	How Often Does the Training Department Produce This Output?					How Well Does the Training Department Produce This Output?				
	Never	Seldom	Occasionally	Often	Very Often	Very Poorly	Poorly	Adequately	Well	Very Well
	1	2	3	4	5	1	2	3	4	5
90. Written or oral briefings to performers, performers' managers, process owners or other stakeholders about the results of performance analysis or cause analysis	1	2	3	4	5	1	2	3	4	5
91. Useful information drawn from performance or cause analysis	1	2	3	4	5	1	2	3	4	5
92. Approaches for choosing appropriate human performance improvement strategies to close performance gaps	1	2	3	4	5	1	2	3	4	5
93. Written and oral briefings to performers, performers' managers, process owners and other stakeholders about the likely impact of change or of a human performance improvement intervention on processes, individuals or the organization	1	2	3	4	5	1	2	3	4	5
94. Problem-solving activities to lead performers, performers' managers, process owners and other stakeholders to discover/forecast the impact of an intervention's implementation on processes, individuals or the organization	1	2	3	4	5	1	2	3	4	5
95. Written and oral briefings to performers, performers' managers, process owners and other stakeholders about the likely impact of multiple interventions on processes, individuals or the organization	1	2	3	4	5	1	2	3	4	5
97. Organizational analyses	1	2	3	4	5	1	2	3	4	5
98. Process analyses	1	2	3	4	5	1	2	3	4	5

	1	2	3	4	5	1	2	3	4	5
99. Individual assessments	1	2	3	4	5	1	2	3	4	5
100. White papers on improvement strategies	1	2	3	4	5	1	2	3	4	5
101. Oral and written briefings to performers, performers' managers, process owners and other stakeholders about possible improvement strategies	1	2	3	4	5	1	2	3	4	5
102. Customer satisfaction information/survey results	1	2	3	4	5	1	2	3	4	5
103. Written or oral goals for human performance improvement	1	2	3	4	5	1	2	3	4	5
104. Performance objectives for interventions	1	2	3	4	5	1	2	3	4	5
105. Facilitated performance objectives	1	2	3	4	5	1	2	3	4	5
107. Persuasive reports to stakeholders about the appropriate intervention(s) to close past, present or future performance gap(s)	1	2	3	4	5	1	2	3	4	5
108. A convincing case made for the need for change	1	2	3	4	5	1	2	3	4	5
109. Organizational sponsorship identified and secured	1	2	3	4	5	1	2	3	4	5
110. Evidence of support obtained through commitment of resources	1	2	3	4	5	1	2	3	4	5
111. Designs/action plans for introducing and consolidating interventions	1	2	3	4	5	1	2	3	4	5
112. Designs/plans for reducing resistance to interventions	1	2	3	4	5	1	2	3	4	5
Subtotal										

Table Appendix I-1 *Continued*

Output	How Often Does the Training Department Produce This Output?					How Well Does the Training Department Produce This Output?				
	Never	Seldom	Occasionally	Often	Very Often	Very Poorly	Poorly	Adequately	Well	Very Well
	1	2	3	4	5	1	2	3	4	5
113. Recommendations to management about management's role in introducing and consolidating change	1	2	3	4	5	1	2	3	4	5
114. Recommendations to workers about their role in introducing and consolidating change	1	2	3	4	5	1	2	3	4	5
115. Communication plans established to keep participants in change and stakeholders of change informed about the progress of the human performance improvement intervention	1	2	3	4	5	1	2	3	4	5
117. Performance improvement interventions effectively monitored with participants and stakeholders	1	2	3	4	5	1	2	3	4	5
118. Human performance improvement evaluation objectives	1	2	3	4	5	1	2	3	4	5
119. Human performance improvement evaluation designs and plans	1	2	3	4	5	1	2	3	4	5
120. Human performance improvement evaluation instruments	1	2	3	4	5	1	2	3	4	5
121. Pre- and post-measures of worker performance	1	2	3	4	5	1	2	3	4	5
122. Evaluation findings, conclusions and recommendations	1	2	3	4	5	1	2	3	4	5
123. Reports to management and workers on the outcomes of human performance improvement strategies	1	2	3	4	5	1	2	3	4	5
Subtotal										

	1	2	3	4	5		1	2	3	4	5
124. Linkage of human performance improvement strategies to other change efforts of the organization	1	2	3	4	5		1	2	3	4	5
125. Linkage of each human performance improvement intervention with other interventions	1	2	3	4	5		1	2	3	4	5
126. Linkage of human performance improvement interventions to organizational plans, goals and objectives	1	2	3	4	5		1	2	3	4	5
127. Linkage of human performance improvement interventions to organizational/business needs	1	2	3	4	5		1	2	3	4	5
128. Work standards/expectations established	1	2	3	4	5		1	2	3	4	5
129. Work standards/expectations communicated	1	2	3	4	5		1	2	3	4	5
130. Linkage of human performance improvement interventions to organizational culture	1	2	3	4	5		1	2	3	4	5
131. Written and oral reports to stakeholders about the progress of an intervention	1	2	3	4	5		1	2	3	4	5
132. Written and oral reports to stakeholders about the progress of an intervention	1	2	3	4	5		1	2	3	4	5
133. Groups successfully observed	1	2	3	4	5		1	2	3	4	5
134. Plans for influencing groups based on knowledge of small group development theory	1	2	3	4	5		1	2	3	4	5
Subtotal											

Table Appendix I-1 *Continued*

Output	How Often Does the Training Department Produce This Output?						How Well Does the Training Department Produce This Output?				
	Never	Seldom	Occasionally	Often	Very Often		Very Poorly	Poorly	Adequately	Well	Very Well
	1	2	3	4	5		1	2	3	4	5
135. Group process observation forms	1	2	3	4	5		1	2	3	4	5
136. Descriptions to group members and individuals about the effects of their behavior on a group or on individuals	1	2	3	4	5		1	2	3	4	5
137. Plans for facilitating group discussions	1	2	3	4	5		1	2	3	4	5
138. Plans for facilitating individual or group decision-making and problem-solving	1	2	3	4	5		1	2	3	4	5
139. Effective interpersonal interactions among participants and stakeholders of interventions	1	2	3	4	5		1	2	3	4	5
140. Feedback to the organization about performance	1	2	3	4	5		1	2	3	4	5
141. Feedback to the organization about progress of interventions	1	2	3	4	5		1	2	3	4	5
142. Feedback to work groups or teams about performance	1	2	3	4	5		1	2	3	4	5
143. Feedback to work groups or teams about progress of interventions	1	2	3	4	5		1	2	3	4	5
144. Feedback to management about performance	1	2	3	4	5		1	2	3	4	5
145. Feedback to management about interventions	1	2	3	4	5		1	2	3	4	5
147. Effective feedback provided to key stakeholder groups, on a continuing basis, about the progress of interventions	1	2	3	4	5		1	2	3	4	5
Subtotal											

Total Scores on the Instrument: Respondents should add the subtotals from both columns from all pages and insert the numbers in the boxes below:

Total	How Often Does the Training Department Produce This Output?	How Well Does the Training Department Produce This Output?

Interpreting the Scores: Respondents should find the scores in the table below that are closest to their scores on the instrument. They should then read the interpretation. When they finish, they should proceed to the next section.

(*text continues on p. 275*)

Table Appendix I-2

How Often Does the Training Department Produce This Output?	Interpretation	How Well Does the Training Department Produce This Output?	Interpretation
735	Perfect score—Your training department is frequently doing human performance improvement work. It is, in effect, a human performance improvement department.	735	Perfect score—Your training department is effectively doing human performance improvement work—at least in your opinion.
588–734	Grade your training department a "B" on "doing human performance improvement work" *frequently*. If the aim is to reinvent the training department, you still have your work cut out for you. More work is needed.	588–734	Grade your training department a "B" on "doing human performance improvement work" *effectively*. If the aim is to reinvent the training department, you still have your work cut out for you. More work is needed.
441–587	Grade your training department a "C" on "doing human performance improvement work" *frequently*. If the aim is to reinvent the training department, you still have much more work to do.	441–587	Grade your training department a "C" on "doing human performance improvement work" *effectively*. If the aim is to reinvent the training department, you still have much more work to do.
440–Lower	Grade your training department a "D" on "doing human performance improvement work" *frequently*. You are just starting.	440–Lower	Grade your training department a "D" on "doing human performance improvement work" *effectively*. You are just starting.

Setting Priorities and Planning for Action: After respondents have interpreted their scores, they should then think about the items they rated as lowest in frequency or effectiveness and should focus their attention on those items. They should then make a list of outputs that the training department should attempt to be giving to the organization. Those outputs should then be listed below. Respondents should then be prepared to discuss those outputs with other members of the organization—such as top managers and key line personnel—so that they understand what it could mean to the organization if the training department focused attention on human performance improvement work and provided those outputs.

Priority (1 = Most Important)	Output(s)

Finally, respondents should prepare an action plan to indicate how the Training Department can begin offering these outputs to the organization over time. They should use the space below to indicate who should do what by when to achieve this (or these) goals:

Action Plan

Figure Appendix I-1   Training department assessment instrument.

Appendix II

Determining Your Optimum Pathway to Development

This instrument is designed to help you or others assess your strengths and areas for growth as you begin your journey to becoming a Human Performance Improvement practitioner. This instrument will also help you identify your priorities for development.

Instructions:

For each HPI competency listed, indicate your current level of aptitude in Column A:

0–Expert—Extremely skilled. Can demonstrate this competency in highly complex situations; could instruct others in the development or application of this competency.

1–Intermediate—Skilled. Can demonstrate this competency in most situations; might require some help in complex situations; could instruct others in the application of this competency in basic situations.

2–Novice—Have some limited experience demonstrating this competency. Would benefit from some help if the situation is not straightforward.

3–None—Cannot, or have never had the opportunity to, demonstrate this competency.

Next, for each HPI competency listed, indicate the importance of demonstrating that competency in your job—now or in the future.

0–N/A—Not applicable to my job.

1–Low—Not that critical to success in my job.

2–Medium—Important to success in my job.

3–High—Extremely critical to success in my job.

Finally, to determine your priorities for development, multiply the number in Column A by the number in Column B. Place the product in Column C.

Table Appendix II-1   Competency Assessment Instrument

Core Competencies	Column A Current Level of Aptitude 0–Expert 1–Intermediate 2–Novice 3–None	Column B Importance to Job 0–N/A 1–Low 2–Medium 3–High	Column C Priority (A × B)
Industry Awareness: Understanding the vision, strategy, goals, and culture of an industry; linking human performance improvement interventions to organizational goals.			
Leadership Skills: Knowing how to lead or influence others positively to achieve desired work results.			
Interpersonal Relationship Skills: Working effectively with others to achieve common goals and exercising effective interpersonal influence.			
Technological Awareness and Understanding: Using existing or new technology and different types of software and hardware; understanding performance support systems and applying them as appropriate.			
Problem-Solving Skills: Detecting performance gaps and helping other people discover ways to close the performance gaps in the present and future; closing performance gaps between actual and ideal performance.			

Systems Thinking and Understanding: Identifying inputs, throughputs, and outputs of a subsystem, system, or suprasystem and applying that information to improve human performance; realizing the implications of interventions on many parts of an organization, process, or individual and taking steps to address any side effects of human performance improvement interventions.				
Performance Understanding: Distinguishing between activities and results; recognizing implications, outcomes, and consequences.				
Knowledge of Interventions: Demonstrating an understanding of the many ways that human performance can be improved in organizational settings; showing how to apply specific human performance improvement interventions to close existing or anticipated performance gaps.				
Business Understandings: Demonstrating awareness of the inner workings of business functions and how business decisions affect financial or nonfinancial work results (McLagan, 1989).				
Organization Understanding: Seeing organizations as dynamic, political economic, and social systems that have multiple goals; using this larger perspective as a framework for understanding and influencing events and change (McLagan, 1989).				

Continued

Table Appendix II-1 *Continued*

Core Competencies	Column A Current Level of Aptitude 0–Expert 1–Intermediate 2–Novice 3–None	Column B Importance to Job 0–N/A 1–Low 2–Medium 3–High	Column C Priority (A × B)
Negotiating/Contracting Skills: Organizing, preparing, overseeing, and evaluating work performed by vendors, contingent workers, or outsourcing agents.			
Buy-in/Advocacy Skills: Building ownership or support for change among affected individuals, groups, and other stakeholders.			
Coping Skills: Knowing how to deal with ambiguity and how to handle the stress resulting from change and from multiple meanings or possibilities.			
Ability to See "Big Picture": Looking beyond details to see overarching goals and results.			
Consulting Skills: Understanding the results that stakeholders desire form a process and providing insight into how efficiently and effectively those results can be achieved.			
Project Management Skills: Planning, costing, organizing, resourcing, and managing complex projects.			

Role Competencies	Column A Current Level of Aptitude 0–Expert 1–Intermediate 2–Novice 3–None	Column B Importance to Job 0–N/A 1–Low 2–Medium 3–High	Column C Priority (A × B)
ANALYST			
Performance Analysis Skills (Front-End Analysis): The process of comparing actual and ideal performance in order to identify gaps or opportunities.			
Needs Analysis Survey Design and Development Skills (Open-Ended and Structured): Preparing written (mail), oral (phone), or electronic (e-mail) surveys using open-ended (essay) and closed (scaled) questions in order to identify human performance improvement needs.			
Competency Identification Skills: Identifying the knowledge and skill requirements of teams, jobs, tasks, roles and work (McLagan, 1989).			
Questioning Skills: Gathering pertinent information to stimulate insight in individuals and groups through use of interviews and other probing methods (McLagan, 1989).			
Analytical Skills (Synthesis): Breaking down the components of a larger whole and reassembling them to achieve improved human performance.			
Work Environment Analytical Skills: Examining work environments for issues or characteristics affecting human performance.			

Table Appendix II-2 *Continued*

Role Competencies	Column A Current Level of Aptitude 0–Expert 1–Intermediate 2–Novice 3–None	Column B Importance to Job 0–N/A 1–Low 2–Medium 3–High	Column C Priority (A × B)
INTERVENTION SPECIALIST			
Performance Information Interpretation Skills: Finding useful meaning from the results of performance analysis and helping performers, performers' managers, process owners, and other stakeholders to do so.			
Intervention Selection Skills: Selecting human performance improvement interventions that address the root cause(s) of performance gaps rather than symptoms or side effects.			
Performance Change Interpretation Skills: Forecasting and analyzing the effects of interventions and their consequences.			

Ability to Assess Relationship Among Interventions: Examining the effects of multiple human performance improvement interventions on parts of an organization, its interactions with customers, suppliers, distributors, and workers.		
Ability to Identify Critical Business Issues and Changes: Determining key business issues and applying that information during the implementation of a human performance improvement intervention.		
Goal Interpretation Skills: Ensuring that goals are converted effectively into actions to close existing or pending performance gaps; getting results despite conflicting priorities, lack of resources, or ambiguity.		

Table Appendix II-2 *Continued*

Role Competencies	Column A Current Level of Aptitude 0–Expert 1–Intermediate 2–Novice 3–None	Column B Importance to Job 0–N/A 1–Low 2–Medium 3–High	Column C Priority (A × B)
CHANGE MANAGER			
Change Implementation Skills: Understanding the nature of individual and organizational change and applying that knowledge to effectively lead organizations successfully through change.			
Change Impetus Skills: Determining what the organization should do to address the cause(s) of a human performance gap at present and in the future.			
Communication Channel, Informal Network, and Alliance Understanding: Knowing how communication moves through an organization by various channels, networks, and alliances; building such channels, networks, and alliances to achieve improvements in productivity and performance.			

Groups Dynamics Process Understanding: Understanding how groups function; influencing people so that group, work, and individuals needs are addressed (McLagan, 1989).		
Process Consultation Skills: Observing individuals and groups for their interactions and the effects of their interactions with others.		
Facilitation Skills: Helping performers, performers' managers, process owners, and stakeholders to discover new insights.		

Table Appendix II-2 *Continued*

Role Competencies	Column A Current Level of Aptitude 0–Expert 1–Intermediate 2–Novice 3–None	Column B Importance to Job 0–N/A 1–Low 2–Medium 3–High	Column C Priority (A × B)
EVALUATOR			
Groups Dynamics Process Understanding, Performance Gap Evaluation Skills: Measuring or helping others to measure the difference between actual performance and ideal performance.			
Ability to Evaluate Results Against Organizational Goals: Assessing how well the results of a human performance improvement intervention match intentions.			
Standard-Setting Skills: Measuring desired results of organizations, processes, or individuals; helping others to establish and measure work expectations.			

Ability to Assess Impact on Culture: Examining the effects of human performance gaps and human performance improvement interventions in shared beliefs and assumptions about "right" and "wrong" ways of behaving and acting in one organizational setting.		
Human Performance Improvement Intervention Reviewing Skills: Finding ways to evaluate and continuously improve human performance improvement interventions before and during implementation.		
Feedback Skills: Collecting information about performance and feeding it back clearly, specifically, and on a timely basis to affected individuals or groups (McLagan, 1989).		

288 Human Performance Improvement

Using Your Results

For Self-Assessments:

Identify all competencies for which you indicated either a 0 or a 1 in Column A. List them below:

_____	_____
_____	_____
_____	_____
_____	_____
_____	_____
_____	_____
_____	_____
_____	_____
_____	_____

These are your strengths. Continue to look for opportunities to exploit these strengths in your organization and to help others develop these competencies.

Review the totals in Column C. Identify the largest four or five numbers. The competencies associated with these scores should be your primary development priority. The next largest four or five scores indicate your secondary development priorities—and so on.

Primary Development Priorities	Secondary Development Priorities
_____	_____
_____	_____
_____	_____
_____	_____

Repeat this self-assessment at least annually, as both your aptitude and the importance of each competency to your job will change.

For Multi-Rater/360-Degree Assessments:

Average the scores found in Column A. Identify all competencies for which you averaged 0–1.5 in Column A. List them below:

_____   _____
_____   _____
_____   _____
_____   _____
_____   _____
_____   _____
_____   _____
_____   _____
_____   _____
_____   _____

Review the totals in Column C. Identify the largest four or five numbers. The competencies associated with these scores should be your primary development priority. The next largest four or five scores indicate your secondary development priorities.

Primary Development Priorities   Secondary Development Priorities

_____   _____
_____   _____
_____   _____
_____   _____
_____   _____
_____   _____
_____   _____
_____   _____
_____   _____

Appendix III

Human Performance Improvement Resource Guide

Using the Resource Guide

The Resource Guide that follows is divided into three sections. Section One identifies a partial list of graduate degree programs that one might choose to enroll in, either part-time or full-time, to acquire the competencies to become an HPI practitioner. Section Two contains a list of recommended readings, workshops, and other development opportunities for a broad overview of HPI. Section Three contains development resources for the 40 competencies in the ASTD HPI Competency Model. For each competency, you will find:

- **Recommended readings:** Current publications that will provide knowledge and the foundation for skill development for the competency.
- **Workshops:** Publicly offered workshops that will help to develop the competency.
- **Self-study options:** Nonclassroom training solutions including self-study text, video, audio, computer-based training (CBT), CD/ROM.
- **Other development opportunities:** A list of nontraditional ways to develop the competency.

Section One: Graduate Degree Programs

Some professionals seeking to transition from training to human performance improvement may choose the academic route. There are many masters and doctorate programs that will provide many of the competencies required for HPI practitioners. This section is a partial list of academic institutions and the degree programs that each offers. Additional degree programs can be found at the following websites:

- www.gradschools.com
- www.usnews.com/usnews/edu/beyond/bchome.htm

For each school you will find:

- Contact information for the school
- General description of the degree program
- Contact information for the degree program

Note: These graduate-degree programs were selected for their appropriateness to the Human Performance Improvement field. This list is not intended to be comprehensive, nor is it intended to endorse or exclude any particular graduate-degree program.

Penn State University Main Campus
301 Keller Building
University Park, PA 16802-3206
Phone: (814) 863-2596
Website: http://www.ed.psu.edu/wfed/

Program Description: The Workforce Education and Development Ph.D. program is offered by the Workforce Education and Development Program at Pennsylvania State University, University Park.

The general focus of the program is preparation for entry into professional positions within the broadly conceived field of workforce education and development, including human resource development or learning and performance in industry, secondary, and postsecondary technical education, and employability programs for special populations. Emphases within the program include training and development/human resources, leadership/administration, school-to-work, and workforce policy analysis.

For More Information:
Edgar I. Farmer
401A Keller Building
University Park, PA 16802
eif1@psu.edu
Phone: (814) 863-3858

Johns Hopkins University
School of Professional Studies in Business and Education
Columbia Center
6740 Alexander Bell Drive
Columbia, MD 21046
Phone: (410) 516-4980
Admissions e-mail: odhr@jhu.edu
Website: http://www.spsbe.jhu.edu/

Program Description: The Master of Science in Organization Development and Strategic Human Resources (ODSHR) is a 42-credit hour program that prepares students for the changing roles and demands of OD and HR professionals, as that of strategic partners. The ODSHR program is also designed for expert practitioners or mid-level managers who represent a myriad of organizations and would like to advance or transition their careers by integrating a cadre of organization development and human resource skills in the public, private, or nonprofit sectors.

The program focuses on core competencies, which integrate organization development and human resource content with an emphasis on strategic human capital and development. The program incorporates building a learning community, an electronic portfolio, and, most importantly, courses and assessments based on the understandings and learning outcomes mentioned above.

Admitted students are required first to complete a set of core courses that provide a common body of knowledge. After completing the core, students must declare their academic concentrations in strategic human resources, organization development, nonprofit, or a general concentration track. In the general concentration track, students develop their own areas of study by selecting courses from the list of ODSHR concentration offerings. Students apply their practical learning in the final degree requirements, Research Methods and Directed Field Work. Students contract with a real organization to provide a service that is reflective of their OD or HR specialization.

For more information, contact the Senior Academic Program Coordinator: Lawrence Waudby, 410-516-4980, email: odhr@jhu.edu, or General Admissions: 410-516-4234

Ohio State University—Columbus
1945 N. High Street
Columbus, OH 43210-1172
Phone: (614) 292-5037

Admissions website: http://gradapply.osu.edu

Website: http://www.education.osu.edu/paes/wde/default.htm

Program Description: The Workforce Development and Education section offers an academic degree program emphasizing adult learning, career and technical education, human resource development, and workforce development policy; conducts research on topics in these areas; and provides professional development opportunities to meet the needs of individuals, organizations and government agencies. The WDE section values scholarly research and quality instruction as a means to model and improve theory and professional practice, nationally and internationally.

The WDE Section offers two undergraduate programs, an M.A. and Ph.D., as well as a range of certificate and licensure options for professionals in Workforce Development and Education. Many of their programs utilize cutting edge technology and is uniquely suited to the needs of working professions. The majority of the classes take place in the evenings.

For More Information:

Dr. David Stein, Associate Professor

WDE Section Head (stein.1@osu.edu)

283 Arps Hall

Columbus, OH 43210

Phone: (614) 292-0988

University of Georgia

College of Education, G-3 Aderhold Hall

Athens, GA 30602

Phone: (706) 542-6446

E-mail: coeinfo@uga.ed

Website: http://www.coe.uga.edu/academic/graduate.html

Program Description: The mission of the Program of Occupational Studies is to prepare and develop professional educators in the public and private sector and to advance the knowledge base of career and technical education, workforce preparation, and professional development through teaching, research, and service.

The Workforce Education program promotes career and technical education and workforce preparation throughout the lifespan by advancing the knowledge base of career and technical education and workforce preparation, preparing professionals for the public and private sectors, and providing quality instruction, research, leadership, service, and policy development.

For More Information:
Workforce Education, Leadership, & Social Foundations
221 River's Crossing, 402 Aderhold Hall
The University of Georgia
Athens, GA 30602
Phone: (706) 542-1682
Fax: (706) 542-4054
E-mail to: welsf@uga.edu

University of Illinois—Urbana
Department of Human Resource Education
University of Illinois at Urbana-Champaign
351 Education Building
1310 South Sixth Street
Champaign, IL 61820
E-mail: hre@uiuc.edu
Phone: (217) 333-0807
Website: http://www.ed.uiuc.edu/hre/index.html

Program Description: As part of a scholarly community in a premier research institution of higher learning, the Department of Human Resource Education engages in forward-looking research, graduate and professional education, and outreach activities for numerous constituencies. In alignment with these aims, the mission of the Department of Human Resource Education is to:

- Create and disseminate new knowledge about human resource education through disciplined inquiry using multiple methodological approaches and theoretical frameworks.
- Faculty and students in the department share a strong commitment to and actively engage in rigorous academic research. Faculty and student researchers place emphasis on theory building, theory validation, and the translation of theoretical knowledge to practical applications. Researchers in the department draw from a variety of fields and disciplines, among them psychology, education, and organization studies and thus play a crucial role in building and expanding the knowledge base of the emerging field of human resource education.
- Provide quality education that provides students with the strong academic foundation needed for improving learning and performance in education, business, health care, military, nonprofit, and government organizations.

- Human Resource Education students will have the ability to lead and facilitate change related to learning and performance as a result of academic experiences in reflective practice, applied processes, and use of technology.
- Enhance the lives and productivity of our many constituencies by providing expertise and assistance through consulting activities, social engagement, and community development.

These constituencies include members of the university and local, state, and global communities that are concerned with improving productivity and fostering lifelong work-based learning through individual and organizational development.

This program offers various masters and doctorate degrees.

For More Information:
Department of Human Resource Education
351 Education Building
University of Illinois
1310 South Sixth Street
Champaign, IL 61820
Phone: (217) 333-0807
Fax: (217) 244-5632
E-mail: hre@uiuc.edu

Virginia Tech
260 Wallace Hall
Blacksburg, VA 24061-0426
Phone: (540) 231-5645
Admissions e-mail: Eaton@VT.EDU
Website: http://www.nvc.vt.edu/alhrd/

Program Description: Virginia Tech's Adult Learning and Human Resource Development Program offers the Master of Science and Doctor of Philosophy Degrees in Human Development for persons working with adults as learners in such setting as business industry, government, military, health care, education, nonprofit organizations, and professional associations. The Program has provided training in Northern Virginia since 1980 based upon five domains of professional practice in ALHRD including facilitation, design, planning, change, and research.

For More Information:
Department of Human Development

ALHRD Program
Virginia Tech—Northern Virginia Center
7054 Haycock Road
Falls Church, VA 22043-2311
Phone: 703-538-8475
Fax: 703-538-8465
E-mail: alhrd@vt.edu

Texas A&M University—College Station
College of Education
College Station, TX 77843-4222
Phone: (409) 845-1044
Website: http://www.cehd.tamu.edu/

Program Description: Texas A&M offers masters and doctoral degree programs in educational human resource development with specializations in adult education and human resource development.

At the Masters or Doctoral level, you will be prepared for professions in public, private, or nonprofit settings. Depending on your specific interests, earning a degree in educational human resource development will provide you, as a student, with a variety of courses and academic experiences beyond foundational, specializations, and research core requirements. The adult education (AE) specialization will allow individuals opportunities to focus on adult education across many contexts, including health care institutions and colleges and universities. The human resource development (HRD) specialization works to improve learning opportunities for adults as faculty positions in colleges and universities, as well as careers in professional organizations, community organizations, and continuing education programs. The HRD specialization also provides individuals with opportunities for international travel, professional presentations, and writing for publication and research. In addition, within the HRD specialization, individuals have the opportunity to participate in a five week training and development certificate program. Participants in the certification program are not required to be admitted to the department.

For More Information:
Dr. Jim Scheurich
Department Head
Department of Educational Administration and Human Resource
Development

Texas A&M University
4226 TAMU
College Station, TX 77843-4226
Phone: (979) 845-2763
Fax: (979) 458-3890
E-mail to: jscheurich@tamu.edu

Colorado State University
Graduate School
Ft. Collins, CO 80523-1005
Phone: (970) 491-6909
Website: www.ColoState.EDU/Depts/Grad

Program Description: The Organizational Performance & Change (OPC) masters program of study is designed for HRD and management professionals who are responsible for optimizing human capital and organizational performance. The course work addresses skill development and understanding related to strategic performance management, and organization change issues and processes.

Graduates currently serve in a variety of HRD strategic planning, training, organization development, staff and program development, career development, evaluation, and professional postsecondary education roles.

For More Information:
Organizational Development and Change (ODC)
School of Education
Education Building
Fort Collins, CO 80523-1588
Phone: (970) 491-1963

Southern Illinois University—Carbondale
Wham Education Building MC4624
Carbondale, IL 62901-4624
Phone: (618) 536-7791
Admissions e-mail: gradschl@siu.edu
Website: http://web.coehs.siu.edu/Public/

Program Description: The workforce education and development concentration is a broad, general leadership and professional development degree that serves individuals having knowledge, experience, and interests in: (a) career education;

(b) career and technical education; (c) public and private sector training and development, and related technical and professional fields; (d) human resource development. Even though many students entering the program have a specific occupational area identity (e.g., business education, health careers education, industrial education), the degree is not awarded in a service area specialty.

For More Information:
Department of Workforce Education and Development
475 Clocktower Drive
Pulliam Hall, Room 212
Mailcode 4605
Southern Illinois University
Carbondale, IL 62901-4605
Phone: (618) 453-3321
Fax: (618) 453-1909
E-mail: wed@siu.edu

Seton Hall University
400 South Orange Avenue
South Orange, NJ 07079
Phone: (973) 761-9000
Website: www.shu.edu

Program Description: The Department of Education Leadership, Management, and Policy offers a Master of Arts in Human Resources Training and Development designed primarily for members of the New Jersey and New York law enforcement communities. Established more than 20 years ago, the program helps students strengthen their professional knowledge and skills, while increasing their capacity for leadership in their respective law enforcement settings. The program is distinctive in that it allows students to attend classes on-campus as well as classes at law enforcement sites in northern and southern New Jersey. In addition to the master's program, the department also offers a certificate program for students who successfully complete 12 credits in either Human Resources Training and Development or Leadership and Management.

For More Information:
Michele Rullo
Phone: (973) 275-2308
E-mail: rullomih@shu.edu

Governor's State University
Office of Admissions, Room D1400
Governors State University
University Park, IL 60466-0975
Phone: (708) 534-5000, ext. 4490
Website: www.govst.edu

Program Description: Human Performance and Training at Governor's State is a hands-on, project-driven masters program designed to develop the skills required of an Instructional Designer. In lieu of tests, students are evaluated on the basis of real-world projects produced during the classes. As in business, deadlines must be met, requiring skills in organizing, prioritizing, and balancing commitments. Completion of the program is equivalent to approximately two years work experience. Graduates leave with a substantial portfolio of works showcasing their talents. Students in the program come from diverse educational backgrounds. Most have full-time careers and/or families, and successfully take one or two courses per trimester. Attending part-time, the necessary 36 credit hours can be completed in about three years. Very few students attempt three classes per trimester.

For More Information:
Communications Department
Governor's State University
University Park, IL 60466-0975
Phone: (708) 534-4080
E-mail: m-lanigan@govst.edu or m-stelni@govst.edu
Website: www.govst.edu/commcentral

Section Two: Comprehensive HPI Resources

This section is for those who do not have the time or inclination to pursue a comprehensive academic solution to their skill and knowledge gaps, but want a broad overview of the human performance improvement field. This part of the resource guide will provide:

- **Recommended readings:** Current publications that will provide an overview of HPI. Descriptions of these books are typically available at www.amazon.com and www.bn.com.

- **Workshops:** Publicly offered workshops that will provide an overview of HPI and, in some cases, begin to develop critical HPI competencies. Descriptions of these workshops are typically available from each vendor's website, which is provided.
- **Self-study options:** Nonclassroom training solutions including self-study text, video, audio, computer-based training (CBT), CD/ROM. Descriptions of these self-study options are typically available from each vendor's website, which is provided.
- **Other development opportunities:** A list of nontraditional ways to understand and gain skills in HPI.

Note: These resources were selected for their appropriateness to the Human Performance Improvement field. This list is not intended to be comprehensive, nor is it intended to endorse or exclude any particular resource.

Recommended Readings

These books were selected for their content and appropriateness for the Human Performance Improvement field. This list is not intended to be comprehensive, nor is it intended to endorse or exclude any particular book or author.

2006 ASTD Training & Performance Source Book
Silberman, Mel (editor)
Alexandria, VA: American Society for Training & Development, 2006
ISBN: 1562864238

HPI Essentials: A Just-the-Facts, Bottom-Line Primer on Human Performance Improvement
Piskurich, George M., Alexandria, VA: American Society for Training & Development. 2002
ISBN: 1562863150

Beyond Training Ain't Performance Fieldbook
Stolvitch, Harold, D., and Keeps, Erica J. Alexandria, VA: American Society for Training & Development. 2006
ISBN: 1562864076

Training Ain't Performance
Stolvitch, Harold D., and Keeps, Erica J. Alexandria, VA: American Society for Training & Development, 2004
ISBN: 1562863673

Telling Ain't Training
Stolvitch, Harold D., and Keeps, Erica J. Alexandria, VA: American Society for Training & Development, 2002
ISBN: 1562863282

Needs Assessment Basics
Tobey, Deborah. Alexandria, VA: American Society for Training & Development, 2005
ISBN: 1562863878

Evaluation Basics
McCain, Don. Alexandria, VA: American Society for Training & Development, 2005
ISBN: 1562863738

Performance Basics
Willmore, Joe. Alexandria, VA: American Society for Training & Development, 2004
ISBN: 1562863703

Human Performance Improvement: Building Practitioner Competence (2nd Edition)
Rothwell, William J., Hohne, Carolyn K., and King, Stephen B.
Elsevier, 2007
ISBN: 978-0-7506-7996-1

Performance Intervention Maps (2nd Edition)
Sanders, Ethan S., and Thiagarajan, Sivasailam
Alexandria, VA: American Society for Training, and Development, 2005
ISBN: 1562864149

Intervention Resource Guide: 50 Performance Improvement Tools
Langdon, Danny G., Whiteside, Kathleen S., and McKenna, Monica M.
San Francisco, CA: Jossey-Bass/Pfeiffer, 1999
ISBN: 0787944017

Peformance Improvement: Make it Happen
Enos, Barry. Boca Raton, FL: CRC, 2000
ISBN: 1574442821

Handbook of Human Performance Technology (3rd Edition)
Pershing, James A. San Francisco, CA: John Wiley & Sons. 2006
ISBN: 0787965308

Advances in Developing Human Resources: Performance Improvement Theory and Practice
Torraco, Richard. San Francisco, CA: Berrett-Koehler Publishers, 2000
ISBN: 1583760113

Human Performance Consulting: Transforming Human Potential into Productive Business Performance (Improving Human Performance)
Pepitone, James S. Houston, TX: Gulf Publishing
ISBN: 0877193525

The Performance Improvement Toolkit: The Guide to Knowledge Based Improvement
Gerst, Robert. Converge Consulting Group, 2002
ISBN: 0968806708

Performance Gap Analysis
Franklin, Maren. Alexandria, VA: American Society of Training and Development, 2006
ISBN: 1562864270

Performance Interventions
Sugrue, Brenda, and Fuller Jim. Alexandria, VA: American Society of Training and Development, 1999
ISBN: 1562861247

Analysis for Improving Performance: Tools for Diagnosing Organizations & Documenting Workplace Expertise
Swanson, Richard A. San Francisco, CA: Berrett-Koehler Publishers, Inc., 1996
ISBN: 1576750019

Handbook of Human Performance Technology: Improving Individual & Organizational Performance Worldwide (2nd Edition)
Stolovitch, Harold D., and Keeps, Erica J. San Francisco, CA: Jossey-Bass Pfeiffer, 1999
ISBN: 0787911089

Performance Consulting: Moving Beyond Training
Robinson, D.G., and Robinson, J.C. San Francisco, CA: Berrett-Koehler Publishers, 1996
ISBN: 1881052842

The Performance Consultant's Fieldbook: Tools and Techniques for Improving Organizations and People
Hale, Judith A. San Francisco, CA: Jossey-Bass Publishers, 1998
ISBN: 0787940194

Improving Performance: How to Manage the White Space on the Organization Chart (2nd Edition)
Rummler, G.A., and Brache, A.P. San Francisco, CA: Jossey-Bass Publishers, 1995
ISBN: 0787900907

ASTD Models for Human Performance Improvement: Roles, Competencies, and Outputs
Rothwell, William J. Alexandria, VA: American Society for Training and Development, 1996
ISBN: 1562860569

The Performance Consulting Toolbook
Nilson, Carolyn. New York, NY: McGraw-Hill, 1999
ISBN: 007047169

Moving from Training to Performance: A Practical Guidebook
Robinson, D.G., and Robinson, J.C. (Editors). Alexandria, VA: American Society for Training and Development, San Francisco: Berrett-Koehler Publishers, 1998
ISBN: 1576750396

From Training to Performance Improvement: Navigating the Transition
Fuller, J., and Farrington, J. San Francisco, CA: Jossey-Bass Pfeiffer, 1999
ISBN: 0787911208

Workshops

These workshops were selected for their content and appropriateness for the Human Performance Improvement field. This list is not intended to be comprehensive, nor is it intended to endorse or exclude any particular workshop.

HPI in Workplace
Length: 3 days   Cost: $1,395 (member), $1,595
Location: Various, contact vendor
American Society for Training & Development

1640 King Street, Box 1443
Alexandria, VA 22313-2043
Telephone: (703) 683-8100
Website: www.astd.org

Analyzing Human Performance

Length: 3 days   Cost: $1,395 (member), $1,595
Location: Various, contact vendor
American Society for Training & Development
1640 King Street, Box 1443
Alexandria, VA 22313-2043
Telephone: (703) 683-8100
Website: www.astd.org

Evaluating Performance Improvement Interventions

Length: 3 days   Cost: $1,395 (member), $1,595
Location: Various, contact vendor
American Society for Training & Development
1640 King Street, Box 1443
Alexandria, VA 22313-2043
Telephone: (703) 683-8100
Website: www.astd.org

Selecting and Managing Interventions

Length: 3 days   Cost: $1,395 (member), $1,595
Location: Various, contact vendor
American Society for Training & Development
1640 King Street, Box 1443
Alexandria, VA 22313-2043
Telephone: (703) 683-8100
Website: www.astd.org

Transition to Human Performance Improvement

Length: 3 days   Cost: $1,395 (member), $1,595
Location: Various, contact vendor
American Society for Training & Development
1640 King Street, Box 1443
Alexandria, VA 22313-2043
Telephone: (703) 683-8100
Website: www.astd.org

Performance Consulting Skills
Length: 2 days   Cost: $1,099
Location: Various, contact vendor
Friesen, Kaye and Associates
13101 Washington Blvd., Suite 431
Los Angeles, CA 90066
Telephone: (213) 236-0641
Website: www.fka.com

Human Resources Consulting: Transitioning to the Future of HR
Length: 3 days   Cost: Contact Vendor
Location: Various, contact vendor
9155 Ft. Fisher Ct.
Burke, VA 22015
Telephone: (703) 425-4259
E-mail: trnsmatr@idsonline.com
Website: www.transitionmatters.com/

Serious Performance Consulting
Length: 2 days   Cost: $995 (members), $1,095
Location: Various, contact vendor
International Society for Performance Improvement
1400 Spring Street, Suite 260
Silver Spring, MD 20910
Telephone: (301) 587-8570
E-mail: registration@ispi.com
Website: www.ispi.org

Building Fluent Performance for Results
Length: 2 days   Cost: $995 (members), $1,095
Location: Various, contact vendor
International Society for Performance Improvement
1400 Spring Street, Suite 260
Silver Spring, MD 20910
Telephone: (301) 587-8570
E-mail: registration@ispi.com
Website: www.ispi.org

Consulting Skills for Trainers: Collaborative Performance Improvement
Length: 3 days   Cost: $1,499
Location: Various, contact vendor

Langevin Learning Services
P.O. Box 1221
Ogdensburg, NY 13669-6221
Telephone: (800) 223-2209
E-mail: training@langevin.com
Website: http://www.langevin.com

Self-Study Options

These self-study options were selected for their content and appropriateness for the Human Performance Improvement field. This list is not intended to be comprehensive, nor is it intended to endorse or exclude any particular self-study option.

What Is Performance Technology? (web-based)
Cost: Free
San Diego State University
Website: coe.sdsu.edu/eet/Articles/hpt/index.htm

Other Development Opportunities

Work Collaboratively with an Experienced HPI Practitioner

This method offers the benefit of accomplishing actual client projects while building competence. Essentially, you want to help conduct all aspects of an HPI project. Your goal is not to provide much input, although based on your past experience you may find that you can. Your goal is to understand the thought processes and actions of the experienced practitioner. What questions do they ask and why? Of whom? What resources do they seek? Who gets involved in the project at each stage and why? How do they collect and analyze the data? How and to whom do they report the results? What interventions do they recommend and why? Basically, all aspects of the project are part of your curriculum for learning. The drawback of this form of development is that it tends to add time to the project. The experienced HPI practitioner, in addition to accomplishing the tasks of the project, must act as a teacher at every point in the project. It also will take a great deal of your time away from the tasks of your current job. This suggestion is probably the most effective way to develop not only a broad perspective on the field of HPI consulting but also will go a long way to develop the numerous competencies associated with HPI.

Seek a Shadow HPI Consultant/Coach

If your organization cannot afford to hire or utilize an experienced HPI consultant to work with you full-time on a performance improvement project, perhaps they could afford to hire or utilize one to guide you through most of the work. This relationship is sometimes referred to as shadow consulting or coaching. Essentially, you would meet, either in-person or via telephone, before every major step of the project and seek advice for how to proceed or receive feedback on tasks completed to date. This process does not work unless you have some level of skills and knowledge to achieve the tasks at hand. This method of development would work well in applying skills and knowledge learned via books, workshops or self-study options.

Section Three: Competency Development Resources

This section is for those who do not have the time or inclination to pursue a comprehensive academic solution to their skill and knowledge gaps and who are looking for more than a broad overview of HPI. This part of the resource guide will provide the following resources for developing each of the 40 competencies in *ASTD Models for Human Performance Improvement:*

- **Recommended readings:** Current publications that will provide knowledge and the foundation for skill development for the competency. Descriptions of these books are typically available at www.amazon.com and www. bn.com.
- **Workshops:** Publicly offered workshops that will help to development the competency. Descriptions of these workshops are typically available from each vendor's website, which is provided.
- **Self-study options:** Nonclassroom training solutions including self-study text, video, audio, computer-based training (CBT), and CD-ROM. Descriptions of these self-study options are typically available from each vendor's website, which is provided.
- **Other development opportunities:** A list of nontraditional ways to develop the competency.

Note: These resources were selected for their appropriateness to the Human Performance Improvement field. This list is not intended to be comprehensive nor is it intended to endorse or exclude any particular resource.

Core Competencies

The following section will provide resources for the 16 Core HPI Competencies.

Industry Awareness

Recommended Readings

> Annual reports
> Amazon.com or barnesandnoble.com, etc.
> Trade journals

Workshops

Contact industry associations and professional societies within your industry to obtain information about industry-specific conferences and workshops.

Other Development Opportunities

- Develop a relationship with a marketing or salesperson in the organization.
- Develop a relationship with a business leader in the organization.
- Review the organization's annual report.
- Explore company websites.
- Interview friends/relatives who work in the industry.
- Search the Internet for newsgroups, chat areas, and bulletin boards.
- Participate in associations and professional organizations.
- Subscribe to industry trade magazines and journals.

Leadership Skills

Recommended Readings

These readings were selected for their appropriateness to the Human Performance Improvement field. This list is not intended to be comprehensive, nor is it intended to endorse or exclude any particular book.

Leadership Development
Russell, Lou. Alexandria, VA: American Society of Training and Development, 2005
ISBN: 1-56286-395-9

Getting Things Done When You Are Not in Charge
Bellman, Geoffery M. San Francisco, CA: Berrett-Koehler 2001
ISBN: 1576751724

Influence Without Authority (2nd Edition)
Cohen, Allen R., and Bradford, David L. Hoboken, NJ: John Wiley & Sons (2005)
ISBN: 0471463302

Power, Influence, and Persuasion: Sell Your Ideas and Make Things Happen
Boston, MA: Harvard Business School Press (2005)
ISBN: 159139631X

Getting It Done: How to Lead When You're Not in Charge
Fisher, Roger, Sharp, Alan, and Richardson, John. New York, NY: HarperBusiness, 1998
ISBN: 0887308422

Reinventing Influence: How to Get Things Done in a World Without Authority
Bragg, Mary. Marshfield, MA: Pitman Publishing Ltd., 1997
ISBN: 0273623133

Power and Influence/Beyond Formal Authority
Kotter, John P. New York, NY: Free Press, 1985
ISBN: 0029183308

Workshops

These workshops were selected for their content and appropriateness for the Human Performance Improvement field. This list is not intended to be comprehensive, nor is it intended to endorse or exclude any particular workshop.

Positive Power & Influence
Length: 2–3 Days   Cost: Contact vendor

Location: Contact vendor
Nashua Office Park
98 Spit Brook Road, Suite 201
Nashua, NH 03062-5737
Telephone: (603) 897-1200
Website: www.smsinc.com
E-mail: info@smsinc.com

Getting Results Without Authority

Length: 3 days   Cost: $1,795 (AMA members), $1,995
Locations: Contact vendor
American Management Association
1601 Broadway
New York, NY 10019
Telephone: (800) 262-9699
Website: www.amanet.org/seminars/CMD2/2532.html

Becoming an Influential Leader: Defining Your Leadership Style

Length: 2 days   Cost: 2,995
Location: Contact vendor
Center for Business Excellence, St. Thomas Graduate School of
Business
Terrence Murphy Hall 166
1000 LaSalle Ave.
Minneapolis, MN 55403-2005
Telephone: (800) 328-6819
Website: http://www.stthomas.edu/cob/centers/cbe/
E-mail: cbe@stthomas.edu

Leadership Development for Human Resource Professionals

Length: 5 days   Cost: $6,600
Location: Colorado Springs, CO
Center for Creative Leadership
P.O. Box 26300
Greensboro, NC 27410-6300
Telephone: (336) 545-2810
Website: www.ccl.org/programs

Additional workshops can be found at www.firstseminar.com
Keywords: Leadership, Influence

Other Development Opportunities

- Seek out role models who exhibit good leadership at various levels of your organization and learn from them.
- Identify those people within your network of friends, family, and colleagues who have consistently won the support of others. Observe their behaviors. Seek advice/mentoring from these individuals.
- Seeking task force assignment that may fall outside your core responsibilities.
- Actively seeking feedback from others and know your limitation and strength, keep open to response to feedbacks.

Interpersonal Relationship Skills

Recommended Readings

These readings were selected for their appropriateness to the Human Performance Improvement field. This list is not intended to be comprehensive, nor is it intended to endorse or exclude any particular book.

How to Lead Work Teams: Facilitation Skills (2nd Edition)
Rees, Fran. San Francisco, CA: Jossey–Bass/Pfeiffer, 2001
ISBN: 0787956910

Human Relations and Your Career (3rd Edition)
Johnson David W. Englewood Cliffs, NJ: Prentice-Hall, 1996
ISBN: 013446253X

Human Relations and Your Career
Johnson, David W. Englewood Cliffs, NJ: Prentice-Hall, 1978
ISBN: 013446253X

People Styles at Work: Making Bad Relationships Good, and Good Relationships Better
Bolton, Robert, and Bolton, Dorothy G. New York, NY:
AMACOM, 1996
ISBN: 0814477232

Interpersonal Skills at Work
Hayes, John. New York, NY: Routledge, 2002
ISBN: 0415227755

Interpersonal Skills at Work (2nd Edition)
Guirdham, Maureen. Englewood Cliffs, NJ: Prentice Hall, 1995
ISBN: 0131495356

Self-Help Stuff That Works: How to Become More Effective with Your Actions and Feel Good More Often
Khan, Adam, and Evans, J.C. Bellevue, WA: YouMe Works, 1999
ISBN: 0962465674

Workshops

These workshops were selected for their content and appropriateness for the Human Performance Improvement field. This list is not intended to be comprehensive, nor is it intended to endorse or exclude any particular workshop.

Interpersonal Communications
The Management Center, St. Thomas Graduate School of Business
Length: 2 day   Cost: $695
Location: Contact vendor
Center for Business Excellence, St. Thomas Graduate School of Business
Terrence Murphy Hall 166
1000 LaSalle Ave.
Minneapolis, MN 55403-2005
Telephone: (800) 328-6819
Website: http://www.stthomas.edu/cob/centers/cbe/

Interpersonal Skills
Length: 3 days   Cost: $1,795 (members), $1,995
Location: Various, contact vendor
American Management Association
1601 Broadway
New York, NY 10019
Telephone: (800) 262-9699
Website: www.amanet.org

Building Better Work Relationships: New Techniques for Results-oriented Communication
Length: 3 days   Cost: $1,795 (members), $1,995
Location: Various, contact vendor
American Management Association

1601 Broadway
New York, NY 10019
Telephone: (800) 262-9699 or (212) 586-8100
E-mail: customerservice@amanet.org
Website: www.amanet.org

Improving Your People Skills
Length: 2 days   Cost: $995
Locations: Various, contact vendor
ILR School, Cornell University
309 Ives Hall
IThaca, NY 14853
Telephone: (212) 340-2874
Website: www.ilr.cornell.edu/mgmtprog

Additional workshops can be found at www.firstseminar.com
Keyword(s): Interpersonal Skills

Other Development Opportunities

Volunteer to run the United Way (or similar) campaign at work.

Technological Awareness and Understanding

Recommended Readings

These readings were selected for their appropriateness to the Human Performance Improvement field. This list is not intended to be comprehensive, nor is it intended to endorse or exclude any particular book.

Business Multimedia Explained: A Manager's Guide to Key Terms and Concepts
Keen, Peter G.W., Mougayer, Walid, and Torregrossa, Tracy. Boston, MA: Harvard Business School Press, 1998
ISBN: 0875848400

Train the Trainer, Volume 5: Applying Technology to Learning
Russo, Cat. Alexandria, VA: American Society for Training and Development, 2001
ISBN: 1562862820

The ASTD Media Selection Tool for Training and Performance Improvement
Marx, Raymond J. Alexandria, VA: American Society for Training and Development, 1999
ISBN: 1562861166

ASTD Models for Learning Technologies: Roles, Competencies, and Outputs
Piskurich, George M., and Sanders, Ethan S. Alexandria, VA: American Society for Training & Development, 1998
ISBN: 1562860836

Microsoft Office 2003 Resource Kit
Microsoft Corporation. Redmond, WA: Microsoft Press 2004
ISBN: 0735618801

Office 2003 All-in-One Desk Reference for Dummies
Weverka, Peter. Hoboken, NJ: Wiley 2003
ISBN: 0764538837

The Internet for Dummies
Levine, John R., Young, Margaret L., and Baroudi, Carol. Hoboken, NJ: Wiley 2005
ISBN: 0764589962

Web-Based Training: Designing e-learning
Driscoll Margaret. San Francisco, CA: Jossey-Bass/Pfeiffer, 2002
ISBN: 0787956198

Multimedia-Based Instructional Design: Computer-Based Training; Web-based Training; Distance Broadcast Training; Performance-Based Solutions (2nd Edition)
Lee, William W., and Owens, Diana L. San Francisco, CA: Jossey-Bass/Pfeiffer, 2000
ISBN: 0787970697

Web-Based Training Cookbook
Hall, Brandon. New York, NY: John Wiley & Sons, 1997
ISBN: 0471180211

Workshops

These workshops were selected for their content and appropriateness for the Human Performance Improvement field. This list is not intended to be comprehensive, nor is it intended to endorse or exclude any particular workshop.

Develop Web-Based Training
Length: 3 days   Cost: $495
Location: Contact vendor
ASK International
Telephone: (800) 547-2476
Website: www.askintl.com

Developing Web-Based Training (WBT) Storyboards
Length: 3 days   Cost: $495
Location: Contact vendor
ASK International
Telephone: (800) 547-2476
Website: www.askintl.com

E-Learning Instructional Design Certificate Program
Length: 2 days   Cost: $895 (member), $1,095
P.O. Box 1567
Merrifield, VA 22116-1567
Telephone: (800) 628 2783

Additional workshops can be found at www.firstseminar.com
Keywords: Microsoft, Computer, Multimedia

Self-Study Options

These self-study options were selected for their content and appropriateness for the Human Performance Improvement field. This list is not intended to be comprehensive, nor is it intended to endorse or exclude any particular self-study option.

Web-Based Training (Internet-based)
Cost: $695
eSOCRATES
425 Pheasant Ridge Road

Lewisburg, PA 17837
Telephone: (570) 523-0030
Website: www.esocrates.com

Microsoft® Office 2003 (Video-based)
Cost: $132.99–$182.99
Business Advantage, Inc.
4900 University Ave.
West Des Moines, IA 50266
Telephone: (800) 305-9044
E-mail: info@businessvideos.com
Website: www.businessvideos.com

Additional self-study options can be found at www.businessvideos.com or www.careertrack.com.

Other Development Opportunities

- Schedule brown-bag seminars over lunch periodically, featuring how individuals are using technology to improve their job performance.
- Interview or mentor with computer-savvy individuals in your workgroup.

Problem-Solving Skills

Recommended Readings

These readings were selected for their appropriateness to the Human Performance Improvement field. This list is not intended to be comprehensive nor is it intended to endorse or exclude any particular book.

101 Creative Problem Solving Techniques: The Handbook of New Ideas for Business
Higgins, James M. Winter Park, FL: New Management Publishing Company, 2005
ISBN: 1883629055

Problem-Solving & Decision-Making Tool Kit
Wildman, Paul, and Warner Jon. Amherst, MA: HRD Press, 2003
ISBN: 0874257212

The Problem Solving Journey: Your Guide for Making Decision and Getting Results
Hoening, Christopher. Project Management Institute, 2000
ISBN: 0738202800

Decision Analysis in Projects
Schuyler, John R. Newtown, PA: Project Management Institute
Publications, 1996
ISBN: 1880410397

Creative Problem Solving (Barrons Business Success Guide)
Noone, Donald J. New York, NY: Barrons Educational Series, 1998
ISBN: 0764104039

Problem Solving for Results
Roth, William, Roth, William F., Voehl, Frank, and Ryder, James. Boca Raton, FL: Saint Lucie Press, 1996
ISBN: 1574440187

The Business Analyzer and Planner: The Unique Process for Solving Problems, Finding Opportunities and Making Better Decisions Every Day
Zambruski, Michael, S. New York, NY: AMACOM, 1998
ISBN: 0814479847

Workshops

These workshops were selected for their content and appropriateness for the Human Performance Improvement field. This list is not intended to be comprehensive, nor is it intended to endorse or exclude any particular workshop.

Problem Solving & Decision Making
Length: 2–3 days   Cost: Contact vendor
Location: Various
Schedule via First Seminar, ID #3241
Website: www.firstseminar.com

Critical Thinking for Problem Solving
Length: 3 days   Cost: $595
Location: Contact vendor
Management Concepts, Inc.
8230 Leesburg Pike, Suite 800

Vienna, VA 22182
Telephone: (703) 790-9595
E-mail: info@mgmtconcepts.com
Website: www.managementconcepts.com

Problem Solving & Decision Making
Length: 2 days   Cost: $995
Location: Various, contact vendor
Cornell University
16 E. 34th Street
New York, NY 10016
Telephone: (212) 340-2819
Website: www.ilr.cornell.edu/mgmtprog

Additional workshops can be found at www.firstseminar.com
Keywords: Problem Solving

Self-Study Options

These self-study options were selected for their content and appropriateness for the Human Performance Improvement field. This list is not intended to be comprehensive, nor is it intended to endorse or exclude any particular self-study option.

Creative Problem Solving (Audio/Text-based)
Cost: $155, $30 for additional workbooks
American Management Association
1601 Broadway
New York, NY 10019
Telephone: (800) 250-5308 or (800) 262-9699
E-mail: cust_serv@amanet.org
Website: www.amanet.org

Practical Problem-Solving Skills in the Workplace (Text-based)
Cost: $139
American Management Association—Extension Institute
1601 Broadway
New York, NY 10019
Telephone: (800) 250-5308 or (800) 262-9699
E-mail: cust_serv@amanet.org
Website: www.amanet.org

Other Development Opportunities

- Observe a colleague facilitate a team through a problem-solving exercise.
- Identify a current problem in your home or workplace, and involve members of your family or workgroup to list potential causes of the problem and corresponding solutions.

Systems Thinking and Understanding

Recommended Readings

These readings were selected for their appropriateness to the Human Performance Improvement field. This list is not intended to be comprehensive, nor is it intended to endorse or exclude any particular book.

The Fifth Discipline: The Art and Practice of the Learning Organization
Senge, Peter M. New York, NY: Doubleday/Currency, 2006
ISBN: 0385517254

The Fifth Discipline Fieldbook: Strategies and Tools for Building a Learning Organization
Senge, Peter M., Kleiner, Art, Roberts, Charlotte, Ross, Rick, and Smith, Bryan (eds.), New York, NY: Doubleday/Currency, 1994
ISBN: 0385472560

The Learning Alliance: Systems Thinking in Human Resource Development
Brinkerhoff, Robert O., and Gill, Stephen J., San Francisco, CA: Jossey-Bass Publishers, 1994
ISBN: 1555427111

System Thinking Basics: From Concepts to Causal Loops
Anderson, Virginia, and Johnson Lauren. Waltham, MA: Pegasus Communications, 1997
ISBN: 1883823129

Seeing Systems: Unlocking the Mysteries of Organizational Life
Oshry, Barry. San Francisco, CA: Berrett-Koehler Publishers, Inc., 1996
ISBN: 1881052990

Workshops

These workshops were selected for their content and appropriateness for the Human Performance Improvement field. This list is not intended to be comprehensive, nor is it intended to endorse or exclude any particular workshop.

Systems Thinking: A Language for Learning and Action™

Length: 3 days   Cost: 1,950 (member), $2,450
Location: Contact vendor
Innovation Associates Organization Learning
Telephone: (508) 435-7999
E-mail: mrginhop@aol.com
Website: www.innovationassociates.com

Beyond Reengineering: Partner-Centered Performance

Length: Contact the vendor   Cost: $375
Location: Various, contact vendor
Systems Thinking Institute
Website: www.skerja.net/systhink/int2.html

The Logical Thinking Process

Length: 6 days   Cost: Contact vendor
Location: Contact vendor
Goal Systems International
111 Hurricane View Lane
Port Angeles, WA 98362
Telephone: (360) 565-8300
Website: www.goalsys.com
E-mail: gsi@goalsys.com

Systems Thinking for Project Managers

Length: 1 day   Cost: $395
Location: Contact vendor
Center for Business Excellence, St. Thomas Graduate School of Business
Terrence Murphy Hall 166
1000 LaSalle Ave.
Minneapolis, MN 55403-2005
Telephone: (800) 328-6819
Website: http://www.stthomas.edu/cob/centers/cbe/

Systems Thinking
Length: 2 days　　　Cost: $1,395
Location: Various, contact vendors
Linkage Incorporated
16 New England Executive Park, Suite 205
Burlington, MA 01803
Telephone: (781) 402-5555
Website: www.linkageinc.com
E-mail: info@linkage.com

Additional workshops can be found at www.firstseminar.com
Keywords: Systems Thinking

Self-Study Options

These self-study options were selected for their content and appropriateness for the Human Performance Improvement field. This list is not intended to be comprehensive, nor is it intended to endorse or exclude any particular self-study option.

Leadership & Systems Thinking (Web-based)
Cost: Contact vendor
The University of the Future
P.O. Box 882493
San Francisco, CA 94188-2493
Telephone: (415) 824-7726
Website: www.futureu.com

Activating the Fifth Discipline with Peter Senge (CD/ROM)
Cost: $295
Videolearning Systems, Inc.
850 Lancaster Avenue
Bryn Mawr, PA 19010
Telephone: (800) 622-3610 or (610) 526-9100
Website: www.videolrn.com

Other Development Opportunities

Go on a scavenger hunt within your organization for process flow maps, if they exist. Collect and study as many as possible. Interview those responsible for producing them.

Performance Understanding

Recommended Readings

These readings were selected for their appropriateness to the Human Performance Improvement field. This list is not intended to be comprehensive, nor is it intended to endorse or exclude any particular book.

Measuring Instructional Results (3rd Edition)
Mager, Robert F. Atlanta, GA: Center for Effective Performance, 1997
ISBN: 1879618168

Measuring Organizational Improvement Impact (Quality Improvement Series)
Chang, Richard Y., and Yong, Paul D. San Francisco, CA: Jossey-Bass Pfeiffer, 1999
ISBN: 0787951013

Measuring Organizational Improvement Impact: A Practical Guide to Successfully Linking Organizational Improvement Measures
Chang, Richard Y., and DeYoung, Paul H. Irvine, CA: Richard Chang Associates Inc., 1996
ISBN: 1883553172

Guidebook for Performance Improvement: Working with Individuals and Organizations
Kaufman, Roger, Thiagarajan, Sivasailam, and MacGillis, Paul.
San Francisco, CA: Jossey-Bass Publishers, 1996
ISBN: 0787903531

Workshops

These workshops were selected for their content and appropriateness for the Human Performance Improvement field. This list is not intended to be comprehensive, nor is it intended to endorse or exclude any particular workshop.

Evaluating Performance Improvement in the Workplace
Length: 3 days   Cost: $1,395 (member), $1,595
Location: Contact vendor
American Society for Training and Development
1640 King Street, Box 1443
Alexandria, VA 22313-2043

Telephone: (800) 628-2783 or (703) 683-8100
Website: www.astd.org

Performance Measurement: Measuring Your Organization's Efforts
Length: 2 days   Cost: $495
Location: Contact vendor
Management Concepts
8230 Leesburg Pike
Vienna, VA 22182
Telephone: (703) 790-9595
E-mail: info@mgmtconcepts.com
Website: www.managementconcepts.com

Additional workshops can be found at www.firstseminar.com
Keywords: Performance, Evaluation

Other Development Opportunities

Identify major initiatives of organizations you are associated with. Determine the results of those initiatives.

Knowledge of Interventions

Recommended Readings

These readings were selected for their appropriateness to the Human Performance Improvement field. This list is not intended to be comprehensive, nor is it intended to endorse or exclude any particular book.

Intervention Resource Guide: 50 Performance Improvement Tools
Langdon, Danny G. Whiteside, Kathleen S., and
McKenna, Monica M. (Editors). San Francisco, CA: Jossey-Bass
Publishers, 1999
ISBN: 0787944017

Organizational Development: Behavioral Science Interventions for Organization Improvement (6th Edition)
French, Wendell L., and Bell, Jr., Cecil H. Englewood Cliffs, NJ:
Prentice Hall College Div, 1999
ISBN: 013242231X

The OD Source Book: A Practitioner's Guide
Frame, Robert M., Hess, Randy K., and Nielsen, Warren. San Diego, CA:
Pfeiffer & Company, 1982
ISBN: 0883901722

50 Ways to Teach Your Learner: Activities and Interventions for Building High-Performance Teams
Rose, Ed, and Buckley, Steve (Contributor). San Francisco, CA:
Jossey-Bass Publishers, 1999
ISBN: 0787945048

Large Group Interventions: Engaging the Whole System for Rapid Change
Bunker, Barbara Benedict, and Alban, Billie T. San Francisco, CA:
Jossey-Bass Publishers, 1996
ISBN: 0787903248

Practicing Organization Development: A Guide for Consultants
Rothwell, William J. San Francisco, CA: Pfeiffer, 2005
ISBN: 0787962384

Future Search: An Action Guide to Finding Common Ground in Organizations and Communities
Weisbord, Marvin R., and Janoff, Sandra. San Francisco, CA:
Berrett-Koehler Publishers, Inc., 1995
ISBN: 1881052125

The Search Conference: A Powerful Method for Planning Organizational Change and Community Action
Emery, Merrelyn, and Purser, Ronald E. San Francisco, CA:
Jossey-Bass Publishers, 1996
ISBN: 078790192X

Intervention Skills: Process Consultation for Small Groups and Teams
Reddy, W. Brendan. San Diego, CA: Pfeiffer & Company, 1995
ISBN: 0883904349

The Guidebook for Performance Improvement: Working with Individuals and Organizations
Kaufman, Roger, Thiagarajan, Sivasailam, and MacGillis, Paul.
San Francisco, CA: Jossey-Bass Publishers, 1996
ISBN: 0787903531

Reengineering the Corporation: A Manifesto for Business Revolution (Collins Business Essentials)
Hammer, Michael, and Champy, James. New York, NY: HarperCollins, 2003
ISBN: 0060559535

Fieldbook of Team Interventions: A Step-by-Step Guide to High-Performance Teams
Eggletson, C. H. Amherst, MA: HRD Press, 1996
ISBN: 087425325X

The Intervention Selector, Designer, & Developer [Quick Reference Guides (DDC)]
Rothwell, William J. Alexandra, VA: ASTD Press, 2000
ISBN: 1562861425

Performance Intervention Maps (2nd Edition)
Sanders, Ethan S., and Thiagarajan Sivasailam. Alexandria, VA: ASTD Press, 2005
ISBN: 1562864149

Workshops

These workshops were selected for their content and appropriateness for the Human Performance Improvement field. This list is not intended to be comprehensive, nor is it intended to endorse or exclude any particular workshop.

Selecting and Managing Interventions
Length: 3 days   Cost: $1,395 (member), $1,595
Location: Contact vendor
American Society for Training and Development
1640 King Street, Box 1443
Alexandria, VA 22313-2043
Telephone: (800) 628-2783 or (703) 683-8100
Website: www.astd.org

Group Process Consultation: A Practical Diagnostic and Intervention Approach
Length: 6 days   Cost: $2,300
Location: Contact vendor
NTL Institute

300 N. Lee Street, Suite 300
Alexandria, VA 22314-2630
Telephone: (800) 777-5227 or (703) 548-1500
E-mail: info@ntl.org
Website: www.ntl.org

Additional workshops can be found at www.firstseminar.com
Keywords: Organizational development, Intervention

Other Development Opportunities

- Interview/mentor with practitioners in the quality, OD, strategic planning departments in your organization.
- Volunteer to lead an intervention for organizations in your community.
- Volunteer your services to a professional association.

Business Understanding

Recommended Readings

These readings were selected for their appropriateness to the Human Performance Improvement field. This list is not intended to be comprehensive, nor is it intended to endorse or exclude any particular book.

The Complete MBA Companion: The Latest in Management Thinking from the World's Leading Business Schools
IMD. Marshfield, MA: Pitman Publishing Ltd, 1997
ISBN: 0273627295

Understanding Business (7th Edition)
Nickels, William G., McHugh, James M., and McHugh, Susan. McGraw-Hill/Irwin, 2004
ISBN: 0072922184

Complete Idiot's Guide to MBA Basics (2nd Edition)
Gorman, Tom. Indianapolis: IN: Alpha Books, 2003
ISBN: 0028644492

The 12-Hour MBA Program: The Key Concepts and Techniques in a Fraction of the Time
Sobel, Milo. Englewood Cliffs, NJ: Prentice Hall Trade, 1993
ISBN: 0130453528

The Ten-Day MBA: A Step-by-Step Guide to Mastering the Skills Taught in America's Top Business Schools
Silbiger, Steven. New York, NY: William Morrow, 1999
ISBN: 0688137881

Workshops

These workshops were selected for their content and appropriateness for the Human Performance Improvement field. This list is not intended to be comprehensive, nor is it intended to endorse or exclude any particular workshop.

Fundamentals of Finance and Accounting for Nonfinancial Managers
Length: 3 days   Cost: $1,795 (members), $1,995
Location: Various, contact vendor
American Management Association
1601 Broadway
New York, NY 10019
Telephone: (800) 262-9699 or (212) 586-8100
E-mail: customerservice@amanet.org
Website: www.amanet.org

Human Resource Business School: Aligning Human Resource to Business Strategies
Length: 6 days   Cost: $4,000
Location: Philadelphia, PA
Wharton Executive Education
255 South 38th Street
Philadelphia, PA 19104-6359
Telephone: (800) 255-3932 or (215) 898-4560
E-mail: execed@wharton.upenn.edu
Website: www.wharton.com/execed

BIZ WIZ®
Length: 1 day   Cost: Contact vendor
Location: Various, contact vendor
The Business Center
120 Westview Lane
Oak Ridge, TN 37830
Telephone: (865) 220-0774
Website: www.bizcenter.com/universal.htm

Certificate in Essentials of Business Administration^{sm} **Seminar**

Length: 4.5 days   Cost: $2,075

Location: Various, contact vendor

Institute for Applied Management & Law, Inc.

610 Newport Center Drive, Suite 1060

Newport Beach, CA 92660

Telephone: (949) 760-1700

Website: www.iaml.com

Non-Financial Manager's Guide to Understanding Financial Statements

Length: 1 days   Cost: $299

Location: Various, contact vendor

National Seminars Group

P.O. Box 419107

Kansas City, MO 64141-6107

Telephone: (800) 258-7246 or (913) 432-7755

E-mail: onsite@natsem.com

Website: www.natsem.com

Additional workshops can be found at www.firstseminar.com and www.alx.org

Keywords: Business, business administration, business and finance, human resource management

Self-Study Options

These self-study options were selected for their content and appropriateness for the Human Performance Improvement field. This list is not intended to be comprehensive, nor is it intended to endorse or exclude any particular self-study option.

BIZ WIZ® Universal (Workbook)

Cost: $53.90 plus shipping

The Business Center

120 Westview Lane

Oak Ridge, TN 37830

Telephone: (865) 220-0774

Website: www.bizcenter.com/universal.htm

A Manager's Guide to Financial Analysis (5th Edition)
Cost: $189
American Management Association—Extension Institute
1601 Broadway
New York, NY 10019
Telephone: (800) 262-9699 or (212) 586-8100
E-mail: customerservice@amanet.org
Website: www.amanet.org

Finance and Accounting for Nonfinancial Managers
(Audio/Text-based)
Cost: $159
American Management Association—Extension Institute
1601 Broadway
New York, NY 10019
Telephone: (800) 262-9699 or (212) 586-8100
E-mail: customerservice@amanet.org
Website: www.amanet.org

Beyond the Basics: Intermediate Finance and Accounting for Nonfinancial Managers
Cost: $139
American Management Association—Extension Institute
1601 Broadway
New York, NY 10019
Telephone: (800) 262-9699 or (212) 586-8100
E-mail: customerservice@amanet.org
Website: www.amanet.org

Fundamentals of Finance for Nonfinancial Managers, Version 2.0
(CD/ROM)
Cost: $265.50 (members), $295
American Management Association
1601 Broadway
New York, NY 10019
Telephone: (800) 262-9699 or (212) 586-8100
E-mail: customerservice@amanet.org
Website: www.amanet.org

Other Development Opportunities

- Interview a business or operations manager.
- Contact your local colleges and universities for an introduction to business course/workshop.
- Request a temporary assignment in a business oriented department like strategic planning, finance or operations.

Organization Understanding

Recommended Readings

These readings were selected for their appropriateness to the Human Performance Improvement field. This list is not intended to be comprehensive, nor is it intended to endorse or exclude any particular book.

Changing Bureaucracies
Medina, William Antonio. New York, NY: Marcel Dekker, Inc., 1982
ISBN: 0824716728

Improving Performance: How to Manage the White Space on the Organization Chart (2nd Edition)
Rummler, G.A., and Brache, A.P. San Francisco, CA: Jossey-Bass Publishers, 1995
ISBN: 0787900907

Behavior in Organizations: Understanding and Managing the Human Side of Work (8th Edition)
Greenberg, Jerald, and Baron, Robert A. Englewood Cliffs, NJ: Prentice Hall, 2002
ISBN: 013066491X

Understanding Organizations (4th Edition)
Handy, Charles. Oxford, UK: Oxford University Press, 1993
ISBN: 0195087321

Reframing Organizations: Artistry, Choice, and Leadership (3rd Edition)
Bolman, Lee G., and Deal, Terrence E.
San Francisco, CA: Jossey- Bass, 2003
ISBN: 0787964271

Workshops

These workshops were selected for their content and appropriateness for the Human Performance Improvement field. This list is not intended to be comprehensive, nor is it intended to endorse or exclude any particular workshop.

Integrating OD Theory and Practice

Length: 6 days   Cost: $2,300

Location: Stowe, VT

NTL Institute

300 North Lee Street, Suite 300

Alexandria, VA 22314-2630

Telephone: (800) 777-5227 or (703) 548-1500

E-mail: info@ntl.org

Website: www.ntl.org

Additional workshops can be found at www.firstseminar.com

Keyword: Organization

Self-Study Options

No self-study options were found for this competency.

Other Development Opportunities

- Attend company orientation programs.
- Establish relationships with functional managers.
- Explore company websites.
- Read company newsletters, press releases, etc.
- Review company organization charts.

Negotiating/Contracting Skills

Recommended Readings

These readings were selected for their appropriateness to the Human Performance Improvement field. This list is not intended to be comprehensive, nor is it intended to endorse or exclude any particular book.

How to Select and Use Consultants: A Client's Guide, 2nd Impression
Kubr, Milan. Geneva, Switzerland: International Labor Office, 1997
ISBN: 9221085171

The Outsourcing Handbook: How to Implement a Successful Outsourcing Process
Power, Mark J., Desouza, Kevin, and Bonifazi, Carlo. Philadelphia, PA: Kogan Page
ISBN: 0749444304

Outsourcing: A Guide to Selecting the Correct Business Unit, Negotiating the Contract, Maintaining Control of the Process
Bragg, Stephen M. New York, NY: John Wiley & Sons, Incorporated, 1998
ISBN: 0471247286

Hiring Independent Contractors: The Employer's Legal Guide (Working with Independent Contractors) (4th Bk & CDR Edition)
Fishman, Stephen, and Delpo, Amy. Berkeley, CA: Nolo, 2003
ISBN: 0873379187

Getting the Most Out of Your Consultant: A Guide to Selection Through Implementation
Fuller, Gordon. Boca Raton, FL: CRC Press, 1998
ISBN: 0849380073

Consultant and Independent Contractor Agreements (5th Edition)
Fishman Stephen. Berkeley, CA: Nolo Press, 2005
ISBN: 1413303730

The Anatomy of Persuasion
Aubuchon, Norbert. New York, NY: AMACOM, 1997
ISBN: 0814479529

Selecting and Working with Consultants: A Guide for Clients
Ucko, Thomas J., and Crisp, Michael G. Menlo Park, CA: Crisp Publications., Inc., 1990
ISBN: 0931961874

Business Negotiating Basics (The Briefcase Books)
Economy, Peter. New York, NY: Irwin Professional Publishing, 1993
ISBN: 155623841X

Outsourcing Training & Education
DeRose, Garry J. Alexandria, VA: American Society for Training and
Development, 1999
ISBN: 1562861123

Workshops

These workshops were selected for their content and appropriateness for the
Human Performance Improvement field. This list is not intended to be comprehensive, nor is it intended to endorse or exclude any particular workshop.

Bargaining and Negotiating: A Learning Laboratory
Length: 4 days   Cost: $5,200–5,400
Location: Contact vendor
University of Virginia
Darden Executive Education
P.O. Box 7186
Charlottesville, VA 22906-7186
Telephone: (877) 833-3974
E-mail: Darden_Exed@virginia.edu
Website: www.darden.virginia.edu

Becoming a Better Negotiator
Length: 3 days   Cost: $1,695
Location: Madison, WI
University of Wisconsin-Madison
Executive Education, School of Business
601 University Avenue
Madison, WI 53706-1035
Telephone: (800) 292-8964 or (608) 441-7357
Website: www.wisc.edu/mi

Additional workshops can be found at www.firstseminar.com
Keywords: Negotiating, Contracting

Self-Study Options

These self-study options were selected for their content and appropriateness for
the Human Performance Improvement field. This list is not intended to be
comprehensive, nor is it intended to endorse or exclude any particular self-study
option.

Interpersonal Negotiations: Breaking Down the Barriers
(Text-based)
Cost: $139
American Management Association
1601 Broadway
New York, NY 10019
Telephone: (800) 262-9699 or (212) 586-8100
E-mail: customerservice@amanet.org or cust_serv@amanet.org
Website: www.amanet.org

Successful Negotiating (text-based)
Cost: $139
American Management Association
1601 Broadway
New York, NY 10019
Telephone: (800) 262-9699 or (212) 586-8100
E-mail: customerservice@amanet.org
Website: www.amanet.org

Other Development Opportunities

- Develop a relationship with a purchasing manager.
- Seek an opportunity to sit in on a contract negotiation.
- Review contracts that have been used in the past in your organization.
- Interview your vendors on their experience with contracts.

Buy-in/Advocacy Skills

Recommended Readings

These readings were selected for their appropriateness to the Human Performance Improvement field. This list is not intended to be comprehensive, nor is it intended to endorse or exclude any particular book.

HRD Survival Skills: Essential Strategies to Promote Training and Development Within Your Organization
Levant, Jessica. Houston, TX: Gulf Publishing Company, 1998
ISBN: 0884152707

Think Like a Lawyer: How to Get What You Want by Using Advocacy Skills
Dudley, Robert J. Chicago, IL: Nelson-Hall Company, 1980
ISBN: 0882295713

Influence: Portable Power for the '90s
Zuker, Elaina. Menlo Park, CA: Crisp Publications, Inc., 1995
ISBN: 1560522755

Influencing Others: Successful Strategies for Persuasive Communication
Nothstine, William. Menlo Park, CA: Crisp Publications, Inc., 1989
ISBN: 093196184X

Selling Skills for HR Professionals: How to Obtain Support for Ideas and New Programs
Markowich, M. Michael. Scottsdale, AZ: American Compensation Association, 1997
ISBN: 1579630529

Workshops

These workshops were selected for their content and appropriateness for the Human Performance Improvement field. This list is not intended to be comprehensive, nor is it intended to endorse or exclude any particular workshop.

Write to Get the Results You Want from Clients, Top Management, and Colleagues
Length: 2 days   Cost: $1,495 (members), $1,695
Location: Contact vendor
The American Management Association
1601 Broadway
New York, NY 10019
Telephone: (800) 262-9699 or (212) 586-8100
E-mail: customerservice@amanet.org
Website: www.amanet.org

Persuasion and Influence Skills for Project Managers
Length: 3 days   Cost: $1,595–$1,795
Location: Madison, WI
University of Wisconsin-Madison
Executive Education, School of Business

601 University Avenue
Madison, WI 53706-1035
Telephone: (800) 292-8964 or (608) 441-7357
Website: www.wisc.edu/mi

Additional workshops can be found at www.firstseminar.com
Keywords: Influence, Persuasion

Other Development Opportunities

Identify someone who frequently is able to generate support for his/her ideas. Find opportunities to observe that person when they are seeking support. Ask that person to be your mentor.

Coping Skills

Recommended Readings

These readings were selected for their appropriateness to the Human Performance Improvement field. This list is not intended to be comprehensive, nor is it intended to endorse or exclude any particular book.

Dancing with Fear: Controlling Stress and Creating a Life Beyond Panic and Anxiety
Foxman, Paul. Alameda: CA, Hunter House, 2006
ISBN: 0897934768

Dancing with Fear: Overcoming Anxiety in a World of Stress and Uncertainty
Foxman, Paul. Northvale, NJ: Jason Aronson Publishers, 1997
ISBN: 0765701502

Harvard Business Review on Managing Uncertainty (The Harvard Business Review Paperback Series)
Boston, MA: Harvard Business School Press, 1999
ISBN: 0875849083

Don't Sweat the Small Stuff at Work: Simple Ways to Minimize Stress and Conflict While Bringing Out the Best in Yourself and Others
Carlson, Richard. Sunnyvale, CA: Hyperion, 1998
ISBN: 0786883367

Workshops

These workshops were selected for their content and appropriateness for the Human Performance Improvement field. This list is not intended to be comprehensive, nor is it intended to endorse or exclude any particular workshop.

Journey Into Relaxation
Cost: Contact vendor
Stress Solutions, Inc.
Telephone: (212) 229-7779
E-mail: info@stress-solutions.com
Website: www.stress-solutions.com/index.htm

Creating Value by Managing the Source of Your Stress
Length: 2 hours–one day   Cost: Contact vendor
Roger Reece Seminars
1425 Market Blvd, Suite 330-250
Roswell, GA 30076 (Atlanta)
Telephone: (770) 642-9298
Email: info@rogerreece.com
Website: www.rogerreece.com/index.html

Additional workshops can be found at www.firstseminar.com.
Keywords: Coping, Stress, Ambiguity

Self-Study Options

These self-study options were selected for their content and appropriateness for the Human Performance Improvement field. This list is not intended to be comprehensive, nor is it intended to endorse or exclude any particular self-study option.

Managing Stress for Mental Fitness (CD/ROM/Audio/Text-based)
Cost: $199 (for site-license)
Thomson Learning Course Technology
Telephone: (800) 354-9706 or (203) 539-8000
E-mail: eSales@thomsonlearning.com
Website: www.courseilt.com

How to Manage Stress (video)
Cost: $199.95
CareerTrack, Inc.

Telephone: (800) 780-8476
Website: www.careertrack.com

Other Development Opportunities

- List 25 things that you're currently tolerating in your life. Identify ways to eliminate half of these tolerances in the next six months.
- Ask to be temporarily assigned into a higher-pressure position, either within your field, or outside of your field.

The Ability to See the Big Picture

Recommended Readings

These readings were selected for their appropriateness to the Human Performance Improvement field. This list is not intended to be comprehensive, nor is it intended to endorse or exclude any particular book.

The Dynamic Enterprise: Tools for Turning Chaos into Strategy and Strategy into Action
Friedman, Lisa, and Gyr, Herman (Contributor). San Francisco, CA:
Jossey Bass Publishers, 1997
ISBN: 0787910147

The 8 Practices of Exceptional Companies: How Great Organizations Make the Most of Their Human Assets
New York, NY: AMACOM, 2005
ISBN: 0814473237

Choosing the Future: The Power of Strategic Thinking
Wells, Stuart. Boston, MA: Butterworth-Heinemann (Trd), 1997
ISBN: 0750698764

Developing Strategic Thought (New edition)
Garratt, Bob. Profile Business, 2003
ISBN: 1861976593

Don't Jump to Solutions: Thirteen Delusions That Undermine Strategic Thinking
Rouse, William B. San Francisco, CA: Jossey-Bass Publishers, 1998
ISBN: 078790998X

Organization Theory: A Strategic Approach (6th Edition)
Hodge, B. J., Anthony, William P., and Gales Lawrence M. Upper Saddle
River, NJ: Prentice Hall
ISBN: 0130330647

**Strategic Thinking and the New Science: Planning in the Midst of Chaos,
Complexity, and Change**
Sanders, T. Irene. New York, NY: Simon & Schuster, 1998
ISBN: 0684842688

Workshops

These workshops were selected for their content and appropriateness for the
Human Performance Improvement field. This list is not intended to be comprehensive, nor is it intended to endorse or exclude any particular workshop.

Strategic Human Resources Planning
Length: 2 days   Cost: $1,095
Location: Contact vendor
ILR School, Cornell University
309 Ives Hall
IThaca, NY 14853
Telephone: (212) 340-2874
Website: www.ilr.cornell.edu/mgmtprog

Tools and Techniques for Thinking and Managing Strategically
Length: 3 days   Cost: $1,895 (members), $2,095
Location: Contact vendor
American Management Association
1601 Broadway
New York, NY 10019
Telephone: (800) 262-9699 or (212) 586-8100
E-mail: customerservice@amanet.org

Additional workshops can be found at www.firstseminar.com
Keyword: Strategic thinking

Self-Study Options

These self-study options were selected for their content and appropriateness for
the Human Performance Improvement field. This list is not intended to be

comprehensive, nor is it intended to endorse or exclude any particular self-study option.

Scenario Thinking: Pathway to the Future (VHS/DVD)
Cost: $195 (rental), $795 (purchase)
LearnCom, Inc.
38 Discovery, Suite 250
Irvine, CA 92618
Telephone: (800) 622-3610
E-mail: sales@learncom.com
Website: ww.learncom.com

Other Development Opportunities

Interview a corporate executive. Determine how they are able to focus on overall goals without getting mired in the details of achieving them.

Consulting Skills

Recommended Readings

These readings were selected for their appropriateness to the Human Performance Improvement field. This list is not intended to be comprehensive, nor is it intended to endorse or exclude any particular book.

Flawless Consulting: A Guide to Getting Your Expertise Used
Block, Peter. San Francisco, CA: Jossey-Bass/Pfeiffer, 1999
ISBN: 0787948039

The Flawless Consulting Fieldbook and Companion: A Guide to Understanding Your Expertise
Block, Peter, and Markowitz, Andrea. San Francisco, CA: Jossey-Bass/Pfeiffer, 2000
ISBN: 0787948047

Organizational Consulting: How to Be an Effective Internal Change Agent
Weiss, Alan. Hoboken, NJ: Wiley & Sons, 2003
ISBN: 0471263788

High-Performance Consulting Skills: The Internal Consultant's Guide to Value-Added Performance
Thomas, Mark. Thorogood, 2004
ISBN: 1854182587

The Business of Consulting: The Basics and Beyond
Biech, Elaine. San Diego, CA: Pfeiffer & Company, 1998
ISBN: 0787940216

The Internal Consultant
Meislin, Marcia C. Menlo Park, CA: Crisp Publications, 1997
ISBN: 1560524170

Secrets of Consulting: A Guide to Giving and Getting Advice Successfully
Weinberg, Gerald M. New York, NY: Dorset House, 1986
ISBN: 0932633013

Workshops

These workshops were selected for their content and appropriateness for the Human Performance Improvement field. This list is not intended to be comprehensive, nor is it intended to endorse or exclude any particular workshop.

Consultation Skills
Length: 6 days   Cost: $2,300
Location: Contact vendor
NTL Institute
300 N. Lee Street, Suite 300
Alexandria, VA 22314-2607
Telephone: (800) 777-5227 or (703) 548-1500
E-mail: info@ntl.org
Website: www.ntl.org

Consulting Skills for HR Professionals
Length: 2 days   Cost: $1,395
Location: Contact vendor
Linkage Incorporated
1 Forbes Road
Lexington, MA 02421
Telephone: (781) 862-3157
Website: www.linkageinc.com

Advanced Consulting: Confidence and Power in Your Approach
Length: 2 days   Cost: $1,395
Location: Contact vendor
Linkage Incorporated
1 Forbes Road
Lexington, MA 02421
Telephone: (781) 862-3157
E-mail: info@linkageein.com
Website: www.linkageinc.com

Corporate Mirror^{sm} Hands-on Training in Organization Development Consulting Skills
Length: 4 days   Cost: $1,695
Location: Contact vendor
Strategic Development, Inc.
Research Triangle Park, NC
Telephone: (800) 849-8326
E-mail: gsmart@strategicdevelopment.com
Website: www.strategicdevelopment.com

Flawless Consulting 1: Contracting
Length: 2 days   Cost: $950
Location: Redbank, NJ
Designed Learning, Inc.
313 South Avenue, Suite 202
Fanwood, NJ 07023
Telephone: (908) 889-0300
E-mail: info@designedlearning.com
Website: www.designedlearning.com

Flawless Consulting 2: Discovery
Length: 2 days   Cost: $950
Location: Redbank, NJ
Designed Learning, Inc.
313 South Avenue, Suite 202
Fanwood, NJ 07023
Telephone: (908) 889-0300
E-mail: info@designedlearning.com
Website: www.designedlearning.com

Flawless Consulting 3: Implementation
Length: 2 days　　　Cost: $950
Location: Redbank, NJ
Designed Learning, Inc.
313 South Avenue, Suite 202
Fanwood, NJ 07023
Telephone: (908) 889-0300
E-mail: info@designedlearning.com
Website: www.designedlearning.com

Advanced Internal Consulting Skills: The "What" and "How" of Attaining Results
Length: 2 days　　　Cost: $1,095
Location: Contact vendor
ILR School, Cornell University
309 Ives Hall
Ithaca, NY 14853
Telephone: (212) 255-2223
Website: www.ilr.cornell.edu/mgmtprog

Additional workshops can be found at www.firstseminar.com
Keyword: Consulting

Other Development Opportunities

- Establish a relationship with an internal and/or external consultant.
- Observe internal/external consultants on the job.
- Think of something that you're knowledgeable or skilled in, and seek an opportunity to share that knowledge with others in a professional manner. (This could be inside or outside of the workplace.)

Project Management Skills

Recommended Readings

These readings were selected for their appropriateness to the Human Performance Improvement field. This list is not intended to be comprehensive, nor is it intended to endorse or exclude any particular book.

Managing Performance Improvement Projects: Preparing, Planning, and Implementing
Fuller, Jim. San Diego, CA: Pfeiffer & Company, 1997
ISBN: 0787909599

ID Project Management: Tools and Techniques for Instructional Designers and Developers
Greer, Michael. Englewood Cliffs, NJ: Educational Technology Publications, 1992
ISBN: 0877782377

Applying Project Management in the Workplace (3rd Edition)
Crow, Jeff. Portland, OR: Blackbird Publishing, 2000
ISBN: 0966046927

The Complete Idiot's Guide to Project Management
Baker, Sunny, Baker, Kim, and Campbell, G. Michael.
Indianapolis, IN: Alpha Books, 2003
ISBN: 1592571190

The Project Manager's Desk Reference
Lewis, James P. New York, NY: McGraw-Hill, 1999
ISBN: 007134750X

Getting a Project Done on Time: Managing People, Time, and Results
Williams, Paul B. New York, NY: AMACOM, 1996
ISBN: 0814402844

Fundamentals of Project Management: Developing Core Competencies to Help Outperform the Competition
Lewis, James P. New York, NY: AMACOM, 2002
ISBN: 0814471323

Additional readings can be found at www.pmi.org

Workshops

These workshops were selected for their content and appropriateness for the Human Performance Improvement field. This list is not intended to be comprehensive, nor is it intended to endorse or exclude any particular workshop.

Project Management for Trainers
Length: 2 days   Cost: $1,199
Location: Contract vendor
Langevin Learning Services
P.O. Box 1221
Ogdensburg, NY 13669-6221
Telephone: (800) 223-2209 or (613) 288-3064
Website: www.langevin.com

Project Management for Everyone (A Nontechnical Approach)
Length: 2 days   Cost: 1,195
Location: Contact vendor
Boston University Corporate Education Center
72 Tyngsboro Road
Tyngsboro, MA 01879-2099
Telephone: (800) 288-7246 or (978) 649-9731 x 255
Website: www.butrain.bu.edu/MDP

Project Management
Length: 1 day   Cost: $199
Location: Contact vendor
Fred Ryor Seminars & Career Track
9757 Metcalf Avenue
Overland Park, KS 66212
Telephone: (800) 780-8476
E-mail: customerservice@pryor.com
Website: www.pryor.com/index_Body.asp

Fundamentals of Effective Project Management
Length: 2 days   Cost: $499
Location: Contact vendor
National Seminars Group
P.O. Box 419107
Kansas City, MO 64141-6107
Telephone: (800) 258-7246 or (913) 432-7755
E-mail: info@natsem.com
Website: www.natsem.com

Improving Your Project Management Skills: The Basics for Success
Length: 3 days   Cost: $1,695 (member), $1,895

Location: Contact vendor
American Management Association
1601 Broadway
New York, NY 10019
Telephone: (800) 262-9699 or (212) 586-8100
E-mail: customerservice@amanet.org
Website: www.amanet.org/index.htm

Project Management
Length: 3 days   Cost: $1,695
Location: Contact vendor
Kepner-Tregoe, Incorporated
Research Road, P.O. Box 704
Princeton, NJ 08542
Telephone: (800) 537-6398 or (609) 921-2806
Website: www.kepner-tregoe.com

Additional workshops can be found at www.firstseminar.com.
Keywords: Project management

Self-Study Options

These self-study options were selected for their content and appropriateness
for the Human Performance Improvement field. This list is not intended to be
comprehensive, nor is it intended to endorse or exclude any particular self-
study option.

Project Management
Cost: $250 (rent), $870 (purchase)
LearnCom Inc.
38 Discovery, Suite 250
Irvine, CA 92618
Telephone: (800) 622-3610
Website: www.learncom.com

Project Management
Cost: $69
Fred Ryor Seminars & Career Track
9757 Metcalf Avenue
Overland Park, KS 66212

Telephone: (800) 780-8476
E-mail: customerservice@pryor.com

Online Project Scope Management
Cost: 695
Boston University Corporate Education Center
72 Tyngsboro Road
Tyngsboro, MA 01879-2099
Telephone: (800) 288-7246 or (978) 649-9731 x 255
Website: www.butrain.bu.edu/MDP

Online Project Human Resource Management
Cost: 695
Boston University Corporate Education Center
72 Tyngsboro Road
Tyngsboro, MA 01879-2099
Telephone: (800) 288-7246 or (978) 649-9731 x 255
Website: www.butrain.bu.edu/MDP

Online Project Time Management
Cost: 695
Boston University Corporate Education Center
72 Tyngsboro Road
Tyngsboro, MA 01879-2099
Telephone: (800) 288-7246 or (978) 649-9731 x 255
Website: www.butrain.bu.edu/MDP

Online Project Cost Management
Cost: 695
Boston University Corporate Education Center
72 Tyngsboro Road
Tyngsboro, MA 01879-2099
Telephone: (800) 288-7246 or (978) 649-9731 x 255
Website: www.butrain.bu.edu/MDP

Online Project Communications Management
Cost: 695
Boston University Corporate Education Center
72 Tyngsboro Road
Tyngsboro, MA 01879-2099

Telephone: (800) 288-7246 or (978) 649-9731 x 255
Website: www.butrain.bu.edu/MDP

Online Project Risk Management
Cost: 695
Boston University Corporate Education Center
72 Tyngsboro Road
Tyngsboro, MA 01879-2099
Telephone: (800) 288-7246 or (978) 649-9731 x 255
Website: www.butrain.bu.edu/MDP

Other Development Opportunities

- Locate and study formalized project plans.
- Solicit the assistance of a mentor/coach for managing a small project.
- Volunteer to assist in the planning of the next major fundraising initiative in your community.
- Volunteer to manage a project for a nonprofit agency.
- Establish a relationship with an experienced project manager. Interview him/her about greatest challenges and how he/she overcomes them.

Change Manager—Change Implementation Skills

Recommended Readings

These readings were selected for their appropriateness to the Human Performance Improvement field. This list is not intended to be comprehensive, nor is it intended to endorse or exclude any particular book.

Managing Transitions: Making the Most of Change (2nd Edition)
Bridges, William. Cambridge, MA: Perseus Books Group, 2003
ISBN: 0738208248

Managing Change and Transition
Boston, MA: Harvard Business School Press, 2003
ISBN: 1578518741

Beyond the Wall of Resistance: Unconventional Strategies That Build Support for Change
Maurer, Rick. Austin, TX: Bard Press, 1996
ISBN: 1885167075

The Dance of Change
Senge, Peter M., Kleiner, Art (Editor), Roberts, Charlotte, Ross, Rick, Roth, George, and Smith, Bryan, New York, NY: Doubleday, 1999
ISBN: 0385493223

Managing the Change Process: A Fieldbook for Change Agents, Team Leaders, and Reengineering Managers
Carr, David K., Kelvin, Hard J., and Trahant, William J. (Contributor). New York, NY: McGraw-Hill, 1996
ISBN: 0070129444

Creating Strategic Change: Designing the Flexible, High-Performing Organization
Pasmore, William A. New York, NY: John Wiley & Sons, Incorporated, 1994
ISBN: 0471597295

The Human Side of Change: A Practical Guide to Organization Redesign (Jossey-Bass Business & Management Series)
Galpin, Timothy J. San Francisco, CA: Jossey-Bass Publishers, 1996
ISBN: 0787902160

The Change Management Handbook: A Road Map to Corporate Transformation
Berger, Lance A., Sikora, Martin J. (Contributor), and Berger, Dorothy R. (Contributor). New York, NY: Irwin Professional Publishing, 1993
ISBN: 1556239750

Real Time Strategic Change
Jacobs, Robert W. San Francisco, CA: Berrett-Koehler Publishers, Inc., 1997
ISBN: 1576750302

The Change Handbook: Group Methods for Shaping the Future
Holman, Peggy, and Devane, Tom (Editors). San Francisco, CA: Berrett-Koehler Publishers, 1999
ISBN: 1576750582

Aftershock: Helping People through Corporate Change
Woodward, Harry, Buchholz, Steve, and Hess, Karen (Editors). New York, NY: John Wiley & Sons, 1997
ISBN: 0471624780

Workshops

These workshops were selected for their content and appropriateness for the Human Performance Improvement field. This list is not intended to be comprehensive, nor is it intended to endorse or exclude any particular workshop.

Facilitating and Managing Complex Systems Change
Length: 7 days   Cost: $2,500
Location: Contact vendor
NTL Institute
300 North Lee Street, Suite 300
Alexandria, VA 22314-2630
Telephone: (800) 777-5227 or (703) 548-1500
E-mail: info@ntl.org
Website: www.ntl.org

Change Leadership: How Leaders Drive Organizational Change
Length: 2 days   Cost: $1,395
Location: Contact vendor
Linkage, Inc.
16 New England Executive Park, Suite 205
Burlington, MA 01803
Telephone: (781) 402-5555
Website: www.linkageinc.com

Implementation: Addressing Barriers and Conflict
Length: 2 days   Cost: $1,095
Location: Contact vendor
ILR School, Cornell University
309 Ives Hall
IThaca, NY 14853
Telephone: (212) 340-2874
Website: www.ilr.cornell.edu/mgmtprog

Leading Organizational Change
Length: 4 days   Cost: $1,800
Location: Potomac, Maryland
NTL Institute
300 North Lee Street, Suite 300
Alexandria, VA 22314-2630

Telephone: (800) 777-5227 or (703) 548-1500
E-mail: info@ntl.org
Website: www.ntl.org

Additional workshops can be found at www.firstseminar.com
Keywords: Change management

Self-Study Options

These self-study options were selected for their content and appropriateness for the Human Performance Improvement field. This list is not intended to be comprehensive, nor is it intended to endorse or exclude any particular self-study option.

Managing Change (VCI CD-ROM)
Cost: $99
Telephone: (800) 442-7477
Website: www.courseilt.com

Change and Leadership: From the Paradigm Mastery Series (video)
Cost: $150 (rental), $495 (purchase)
LearnCom Inc.
38 Discovery, Suite 250
Irvine, CA 92618
Telephone: (800) 622-3610
Website: www.learncom.com

Changes!
Cost: $130, $550
LearnCom Inc.
38 Discovery, Suite 250
Irvine, CA 92618
Telephone: (800) 622-3610
Website: www.learncom.com

Days of Changes
Cost: $195, $495
LearnCom Inc.
38 Discovery, Suite 250
Irvine, CA 92618
Telephone: (800) 622-3610
Website: www.learncom.com

Lead the Change: From the New Workplace Series
Cost: $295 (rental), $945 (purchase)
LearnCom Inc.
38 Discovery, Suite 250
Irvine, CA 92618
Telephone: (800) 622-3610
Website: www.learncom.com

Make the Change: From the New Workplace Series
Cost: Cost: $295(rental), $945 (purchase)
LearnCom Inc.
38 Discovery, Suite 250
Irvine, CA 92618
Telephone: (800) 622-3610
Website: www.learncom.com

Other Development Opportunities

- Identify a change that impacts you or those around you. Study your own and others' reactions to it. If you're feeling resistant, identify those factors that are responsible for your feelings of opposition.
- Identify changes that occurred around you in the past 5 years. Determine what elements of those changes were most difficult. What lead to your eventual acceptance of the change? What was done well to gain your acceptance? What could have been done differently?

Change Manager—Change Impetus Skills

Recommended Readings

These readings were selected for their appropriateness to the Human Performance Improvement field. This list is not intended to be comprehensive, nor is it intended to endorse or exclude any particular book.

Developing Business Strategies (6th Edition)
Aaker David A. New York, NY: John Wiley & Sons., 2001
ISBN: 0471064114

Strategic Planning: What Every Manager Must Know
Steiner, George Albert. New York, NY: Free Press, 1997
ISBN: 0684832453

Applied Strategic Planning: A Comprehensive Guide
Goodstein, Leonard, Nolan, Timothy (Contributor), and Pfeiffer, J.
William. New York, NY: McGraw-Hill, 1993
ISBN: 0070240205

Beyond Strategic Vision: Effective Corporate Action with Hoshin Planning
Cowley, Michael, and Domb, Ellen. Boston, MA: Butterworth-Heinemann
(Trd), 1997
ISBN: 0750698438

Workshops

These workshops were selected for their content and appropriateness for the
Human Performance Improvement field. This list is not intended to be comprehensive, nor is it intended to endorse or exclude any particular workshop.

Diagnosing Organizations with Impact
Length: 6 days   Cost: $2,300
Location: Alexandria, VA
NTL Institute
300 N. Lee Street, Suite 300
Alexandria, VA 22314-2607
Telephone: (800) 777-5227 or (703) 548-1500
E-mail: info@ntl.org
Website: www.ntl.org

Strategic Human Resource Planning
Length: 5 days   Cost: $7,800 (includes meals/lodging)
Location: Ann Arbor, MI
University of Michigan, Ross School of Business
Executive Education
1000 Oakbrook Drive
Ann Arbor, MI 48109-6794
Telephone: (734) 763-1000
E-mail: um.exec.ed@umich.edu
Website: www.execed.bus.umich.edu/execdev/default.aspx

Strategic Human Resources Planning
Length: 2 days   Cost: $1,095

Location: Various, contact vendor
ILR School, Cornell University
309 Ives Hall
IThaca, NY 14853
Telephone: (212) 340-2874
Website: www.ilr.cornell.edu/mgmtprog

Additional workshops can be found at www.firstseminar.com
Keyword: Consulting

Self-Study Options

These self-study options were selected for their content and appropriateness for the Human Performance Improvement field. This list is not intended to be comprehensive, nor is it intended to endorse or exclude any particular self-study option.

Mastering Revolutionary Change with Noel Tichy and Stratford Sherman

Cost: $375 (rental), $1,900 (purchase)
LearnCom Inc.
38 Discovery, Suite 250
Irvine, CA 92618
Telephone: (800) 622-3610
Website: www.learncom.com

How to Develop the Strategic Plan (3rd Edition)

Cost: $159
American Management Association
1601 Broadway
New York, NY 10019
Telephone: (800) 262-9699 or (212) 586-8100
E-mail: customerservice@amanet.org
Website: www.amanet.org

Other Development Opportunities

- Keep up-to-date with the trends that might impact your company/clients. Read industry journals and magazines.
- Create a strategic plan for your career/life. Consider the factors that could/should influence such a plan.

Change Manager—Communication Channel, Informal Network and Alliance Understanding

Recommended Readings

These readings were selected for their appropriateness to the Human Performance Improvement field. This list is not intended to be comprehensive nor is it intended to endorse or exclude any particular book.

Corporate Networking: Building Channels for Information and Influence
Mueller, Robert K. New York, NY: Free Press, 1986
ISBN: 0029221501

Make Your Mark: Influencing Across Your Organization
Craig, Sue. New York, NY: McGraw-Hill, 1998
ISBN: 0077091590

Business Partnering for Continuous Improvement: How to Forge Enduring Alliances Among Employees, Suppliers & Customers
Poirier, Charles C., and Houser, William F. (Contributor). San Francisco, CA: Berrett-Koehler, 1993
ISBN: 1881052109

Communicating Change: How to Win Employee Support for New Business Directions
Larkin, Sandar (Contributor), and Larkin, T.J., New York, NY: McGraw-Hill, 1994
ISBN: 0070364524

Workshops

These workshops were selected for their content and appropriateness for the Human Performance Improvement field. This list is not intended to be comprehensive, nor is it intended to endorse or exclude any particular workshop.

Cross-Functional Communication: Strategies for Workplace Effectiveness
Length: 3 days   Cost: $1,795 (member), $1,995
Location: Contact vendor
American Management Association
1601 Broadway
New York, NY 10019

Telephone: (800) 262-9699 or (212) 586-8100
E-mail: customerservice@amanet.org
Website: www.amanet.org

Leading Through Communication: The Linkage Communication Clinic
Length: 3 days   Cost: $2,495
Linkage, Inc.
16 New England Executive Park Suite 205
Burlington, MA 01803
Telephone: (781) 402-5555
Website: www.linkageinc.com

Additional workshops can be found at www.firstseminar.com
Keywords: Communication, networking

Self-Study Options

These self-study options were selected for their content and appropriateness for the Human Performance Improvement field. This list is not intended to be comprehensive, nor is it intended to endorse or exclude any particular self-study option.

Office Policy: Not Necessary the Truth
Cost: $195 (rental), $695 (purchase)
LearnCom Inc.
38 Discovery, Suite 250
Irvine, CA 92618
Telephone: (800) 622-3610
Website: www.learncom.com

Communication in the Workplace Series (Video-based)
Cost: Check website, search product under "Communication" category
LearnCom Inc.
38 Discovery, Suite 250
Irvine, CA 92618
Telephone: (800) 622-3610
Website: www.learncom.com

Communication (Video)
Cost: $64.99
Alliance Training and Consulting, Inc.

8900 Indian Creek Parkway, Suite 270
Overland Park, KS 66210
Telephone: (877) 385-5515 or (913) 385-5515
E-mail: info@alliancetac.com
Website: www.alliancetac.com

Other Development Opportunities

- Identify the paths of communication in your organization. How do you learn about vital company information? What formal means of communication are used? What informal means of communication are used?
- Interview friends/relatives about the paths of communication in their organizations.

Change Manager—Group Dynamics Process Understanding

Recommended Readings

These readings were selected for their appropriateness to the Human Performance Improvement field. This list is not intended to be comprehensive, nor is it intended to endorse or exclude any particular book.

Team Work and Group Dynamics
Stewart, Greg L., Sims, Henry P., and Manz, Charles C. New York, NY: John Wiley & Sons, 1998
ISBN: 0471197696

Group Dynamics (4th Edition)
Forsyth, Donelson R. Belmont, CA: Wadsworth, 2005
ISBN: 0534368220

Success Through Teamwork: A Practical Guide to Interpersonal Team Dynamics (High-Performance Team Series)
Chang, Richard Y. San Francisco, CA: Jossey-Bass, 1999
ISBN: 0787951110

How Teamwork Works: The Dynamics of Effective Team Development
Syer, John, and Connolly, Christopher (Contributor). New York, NY:
McGraw-Hill, 1996
ISBN: 0077079426

**Paradoxes of Group Life: Understanding Conflict, Paralysis, and
Movement in Group Dynamics**
Smith, Kenwyn K., and Berg, David N. San Francisco, CA: Jossey-Bass Inc.,
Publishers, 1997
ISBN: 078793948X

Workshops

These workshops were selected for their content and appropriateness for the
Human Performance Improvement field. This list is not intended to be
comprehensive, nor is it intended to endorse or exclude any particular
workshop.

Facilitating and Managing Complex Systems Change
Length: 7 days   Cost: $2,500
Location: Various, contact vendor
NTL Institute
300 N. Lee Street, Suite 300
Alexandria, VA 22314-2630
Telephone: (800) 777-5227 or (703) 548-1500
E-mail: info@ntl.org
Website: www.ntl.org

Chartering Teams to High Performance
Length: 1 day   Cost: $995
Boston University Corporate Education Center
72 Tyng Road
Tyngsboro, MA 01879-2099
Telephone: (800) 288-7246 or (978) 649-9731
Website: www.butrain.bu.edu/MDP

ACP—The Advanced Consultant
Cost: Contact vendor
Location: Contact vendor

Numerof & Associates, Inc.
Four CityPlace Drive, Suite 430
St. Louis, MO 63141
Telephone: (314) 997-1587
E-mail: info@nai-consulting.com

Additional workshops can be found at www.firstseminar.com
Keywords: Group dynamics, team dynamics

Self-Study Options

These self-study options were selected for their content and appropriateness for the Human Performance Improvement field. This list is not intended to be comprehensive, nor is it intended to endorse or exclude any particular self-study option.

Team Work at Work
Cost: $195 (rental), $695 (purchase)
LearnCom Inc.
38 Discovery, Suite 250
Irvine, CA 92618
Telephone: (800) 622-3610
Website: www.learncom.com

How to Build High-Performance Teams (text-based)
Cost: $139
American Management Association
1601 Broadway
New York, NY 10019
Telephone: (800) 262-9699 or (212) 586-8100
E-mail: customerservice@amanet.org

Making Teams Work: How to Form, Measure, and Transition Today's Teams
Cost: $139
American Management Association
1601 Broadway
New York, NY 10019
Telephone: (800) 262-9699 or (212) 586-8100
E-mail: customerservice@amanet.org

Human Factors and Team Dynamics for Project Management (Web-based)
Cost: $725
UC Berkeley Extension
1995 University Ave.
Berkeley, CA 94720-7000
Telephone: (888) 827-6278 or (510) 642-7343
Email: info@unex.berkeley.edu
http://www.unex.berkeley.edu/

Prime Team Building (CD)
Cost: $310
PrimeLearning Group Ltd.
410 Park Avenue, 15th Floor
New York, NY 10022
Telephone: (917) 210-9173

Tearing Down Walls (Video)
Cost: $695
Employee University
Telephone: (888) 215-8532
Website: www.employeeuniversity.com

Other Development Opportunities

- Join and actively participate in associations and professional organizations. Observe how those groups interact to accomplish goals.
- Identify groups/teams within your organization that are known for consistently producing results. Observe them in action.
- Identify groups/teams within your organization that are known to be struggling. Observe them in action.

Change Manager—Process Consultation Skills

Recommended Readings

These readings were selected for their appropriateness to the Human Performance Improvement field. This list is not intended to be comprehensive, nor is it intended to endorse or exclude any particular book.

Process Consultation Revisited: Building the Helping Relationship
Schein, Edger H. Upper Saddle River, NJ: Prentice Hall. 1998
ISBN: 020134596X

Process Consultation: Its Role in Organization Development (2nd Edition)
Schein, Edger H. Upper Saddle River, NJ: Prentice Hall, 1988
ISBN: 0201067366

Process Consultation, Volume 2: Lessons for Managers and Consultants
Schein, Edger H. Upper Saddle River, NJ: Prentice Hall, 1987
ISBN: 0201067447

Group Performance and Interaction
Parks, Craig D., and Sanna, Lawrence J. Boulder, CO: Westview Press, 1998
ISBN: 0813333199

Intervention Skills: Process Consultation for Small Groups and Teams
Reddy, W. Brendan. San Diego, CA: Pfeiffer & Company, 1995
ISBN: 0883904349

Workshops

These workshops were selected for their content and appropriateness for the Human Performance Improvement field. This list is not intended to be comprehensive, nor is it intended to endorse or exclude any particular workshop.

Group Process Consultation: A Practical Diagnostic and Intervention Approach
Length: 6 days   Cost: $2,300
Location: Potomac, MD
NTL Institute
300 N. Lee Street, Suite 300
Alexandria, VA 22314-2630
Telephone: (800) 777-5227 or (703) 548-1500
E-mail: info@ntl.org
Website: www.ntl.org

Additional workshops can be found at www.firstseminar.com
Keywords: Process consultation, groups

Self-Study Options

These self-study options were selected for their content and appropriateness for the Human Performance Improvement field. This list is not intended to be comprehensive, nor is it intended to endorse or exclude any particular self-study option.

Twelve Angry Men: Teams that Don't Quit (Video-based)
Cost: $225 (rental), $795 (purchase)
LearnCom Inc.
38 Discovery, Suite 250
Irvine, CA 92618
Telephone: (800) 622-3610
Website: www.learncom.com

Other Development Opportunities

- Join and actively participate in associations and professional organizations. Observe how those groups interact to accomplish goals.
- Identify groups/teams within your organization that are known for consistently producing results. Observe them in action.
- Identify groups/teams within your organization that are known to be struggling. Observe them in action.

Change Manager—Facilitation Skills

Recommended Readings

These readings were selected for their appropriateness to the Human Performance Improvement field. This list is not intended to be comprehensive, nor is it intended to endorse or exclude any particular book.

The Facilitator's Fieldbook (2nd Edition)
Justice, Tom, and Jamieson David W. New York, NY: AMACOM, 2006

The Skilled Facilitator Fieldbook: Tips, Tools, and Tested Methods for Consultants, Facilitators, Managers, Trainers, and Coaches
Schwarz, Roger, Davidson, Anne, Carlson, Peg, and McKinney Sue. San Francisco, CA: Jossey-Bass, 2005
ISBN: 0787964948

Facilitating with Ease!: Core Skills for Facilitators, Team Leaders and Members, Managers, Consultants, and Trainers
Bens Ingrid. San Francisco, CA: Jossey-Bass, 2005
ISBN: 0787977292

The Skilled Facilitator (2nd Edition)
Schwarz, Roger. San Francisco, CA: Jossey-Bass, 2002
ISBN: 0787947237

Facilitating Work Teams: Twenty Simulation Exercises
Johnson, Dora B. Amherst, MA: Human Resource Development Press, 1994
ISBN: 0874259835

Facilitation Skills for Team Leaders
Martin, Charles L., and Hackett, Donald. Menlo Park, CA: Crisp Publications, 1993
ISBN: 1560521996

Workshops

These workshops were selected for their content and appropriateness for the Human Performance Improvement field. This list is not intended to be comprehensive, nor is it intended to endorse or exclude any particular workshop.

Essential Facilitation
Length: 3 days   Cost: $1,995
Location: Various, contact vendor
Interaction Associates
625 Mount Auburn Street, Suite 3
Cambridge, MA 02138
Telephone: (617) 234-2700
Website: www.interactionassociates.com

Facilitating Change
Length: 3 days   Cost: $1,995
Location: Contact vendor
Interaction Associates
625 Mount Auburn Street, Suite 3
Cambridge, MA 02138
Telephone: (617) 234-2700
Website: www.interactionassociates.com

Group Facilitation
Length: 3 days   Cost: $625
Location: Washington, DC
Management Concepts
8230 Leesburg Pike, Suite 800
Vienna, VA 22182
Telephone: (703) 790-9595
E-mail: info@mgmtconcepts.com
Website: www.managementconcepts.com

Additional workshops can be found at www.firstseminar.com
Keyword: Facilitation

Self-Study Options

These self-study options were selected for their content and appropriateness for the Human Performance Improvement field. This list is not intended to be comprehensive, nor is it intended to endorse or exclude any particular self-study option.

Facilitation Skills for Team Leaders (CBT/Text-based)
Cost: $39.94
Crisp Publications
Telephone: (800) 442-7477
E-mail: courseiltcrisp@thomsonlearning.com
Website: www.courseilt.com

How to Be an Effective Facilitator (Text-based)
Cost: $139
1601 Broadway
New York, NY 10019
Telephone: (800) 262-9699 or (212) 586-8100
E-mail: customerservice@amanet.org
Website: www.amanet.org

How to Lead a Team: Team Facilitation and Decision Making
Cost: $59
Fred Pryor Seminars & CareerTrack
9757 Metcalf Avenue
Overland Park, KS 66212

Telephone: (800) 780-8476
E-mail: pryoronsite@pryor.com
Website: www.pryor.com

Effective Facilitation Tools™: Training to Keep a Group Focused, Motivated and Moving Forward (Video-based)
Cost: $249.95
Fred Pryor Seminars & CareerTrack
9757 Metcalf Avenue
Overland Park, KS 66212
Telephone: (800) 780-8476
E-mail: pryoronsite@pryor.com
Website: www.pryor.com

Facilitate! (Video-based)
Cost: $150 (rental), $495 (to purchase)
LearnCom Inc.
38 Discovery, Suite 250
Irvine, CA 92618
Telephone: (800) 622-3610
Website: www.learncom.com

The Complete Guide to Facilitation (CD-ROM)
Cost: $125
GeoLearning, Inc.
Regency West 5, Suite 100, 4500 Westown Parkway
West Des Moines, IA 50266-6717
Telephone: (800) 970-9903 or (515) 222-9903
E-mail: coreenw@geolearning.com
Website: www.geolearning.com

Other Development Opportunities

- Observe an experienced team facilitator.
- Volunteer to lead a team; work with an experienced facilitator to plan each meeting's agenda and exercises.

Evaluator

This section provides a list of resources to develop the six Evaluator role competencies.

Evaluator—Performance Gap Evaluation Skills

Recommended Readings

These readings were selected for their appropriateness to the Human Performance Improvement field. This list is not intended to be comprehensive, nor is it intended to endorse or exclude any particular book.

How to Make Performance Evaluations Really Work: A Step-by-Step Guide Complete with Sample Words, Phrases, Forms, and Pitfalls to Avoid
Shepard, Glenn. Hoboken: NJ: John Wiley & Sons, 2005
ISBN: 0471739634

Measuring Performance: Using the New Metrics to Deploy Strategy and Improve Performance (2nd Edition)
Frost, Bob. Dallas, TX: Measurement International, 2000
ISBN: 0970247117

The HR Scorecard: Linking People, Strategy, and Performance
Becker, Brian E., Huselid, Mark A., and Ulrich, Dave.
Boston, MA: Harvard Business School Press, 2001
ISBN: 1578511364

The Basics of Performance Measurement
Harbour, Jerry L. New York, NY: Quality Resources, 1997
ISBN: 0527763284

Harvard Business Review on Measuring Corporate Performance (Harvard Business Review Series)
Harvard Business School, Boston, MA: Harvard Business School Press, 1998
ISBN: 0875848826

Performance Drivers: A Practical Guide to Using the Balanced Scorecard
Olve, Nils-Goran, Roy, Jan, and Wetter, Magnus. New York, NY: John Wiley & Sons, 1999
ISBN: 0471986232

Performance Measurement and Evaluation
Holloway, Jacky, Lewis, Jenny, and Mallory, Geoff (Editors). Thousand Oaks, CA: Sage Publications, 1995
ISBN: 0803979592

Analyzing Qualitative Data
Bryman, Alan, and Burgess, Robert G. New York, NY: Routledge, 1994
ISBN: 041506063X

Workshops

These workshops were selected for their content and appropriateness for the Human Performance Improvement field. This list is not intended to be comprehensive, nor is it intended to endorse or exclude any particular workshop.

Performance Measurement Workshop
Length: 3 days   Cost: $635
Location: Contact vendor
Management Concepts
8230 Leesburg Pike, Suite 800
Vienna, VA 22182
Telephone: (703) 790-9595
E-mail: info@mgmtconcepts.com
Website: www.managementconcepts.com

Statistics Made Simple
Length: 5 days   Cost: $830
Location: Vienna, VA; Washington, DC
Management Concepts
8230 Leesburg Pike, Suite 800
Vienna, VA 22182
Telephone: (703) 790-9595
E-mail: info@mgmtconcepts.com
Website: www.managementconcepts.com

Additional workshops can be found at www.firstseminar.com
Keywords: Measurement, performance measurement, statistics

Self-Study Options

These self-study options were selected for their content and appropriateness for the Human Performance Improvement field. This list is not intended to be comprehensive, nor is it intended to endorse or exclude any particular self-study option.

Introduction to Statistics (CD-ROM, text-based)
Cost: Contact vendor
ITC Learning Corporation
1616 Anderson Road, Suite 109
McLean, VA 22102
Telephone: (800) 638-3757
E-Mail: learning@itclearning.com
Website: www.itclearning.com

Applied Quantitative Analysis (Web-based)
Length: 12 weeks   Cost: $845
The Graduate School of America
330 2nd Ave. S., Suite 550
Minneapolis, MN 55401
E-mail: tgsainfo@tgsa.edu
Telephone: (800) 987-1133 or (612) 339-8650
Website: www.tgsa.edu

Other Development Opportunities

- Establish a relationship with a statistician.
- Establish a relationship with a financial analyst.
- Ask a statistician to coach/mentor you through a simple workplace or community study.
- Identify your company's performance targets. Determine what measures are in place to gauge performance against those targets.

Evaluator—Ability to Evaluate Against Organizational Goals

Recommended Readings

These readings were selected for their appropriateness to the Human Performance Improvement field. This list is not intended to be comprehensive, nor is it intended to endorse or exclude any particular book.

Evaluating Training Programs: The Four Levels (3rd Edition)
Kirkpatrick, Donald L., and Kirkpatrick James D. San Francisco, CA:
Berrett-Koehler Publishers, 2005
ISBN: 1576753484

Measuring Organizational Improvement Impact
Chang, Richard Y., and DeYoung, Paul H. San Francisco, CA: Jossey-Bass
Peiffer, 1999
ISBN: 0787951013

**Measuring Organizational Improvement Impact: A Practical Guide to
Successfully Linking Organizational Improvement Measures**
Chang, Richard Y., and DeYoung, Paul H. Irvine, CA: Richard
Chang Associates Inc, 1996
ISBN: 1883553172

**Return on Investment in Training and Performance Improvement
Programs (2nd Edition)**
Phillips Jack J. Burlington, MA: Butterworth-Heinemann, 2003
ISBN: 0750676019

**How to Measure Training Results: A Practical Guide to Tracking the Six
Key Indicators**
Phillips, Jack, and Stone Ron. New York, NY: McGraw-Hill, 2002
ISBN: 0071387927

**Measuring the Impact of Training: A Practical Guide to Calculating
Measurable Results**
Wade, Pamela A. Irvine, CA: Richard Chang Associates Inc, 1998
ISBN: 1883553369

**Handbook of Training Evaluation and Measurement Methods
(Improving Human Performance Series)**
Phillips, Jack J. Houston, TX: Gulf Publishing Company, 1997
ISBN: 0884153878

**The Bottom Line on ROI: Basics, Benefits, & Barriers to Measuring
Training & Performance Improvement**
Phillips, Patricia Pulliam. Atlanta, GA: CEP, 2002
ISBN: 1879618257

Measuring Performance for Business Results
Zairi, M. Chapman & Hall, 1994
ISBN: 0412574004

**Accountability in Human Resource Management: Techniques for
Evaluating the Human Resource Function and Measuring Bottom-Line
Contribution**

Phillips, Jack J. Houston, TX: Gulf Publishing Company, 1996
ISBN: 0884153967

Workshops

These workshops were selected for their content and appropriateness for the Human Performance Improvement field. This list is not intended to be comprehensive, nor is it intended to endorse or exclude any particular workshop.

Program Evaluation
Length: 3 days   Cost: $695
Location: Vienna, VA
Management Concepts
8230 Leesburg Pike, Suite 800
Vienna, VA 22182
Telephone: (703) 790-9595
E-mail: info@mgmtconcepts.com
Website: www.managementconcepts.com

Analytical Techniques for Budget-Performance Integration Using Microsoft Excel
Length: 4 days   Cost: $785
Location: Contact vendor
Management Concepts
8230 Leesburg Pike, Suite 800
Vienna, VA 22182
Telephone: (703) 790-9595
E-mail: info@mgmtconcepts.com
Website: www.managementconcepts.com

Managing and Appraising Employee Performance
Length: 2 days   Cost: $520
Location: Contact vendor
Management Concepts
8230 Leesburg Pike, Suite 800
Vienna, VA 22182
Telephone: (703) 790-9595
E-mail: info@mgmtconcepts.com
Website: www.managementconcepts.com

Additional workshops can be found at www.firstseminar.com.
Keywords: Program evaluation, evaluation

Self-Study Options

No self-study options were found for this competency.

Other Development Opportunities

- Identify interventions that have been implemented in your organization in the past. Determine if measures were established to gauge their success. If so, determine if they were successful. Why/why not?
- Identify current change initiatives in your organization. Determine if performance measures currently exist for these. Determine who identified those measures and who is responsible for obtaining the data.
- Become an advocate for the use of performance measures with all HPI interventions.

Evaluator—Standard Setting Skills

Recommended Readings

These readings were selected for their appropriateness to the Human Performance Improvement field. This list is not intended to be comprehensive, nor is it intended to endorse or exclude any particular book.

Benchmarking: The Search for Industry Best Practices That Lead to Superior Performance
Camp, Robert C. Milwaukee, WI: American Society for Quality, 1989
ISBN: 0873890582

Business Process Benchmarking: Finding and Implementing Best Practices
Camp, Robert C. New York, NY: Quality Resources, 1995
ISBN: 0873892968

Benchmarking for Competitive Advantage (2nd Edition)
Bendell, Tony, Boulter, Louise, and Goodstadt, Paul.
Pitman Publishing, 1997
ISBN: 0273626345

Benchmarking for Competitive Advantage
Boxwell, Jr., Robert J. New York, NY: McGraw-Hill, 1994
ISBN: 0070068992

The Benchmarking Workout: A Toolkit to Help You Construct a World-Class Organization
Bendell, Tony, Boulter, Louise (Contributor), and Gatford, Kerry. London, UK: Financal Times Management, 1997
ISBN: 0273626353

High-Performance Benchmarking: 20 Steps to Success
Harrington, H. James, and Harrington, James S. (Contributor). New York, NY: McGraw-Hill, 1996
ISBN: 007026774X

Make Success Measurable!: A Mindbook-Workbook for Setting Goals and Taking Action
Smith, Douglas K. New York, NY: John Wiley & Sons, 1999
ISBN: 0471295590

Workshops

These workshops were selected for their content and appropriateness for the Human Performance Improvement field. This list is not intended to be comprehensive, nor is it intended to endorse or exclude any particular workshop.

Benchmarking
Length: 2 days   Cost: $520
Location: Washinton, DC
Management Concepts
8230 Leesburg Pike, Suite 800
Vienna, VA 22182
Telephone: (703) 790-9595
E-mail: info@mgmtconcepts.com
Website: www.managementconcepts.com

Performance Measurement Workshop
Length: 3 days   Cost: $675
Location: Contact vendor
Management Concepts
8230 Leesburg Pike, Suite 800

Vienna, VA 22182
Telephone: (703) 790-9595
E-mail: info@mgmtconcepts.com
Website: www.managementconcepts.com

Strategic Planning
Length: 3 days   Cost: $1,895 (member), $2,095
American Management Association
1601 Broadway
New York, NY 10019
Telephone: (800) 262-9699 or (212) 586-8100
E-mail: customerservice@amanet.org
Website: www.amanet.org

Strategic Planning Tools, Techniques and Implementation
Length: 2 days   Cost: $1,695 (member), $1,895
American Management Association
1601 Broadway
New York, NY 10019
Telephone: (800) 262-9699 or (212) 586-8100
E-mail: customerservice@amanet.org
Website: www.amanet.org

Fundamentals of Strategic Planning
Length: 2 days   Cost: $1,595 (member), $1,795
American Management Association
1601 Broadway
New York, NY 10019
Telephone: (800) 262-9699 or (212) 586-8100
E-mail: customerservice@amanet.org
Website: www.amanet.org

Additional workshops can be found at www.firstseminar.com
Keywords: Benchmarking, measuring goals, strategic planning

Self-Study Options

These self-study options were selected for their content and appropriateness for the Human Performance Improvement field. This list is not intended to be comprehensive, nor is it intended to endorse or exclude any particular self-study option.

Developing Performance Standards: From the Supervision Series (CD-ROM)

Cost: $1,500
LearnCom Inc.
38 Discovery, Suite 250
Irvine, CA 92618
Telephone: (800) 622-3610
Website: www.learncom.com

Managing and Achieving Organizational Goals (Text-based)

Cost: $139
American Management Association
1601 Broadway
New York, NY 10019
Telephone: (800) 262-9699 or (212) 586-8100
E-mail: customerservice@amanet.org
Website: www.amanet.org

Strategic Management: Analyzing Strategic Options

Cost: Contact vendor
NETg
14624 N. Scottsdale Rd., Suite 300
Scottsdale, AZ 85254
Telephone: (877) 688-3717 or (480) 315-4000
Website: www.netg.com

Strategic Management Series

Cost: Contact vendor
NETg
14624 N. Scottsdale Rd., Suite 300
Scottsdale, AZ 85254
Telephone: (877) 688-3717 or (480) 315-4000
Website: www.netg.com

Other Development Opportunities

- Volunteer with a local community organization. Help them create short-term goals and objectives. Establish interim measures for those goals and objectives.

■ Identify 3 work teams who are known for their consistent high level of achievement. Observe each. Determine what they have in common.

Evaluator—Ability to Assess Impact on Culture

Recommended Readings

These readings were selected for their appropriateness to the Human Performance Improvement field. This list is not intended to be comprehensive, nor is it intended to endorse or exclude any particular book.

Corporate Culture and Performance
Kotter, John P., and Heskett, James L. (Contributor). New York, NY:
Free Press, 1992
ISBN: 0029184673

The Corporate Culture Survival Guide
Schein, Edgar H. San Francisco, CA: Jossey-Bass, 1999
ISBN: 0787946990

Organizational Culture and Leadership (Jossey-Bass Business & Management, 3rd Edition)
Schein, Edgar H. San Francisco, CA: Jossey-Bass, 2004
ISBN: 0787975974

Corporate Cultures: The Rites and Rituals of Corporate Life
Deal, Terrence E., and Kennedy Allan A. New York, NY: Perseus Books Group, 2000
ISBN: 0738203300

The Character of a Corporation: How Your Company's Culture Can Make or Break Your Business
Goffee, Robert, and Jones, Gareth. New York, NY: HarperBusiness, 1998
ISBN: 088730902X

Corporate Culture Team Culture: Removing the Hidden Barriers to Team Success
Sherriton, Jacalyn, Stern, James L. (Contributor), and Hickey Adrienne (Editor). New York, NY: AMACOM, 1996
ISBN: 0814403247

The Culture of Success: Building a Sustained Competitive Advantage by Living Your Corporate Beliefs
Zimmerman, John, Sr., and Tregoe, Benjamin (Contributor). New York, NY: McGraw-Hill, 1997
ISBN: 0070730083

Diagnosing and Changing Organizational Culture: Based on the Competing Values Framework (The Jossey-Bass Business & Management Series, Revised Edition)
Cameron, Kim S., and Quinn, Robert E. San Francisco, CA: Jossey-Bass, 2005
ISBN: 0787982830

Diagnosing and Changing Organizational Culture: Based on the Competing Values Framework (Addison-Wesley Series on Organization Development)
Cameron, Kim S., and Quinn, Robert E. Reading, MA: Addison-Wesley Publishing Company, 1998
ISBN: 0201338718

Workshops

These workshops were selected for their content and appropriateness for the Human Performance Improvement field. This list is not intended to be comprehensive, nor is it intended to endorse or exclude any particular workshop.

The Human and Cultural Aspects of M&A
Length: 1 days   Cost: $995 (member), $1,095
Location: Various, contact vendor
American Management Association
1601 Broadway
New York, NY 10019
Telephone: (800) 262-9699 or (212) 586-8100
E-mail: customerservice@amanet.org
Website: www.amanet.org

Moving from an Operational Manager to a Strategic Thinker
Length: 2 days   Cost: $1,595 (member), $1,795
Location: Various, contact vendor
American Management Association

1601 Broadway
New York, NY 10019
Telephone: (800) 262-9699 or (212) 586-8100
E-mail: customerservice@amanet.org
Website: www.amanet.org

Additional workshops can be found at www.firstseminar.com
Keywords: Corporate culture, organizational culture, values

Self-Study Options

These self-study options were selected for their content and appropriateness for the Human Performance Improvement field. This list is not intended to be comprehensive, nor is it intended to endorse or exclude any particular self-study option.

Planning and Managing Change (text-based)
Cost: $159
American Management Association
1601 Broadway
New York, NY 10019
Telephone: (800) 262-9699 or (212) 586-8100
E-mail: customerservice@amanet.org
Website: www.amanet.org

Other Development Opportunities

- Identify the attributes of the culture in your workplace.
- Identify the attributes of the culture in your social organizations.
- Identify your values and beliefs. Determine if they are in sync with the organizations you are a part of.
- Identify any shifts in culture that you have witnessed. Determine what events/changes led to these shifts.
- Think of a change of routine behavior that you'd like to see in your household (i.e., beds always made, dishes always washed immediately after dinner, garage remaining clear of clutter, etc.). Begin the process of instilling this new "culture" in your household.

Evaluator—Human Performance Improvement Intervention Reviewing Skills

Recommended Readings

These readings were selected for their appropriateness to the Human Performance Improvement field. This list is not intended to be comprehensive, nor is it intended to endorse or exclude any particular book.

Accountability in Human Resource Management (Improving Human Performance Series)
Phillips, Jack J. Houston, TX: Gulf Publishing Company, 1996
ISBN: 0884153967

Continuous Improvement Tools: A Practical Guide to Achieve Quality Results Volume 1 (Rev Edition)
Chang, Richard Y., and Niedzwiecki, Matthew E. San Francisco, CA: Pfeiffer, 1999
ISBN: 0787950807

Continuous Improvement Tools, Quality Improvement Series (Rev Edition)
Chang, Richard Y., and Niedzwiecki, Matthew E. San Francisco, CA: Pfeiffer, 1999
ISBN: 0787950815

Evaluating Training Programs: The Four Levels (3rd Edition)
Kirkpatrick, Donald L., and Kirkpatrick, James D. San Francisco, CA: Berrett-Koehler, 2005
ISBN: 1576753484

In Action: Measuring Return on Investment, Volume 3
Phillips, Jack J., and Phillips, Patricia Pulliam. Alexandria, VA: ASTD Press, 2001
ISBN: 156286288X

Linking Learning and Performance: A Practical Guide to Measuring Learning and On-the-Job Application (Improving Human Performance)
Hodges, Toni. San Francisco, CA: Butterworth-Heinemann, 2001
ISBN: 0750674121

Return on Investment in Training and Performance Improvement Programs (Improving Human Performance, 2nd Edition)
Phillips, Jack J. San Francisco, CA: Butterworth-Heinemann, 2003
ISBN: 0750676019

Handbook of Training Evaluation and Measurement Methods (Improving Human Performance Series)
Phillips, Jack J. Houston, TX: Gulf Publishing Company, 1997
ISBN: 0884153878

Workshops

These workshops were selected for their content and appropriateness for the Human Performance Improvement field. This list is not intended to be comprehensive, nor is it intended to endorse or exclude any particular workshop.

Program Evaluation
Length: 3 days   Cost: $695
Location: Vienna, VA
Management Concepts
8230 Leesburg Pike, Suite 800
Vienna, VA 22182
Telephone: (703) 790-9595
E-mail: info@mgmtconcepts.com
Website: www.managementconcepts.com

Additional workshops can be found at www.firstseminar.com
Keywords: Continuous improvement

Self-Study Options

These self-study options were selected for their content and appropriateness for the Human Performance Improvement field. This list is not intended to be comprehensive, nor is it intended to endorse or exclude any particular self-study option.

Building a Framework for Continuous Improvement (CD-ROM)
Cost: Contact vendor
GeoLearning, Inc.
4600 Westown Parkway, Suite 301

West Des Moines, IA 50266
Telephone: (800) 970-9903 or (515) 222-9903
E-mail: info@geolearning.com
Website: www.geolearning.com

Using Tools for Continuous Improvement (CD-ROM)
Cost: Contact vendor
GeoLearning, Inc.
4600 Westown Parkway, Suite 301
West Des Moines, IA 50266
Telephone: (800) 970-9903 or (515) 222-9903
E-mail: info@geolearning.com
Website: www.geolearning.com

Other Development Opportunities

- Establish a relationship with a quality consultant (internal or external).
- Become a part of a quality improvement effort, either in your company or in a community organization.
- Identify interventions that were implemented in your organization that may not have been very successful. Determine what could have made them more successful.
- Look for opportunities to apply quality improvement tools.

Evaluator—Feedback Skills

Recommended Readings

These readings were selected for their appropriateness to the Human Performance Improvement field. This list is not intended to be comprehensive, nor is it intended to endorse or exclude any particular book.

Designing Feedback: Performance Measures for Continuous Improvement (Crisp Management Library)
Thor, Carl G. Menlo Park, CA: Crisp Publications, 1998
ISBN: 1560524685

Coaching through Effective Feedback: A Practical Guide to Successful Communication (Management Skills Series)
Jerome, Paul J. San Francisco: Pfeiffer, 1999
ISBN: 0787951072

Job Feedback: Giving, Seeking, and Using Feedback for Performance Improvement (2nd Edition)
London, Manuel. Mahwah, NJ: LEA, 2003
ISBN: 0805844945

Workshops

These workshops were selected for their content and appropriateness for the Human Performance Improvement field. This list is not intended to be comprehensive, nor is it intended to endorse or exclude any particular workshop.

Data Collection Techniques
Length: 5 days   Cost: $850
Location: Vienna, VA; Washington, DC
Management Concepts
8230 Leesburg Pike, Suite 800
Vienna, VA 22182
Telephone: (703) 790-9595
E-mail: info@mgmtconcepts.com
Website: www.managementconcepts.com

Data Analysis and Interpretation
Length: 4 days   Cost: $725
Location: Vienna, VA; Washington, DC
Management Concepts
8230 Leesburg Pike, Suite 800
Vienna, VA 22182
Telephone: (703) 790-9595
E-mail: info@mgmtconcepts.com
Website: www.managementconcepts.com

Statistics Made Simple
Length: 5 days   Cost: $795
Location: Washington, DC
Management Concepts
8230 Leesburg Pike, Suite 800
Vienna, VA 22182
Telephone: (703) 790-9595
E-mail: info@mgmtconcepts.com
Website: www.managementconcepts.com

Communicating & Presenting for Management Success
Length: 3 days   Cost: $1,495
Location: Contact vendor
Boston University Corporate Education Center
72 Tyngsboro Road
Tyngsboro, MA 01879-2099
Telephone: (800) 288-7246 or (978) 649-9731 X 243
Website: www.butrain.bu.edu/MDP

Additional workshops can be found at www.firstseminar.com
Keywords: Technical data, technical presentations, feedback, performance feedback, technical writing

Self-Study Options

These self-study options were selected for their content and appropriateness for the Human Performance Improvement field. This list is not intended to be comprehensive, nor is it intended to endorse or exclude any particular self-study option.

Effective Presentation Skills (3rd Edition + CBT)
Cost: $39.95
Thomson Learning Course Technology
Telephone: (800) 354-9706 or (203) 539 8000
E-mail: eSales@thomsonlearning.com
Website: www.courseilt.com

Giving and Receiving Feedback (VCI CD-ROM)
Cost: $99
Thomson Learning Course Technology
Telephone: (800) 354-9706 or (203) 539-8000
E-mail: eSales@thomsonlearning.com
Website: www.courseilt.com

Other Development Opportunities

- Locate and review executive summary reports for performance improvement efforts in your organization.
- Page through journals and magazines. Identify techniques used to convey data in an easily understood manner.
- Identify opportunities to provide feedback to individuals about their performance.

Index

About the Authors

William J. Rothwell, Ph.D., is Professor of Workplace Learning and Performance in the Workforce Education and Development Program, part of the Department of Learning and Performance Systems, on the University Park Campus of Pennsylvania State University. He was previously Assistant Vice President and Management Development Director for the Franklin Life Insurance Company in Springfield, Illinois, and Training Director for the Illinois Office of Auditor General. He has worked full time in human performance improvement from 1979 to the present, thus combining real-world experience with academic and consulting experience. As President of Rothwell & Associates (see www.rothwell associates.com), a private consulting firm, he numbers over 32 multinational corporations on his client list.

Rothwell's latest publications include Rothwell, W., Butler, M., Hunt, D., Li, J., Maldonado, C., Peters, K., with Kingstern, J. (Eds.). (2006). *The Handbook of Training Technologies*. San Francisco: Pfeiffer; Rothwell, W., Prescott, R., and Taylor, M. (2005). *Strategic Human Resource Leader: How to Prepare Your Organization for the Six Key Trends Shaping the Future*. Mumbai: Jaico Publishing House; Rothwell, W. (2005). *Effective Succession Planning: Ensuring Leadership Continuity and Building Talent from Within*. 3rd ed. New York: Amacom; Rothwell, W., Jackson, R., Knight, S., Lindholm, J. with Wang, A., and Payne, T. (2005). *Career Planning and Succession Management: Developing Your Organization's Talent—For Today and Tomorrow*. Westport, CT: Greenwood Press; Rothwell, W., and Sullivan, R. (Eds.). (2005). *Practicing Organization Development: A Guide for Consultants*. 2nd ed. San Francisco: Pfeiffer & Co.; Rothwell, W., and Kazanas, H. (2005). *Strategic Planning for Human Resources*. Mumbai, India: Jaico Publishing House; Rothwell, W., Donahue, W., and Park, J. (2005). *Creating In-House Sales Training and Development Programs*. [Translation.] Beijing:

Publishing House of the Electronics Industry; Rothwell, W. (2005). *Beyond Training and Developing: The Groundbreaking Classic.* 2nd ed. New York: Amacom; Bernthal, P., Colteryahn, K., Davis, P., Naughton, J., Rothwell, W., and Wellins, R. (2004). *Mapping the Future: Shaping New Workplace Learning and Performance Competencies.* Alexandria, VA: The American Society for Training and Development; Rothwell, W., and Kazanas, H. (2004). *Improving On-the-Job Training: How to Establish and Operate a Comprehensive OJT Program.* 2nd ed. San Francisco: Pfeiffer and Company; Rothwell, W., Gerity, G., and Gaertner, E. (Eds.). (2004). *Linking Training to Performance: A Guide for Workforce Developers.* Washington, DC: American Association of Community Colleges; and, Dubois, D., and Rothwell, W. (2004). *Competency-Based Human Resource Management.* Palo Alto, CA: Davies-Black Publishing.

Rothwell can be reached at 305A Keller Building, University Park, PA 16802, (814) 863-2581, or by e-mail at wjr9@psu.edu.

Carolyn K. Hohne is a performance improvement consultant with over 19 years experience in the field of human performance improvement. As president of Hohne Consulting, LLC, she collaboratively works with clients to improve business results through people.

Hohne helps her clients identify the workforce implications of their business strategies. In addition, she has expertise in the design and development of structured learning events for audiences ranging from technical and manufacturing employees to business executives. She has helped many clients integrate training evaluation into their training curriculum. Hohne has also assisted organizations with the implementation of performance management systems, design and analysis of surveys, game simulations, and the implementation of team-based multisource feedback systems.

Hohne has an M.S. in Instructional Technology and has designed and developed numerous multimedia training programs. She has helped clients successfully integrate technology-based learning into their overall training strategy.

Carolyn has presented on training and performance consulting topics at several national conferences including the Computer-Based Training Conference, the National Industrial Hygiene Conference, the International Society for Performance Improvement International (ISPI) Conferences, American Society for Training and Development's (ASTD) National Technical Skills Training Conferences, ASTD's National Tech-Knowledge Conferences, and the ASTD's International Conferences. In addition, her work has been featured in articles in the *Los Angeles Times* and Dartnell Corporation's *Successful Supervisor* subscription newsletter.

Carolyn is a certified bicycling instructor for the League of American Bicyclists, teaching cyclists of all ages and abilities how to ride safely on the roads for enjoyment and/or transportation.

Hohne can be reached at 17 Marriott Drive, Suite 204, Lumberton, NJ 08048, (609) 265-7700 or by e-mail at chohne@hohneconsulting.com, or visit www. hohneconsulting.com.

Stephen B. King, Ph.D., is Chief Learning Officer, Learning and Organization Development for Constellation Energy. In August 2003, Steve joined Constellation Energy, a Fortune #125 integrated energy company based in Baltimore, Maryland, to lead the Learning & Organization Development function. Recent initiatives and responsibilities include: employee engagement survey and action planning, enterprisewide career development initiative, portal accessible Constellation Learning Center, executive talent assessment and succession management, building change management capability, leadership and executive development, learning technologies, and various learning, OD, and performance improvement.

Prior to joining Constellation Energy, Steve was the Executive Director of the Leadership & Management division of Management Concepts, a global learning and development consulting organization providing an array of leadership and management development solutions, such as training, executive coaching, leadership development, 360-assessments, and action learning to Fortune 500 and government sector clients. Before joining Management Concepts, he was an independent learning and performance consultant providing services to diverse clients including Motorola, FedEx, and the American Society for Training and Development. Steve began his career with Worthington Industries Inc., headquartered in Columbus, Ohio. He served in a variety of operations, project management, quality improvement, and learning and leadership development roles.

Steve received his Bachelor of Science in Business (Operations Management) from Ohio State University. He also received his Masters in Adult Education from Ohio State University. Continuing his education at Pennsylvania State University, Steve received his Ph.D. in Human Resource and Organization Development.

Steve was profiled in the June 2005 issue of *Chief Learning Officer* magazine, and he has delivered a number of learning and development presentations at professional conferences and industry events. Steve is on the adjunct faculty at Johns Hopkins and George Washington University teaching graduate courses in human resources and organization development in the U.S. and in Asia, and has also coauthored several books, articles, and professional publications. In 2006, he was invited to serve on an advisory committee for a learning executive graduate program being codeveloped by the University of Pennsylvania's Wharton School of Business and Graduate School of Education.

Constellation Energy (www.constellation.com), a FORTUNE 200 company based in Baltimore, is the nation's largest competitive supplier of electricity to large commercial and industrial customers and the nation's largest wholesale power seller. In 2005, the combined revenues of the integrated energy company totaled $17.1 billion.